Praise

50 Succes

"This incredible book gives you the very best of success literature ever written—in one easy book that you can read and reread for years. I hope it sells a million!"

Brian Tracy, author of No Excuses!: The Power of Self-Discipline

"A highly readable collection! *50 Success Classics* presents a smorgasbord of some of the best thinking on what success really means."

Ken Blanchard, co-author of The One Minute Manager® *and* Leading at a Higher Level

"I can't imagine anyone needing any other success book after reading *50 Success Classics*. It has every piece of wisdom you'll ever need to make your life extraordinary."

Cheryl Richardson, author of Take Time for Your Life

"I only wish this book had been available years ago—it could have saved me countless hours sifting through the dross by instead pointing me to the really inspirational works. Very highly recommended."

Jim Ewan, Vice-President of The Speakers Association

"If you want to read the core empowering message contained in the top 50 books on reaching success—get this book today!"

Zev Saftlas, author of Motivation That Works

This new and updated edition first published in 2017 by Nicholas Brealey Publishing
An imprint of John Murray Press
First edition published in 2003

An Hachette UK company

23 22 21 20 19 18 17   1 2 3 4 5 6 7 8 9 10

British Library Cataloguing-in-Publication Data
A catalogue record for this book is available from
the British Library and the Library of Congress.

ISBN 978-1-473-65835-6
eBook (UK) ISBN 978-1-857-88476-0
eBook (US) ISBN 978-1-473-64449-6

Printed and bound in the United States of America

John Murray Press policy is to use papers that are natural, renewable
and recyclable products and made from wood grown in sustainable forests.
The logging and manufacturing processes are expected to conform
to the environmental regulations of the country of origin.

Nicholas Brealey Publishing
John Murray Press
Carmelite House
50 Victoria Embankment
London EC4Y 0DZ
Tel: 020 3122 6000

Nicholas Brealey Publishing
Hachette Book Group
Market Place Center, 53 State Street
Boston, MA 02109, USA
Tel: (617) 263 1834

www.nicholasbrealey.com
www.butler-bowdon.com

50 Success Classics

Second Edition

Your shortcut to the most important ideas on motivation, achievement, and prosperity

Tom Butler-Bowdon

NICHOLAS BREALEY
PUBLISHING
London · Boston

Contents

CONTENTS

Preface

Second edition

*"In the last analysis, the essential thing is the life of the
individual. This alone makes history, here alone do the great
transformations take place, and the whole future, the whole
history of the world, ultimately springs as a gigantic summation
from these hidden sources in individuals."*

Carl Jung

5*0 Success Classics* was my second book, after *50 Self-Help
Classics*. The latter book contained a list of 50 extra books at
the end, many of which were not self-help as such but motivational titles that were gunning for the reader's worldly success. There
were enough classics in this area to warrant a book on its own, so I
set about writing one. First published in 2004, in the years since *50
Success Classics* has gone through many reprints and been translated
into 17 languages.

In the original edition I was keen to go back and assess the earliest
writings in the success genre, from Benjamin Franklin (*The Way to
Wealth*) to Orison Swett Marden (founder of *Success* magazine), and
from Horatio Alger, author of scores of entertaining and inspiring
poor-boy-made-good stories, to Russell Conwell, who preached his
famous *Acres of Diamonds* success parable to thousands of rapt audiences. The fields of success and motivation are historically American,
so I also enjoyed including commentaries on *The Art of Worldly
Wisdom*, consisting of brilliant aphorisms from seventeenth-century
Spanish priest Baltasar Gracian, and on ancient China's Sun Tzu and
the counterintuitive strategies of the *Art of War*.

Yet the heart of the success literature is for me the mid-twentieth-
century classics, from Napoleon Hill's enduring *Think and Grow
Rich* (1937) to Claude M. Bristol's powerful and fascinating *The
Magic of Believing* (1948) and David Schwartz's *The Magic of*

Thinking Big (1959). Schwartz's title entered the public idiom and just seeing the cover of the book can make you raise your sights. This period also spans the comforting, wise voice of Florence Scovel Shinn (*The Secret Door to Success*, 1940) and the cracking prosperity wisdom of Catherine Ponder (*The Dynamic Laws of Prosperity*, 1962).

My publisher Nicholas Brealey was quite right when he pointed out that I couldn't write a book about success without including the life stories of successful people, so we made space for the autobiographies of Andrew Carnegie, Henry Ford, Nelson Mandela, Sam Walton, and John Paul Getty, and profiles of Abraham Lincoln, Eleanor Roosevelt, Ernest Shackleton, and Warren Buffett, among others.

The 1980s and 1990s were a boom time for the success genre, with Anthony Robbins's *Unlimited Power* (1986), Stephen Covey's *The 7 Habits of Highly Effective People* (1989), and Spencer Johnson's *Who Moved My Cheese?* (1998), so I made sure the book gave them ample treatment. Though the odd example has dated, these are books that can still be read with great profit.

Times move on though, and as the genre continues to develop I am keen to recognize the fact with an updated, revised edition. One thing that has changed since the first edition is that strategies for success, which were once the preserve of folk wisdom, parents, bosses, and motivational speakers, have become the subject of mainstream academic research. Two great examples, which I include in this edition, are psychologist Angela Duckworth's investigation of the concept of "grit," which tells us much about what makes people successful irrespective of intelligence, grades, or even life circumstances, and organizational psychologist Adam Grant's research into the long-term benefits of being a "giver" in the workplace, which contradicts the idea that success comes from selfish ambition.

In this new edition I also wanted to go beyond tips, ideas, and advice to cover *theories* of success. In this respect, Malcolm Gladwell's *Outliers: The Story of Success* has been important in the way it goes beyond past explanations of the "self-made" person to offer a more well-rounded environmental and social view of how success happens. For the most part his book is convincing, yet I believe that he goes too far in reducing the role of human agency and free will. The fact that life is not just about good opportunities but having the guts or wisdom to seize them, despite the waves this can create, is really the essence of success. It is about not only making a contribution within the milieu in which we find ourselves, but acting to *change* that environment—and transforming ourselves in the process. McDonald's founder Ray Kroc and Apple's Steve Jobs are sterling examples of this, and as an antidote to the Gladwellian view of success I include commentaries on Kroc's *Grinding It Out* and Schlender and Tetzeli's insightful *Becoming Steve Jobs*. And as Gladwell makes much of the example of Bill Gates in his book, I thought it worthwhile to include a commentary on *Hard Drive*, a classic profile of Gates and the early years of Microsoft.

This edition also covers popular success writing of the last few years that has made an impact, including Gary Keller's *The One Thing*, which helps readers to see the power of focusing on the one act or activity we can do at any given moment to make a difference, and Darren Hardy's *The Compound Effect*, which reminds us that it is time and application, not inspiration, that are the reliable paths to success.

My hope is that the combination of psychological science and success philosophy, combined with close observation of how real people advance in real life, will result in a *discipline* of success. Such a conversion would not be dissimilar to the way that, for instance, management moved from being a collection of subjective epithets on how to organize people and production, into an objective discipline. This book is one early contribution toward that.

There are many ways to define success, but for me the simplest and best is "fulfillment of potential." While it is easy to get distracted by various external measures and trappings, what matters is whether we feel we are growing and learning to become everything we can be. Family, community, and institutions may shape our expectations, and circumstances can allow our abilities and interests to flower, but ultimately our journeys of aspiration and accomplishment are our own. You are likely to be the best judge of whether your promise is being fulfilled and this book aims to help you see what may be possible. When thinking about success it is hard to go past the truth of Carl Jung's view: the individual has power, usually much more than he or she imagines.

Tom Butler-Bowdon

Acknowledgments

Success never happens in a vacuum and that includes the writing of this book. My work would go nowhere without a great team who help with editorial direction, editing of the manuscript, sales, publicity, and language rights.

50 Success Classics was originally commissioned by Nicholas Brealey. The new edition took shape at my new publisher Hachette. I thank commissioning editor Holly Bennion, sales manager Ben Slight and editorial assistant Louise Richardson, the rights team headed by Joanna Kaliszewska, and designer Joanne Myler who came up with the great new cover. Thanks for your work championing the 50 Classics series, along with Hachette offices in the United States, Australia, the Far East, and India.

I salute all the writers and figures in the success field that have come before, from Orison Swett Marden to Stephen R. Covey, and am grateful for the ideas of the living authors included in the book. Together these contributions help move us towards a genuine discipline of success.

The book is dedicated to my mother, Marion Butler-Bowdon, who was a model of success.

Introduction

We desire success almost as much as we need to breathe. From the moment we are born we want to do more, get more, be more. While we may have a mental picture of success as striving hard toward perfection, in truth it is more natural. Success can be described as the courage to let out the potent dreams and potentialities already in us, simply to give them air. Most people don't do this because it seems dangerous, it is not routine. Yet those who have gone this way do see it simply as the normal path of life. It feels more like home, a place that should be everyone's experience.

Sometimes the urge for more is drummed out of us by upbringing or culture, so you may have felt compelled to lower your expectations and settle for a less extraordinary life. If, however, you have recently resurrected your desire to succeed, this book is for you.

Authentic achievement

My previous book, *50 Self-Help Classics*, was concerned with the search for authentic happiness and a sense of purpose. *50 Success Classics* is about authentic or meaningful *achievement*.

Only you will know whether you have achieved your aims in life. Some people spend their life climbing up a ladder, to paraphrase Joseph Campbell, only to find it was up against the wrong wall. This is why the term *authentic* is used: doing something or becoming something that expresses your full personality and abilities in the most noble way. Success is not an event or a result in isolation, but an expression of the best that is within you. The world provides endless possibilities for making it more efficient, more humane, more beautiful. It is up to you to find your niche.

Real achievement is not concerned with winning for the sake of it. As Timothy Gallwey puts it:

"Winning is overcoming obstacles to reach a goal, but the value in winning is only as great as the value of the goal reached."

1

INTRODUCTION

You need to make a distinction between a compulsion to succeed for the sake of winning and the desire for enduring achievements that will enrich your life and the lives of others. Authentic and lasting success utilizes the resources of the world to the greatest effect and with the minimum of waste.

Characteristics of successful people

What makes a person successful? What makes them motivated, prosperous, a great leader? These questions fired the writing of each book covered in this selection, and it is possible to draw out some common threads as answers. The following is only a brief and partial list, but it may whet your appetite to discover for yourself some of the principles of success.

Optimism

Optimism is power. This is a secret discovered by all who succeed against great odds. Nelson Mandela, Ernest Shackleton, Eleanor Roosevelt—all admitted that what got them through tough times was an ability to focus on the positive. They understood what Claude Bristol called "the magic of believing." Yet great leaders also have an unusual ability to face up to stark reality, so creating a single powerful attribute: tough-minded optimism.

Optimistic people tend to succeed not simply because they believe that everything will turn out right, but because the expectation of success makes them work harder. If you expect little, you will not be motivated even to try.

A definite aim, purpose, or vision

Success requires a concentration of effort. Most people disperse their energies over too many things and so fail to be outstanding in anything. In the words of Orison Swett Marden:

"The world does not demand that you be a lawyer, minister, doctor, farmer, scientist, or merchant; it does not dictate what you shall do, but it does require that you be a master in whatever you undertake."

So to be successful, you must have higher aims and goals and doggedly pursue their realization.

2

Willingness to work
Successful people are willing to engage in drudgery in the cause of something marvelous. The greater part of genius is the years of effort invested to solve a problem or find the perfect expression of an idea. With hard work you acquire knowledge about yourself that idleness never reveals.

A law of success is that, once first achieved, it can create a momentum that makes it easier to sustain. As the saying goes, "Nothing succeeds like success."

Discipline
Enduring success is built on discipline, an appreciation that you must give yourself orders and obey them. Like compound interest, this subject may be boring, but its results in the long term can be spectacular.

Great achievers know that while the universe is built by atoms, success is built by minutes; they are masters when it comes to their use of time.

An integrated mind
Successful people have a good relationship with their unconscious or subconscious mind. They trust their intuition, and because intuitions are usually right, they seem to enjoy more luck than others. They have discovered one of the great success secrets: When trusted to do so, the nonrational mind solves problems and creates solutions.

Prolific reading
Look into the habits of the successful and you will find that they are usually great readers. Many of the leaders and authors covered here attribute the turning point in their lives to picking up a certain book. If you can read about the accomplishments of those you admire, you cannot help but lift your own sights. Anthony Robbins remarked that "success leaves clues," and reading is one of the best means of absorbing such clues.

Curiosity and the capacity to learn are vital for achievement, thus the saying "leaders are readers." The person who seeks growth, Dale Carnegie said, "must soak and tan his mind constantly in the vats of literature."

Risk taking
The greater the risk, the greater the potential success. Nothing ventured, nothing gained. Be action oriented.

Realizing the power of expectation

Successful people expect the best and they generally get it, because expectations have a way of attracting to you their material equivalent.

Since your life corresponds pretty much to the expectations you have of it, the achiever will argue, why not think big instead of small?

Mastery

Advanced beings can turn any situation to their advantage. They are "masters of their souls, captains of their fate."

When other parties are involved, they will seek solutions in which gains are maximized for all. In the words of Catherine Ponder:

"You do not have to compromise in life, if you are willing to let go of the idea of compromise."

Well-roundedness

Achievements mean little if we are not a success *as a person*. The capacities to love, listen, and learn are vital for our own well-being, and without them it is difficult to have the fulfilling relationships that we need to both renew us and inspire achievement.

A quick tour of the literature

Below is an overview of titles covered in *50 Success Classics*, divided into four categories:

❖ Motivation
❖ Fulfilling your potential
❖ Prosperity
❖ Leadership

Motivation

Horatio Alger *Ragged Dick*
Frank Bettger *How I Raised Myself from Failure to Success in Selling*
Claude M. Bristol *The Magic of Believing*
Stephen R. Covey *The 7 Habits of Highly Effective People*
Les Giblin *How to Have Confidence and Power in Dealing with People*
Darren Hardy *The Compound Effect*

Gary Keller *The One Thing*
Orison Swett Marden *Pushing to the Front*
Anthony Robbins *Unlimited Power*
David J. Schwartz *The Magic of Thinking Big*
Florence Scovel Shinn *The Secret Door to Success*
Brian Tracy *Maximum Achievement*

When we think of success writing it is often the motivational classics that first come to mind, and the titles in this selection represent the historical development of the genre.

Horatio Alger and Orison Swett Marden grandfathered the modern success movement in the nineteenth century, Alger with his entertaining and instructional stories of poor boys made good and Marden with his encyclopedic treatment of success based on the lives of great people. Both prolific, these writers raised the sights of a couple of generations, but what may be surprising is how inspiring they still are today. If you are lukewarm about contemporary success writing, these older-style success books are a rich vein to tap. In the 1920s the books of Florence Scovel Shinn, extraordinary in the way they provide peace of mind in times of challenge, began to find eager readers.

After the Second World War, people naturally turned their thoughts to prosperity and "getting ahead." Millions had not had the opportunity of advanced education and had to pull themselves up by their bootstraps. They were inspired by titles such as Frank Bettger's *How I Raised Myself from Failure to Success in Selling* (1947), which with its timeless principles of selling is still widely read today. Published a year later, Claude Bristol's idiosyncratic meditation on "believing to succeed," *The Magic of Believing*, has also had amazing staying power. But perhaps the greatest success book of the postwar period, although not published until 1959, was Schwartz's *The Magic of Thinking Big*. Its references are mostly to corporate life in 1960s suburban America, but its universal theme that "the size of your success is measured by the size of your belief" quickly made it one of the landmarks in the motivational field.

Although Dale Carnegie's speaking classes had been running for some time, it was only in the 1970s and 1980s that success became its own industry, driven by seminars and bestsellers. Figures such as Zig Ziglar, Denis Waitley, Jim Rohn, Og Mandino, Tom Hopkins, and Brian Tracy became pillars of the motivational profession.

INTRODUCTION

At the end of the 1980s, Stephen Covey, who had studied 200 years of success literature for his doctorate, published *The 7 Habits of Highly Effective People*. Its character-based personal development in the style of a business book attracted a huge audience, and it could be said that Covey revived the success genre and gave it new gravitas. Meanwhile, a young Californian named Anthony Robbins was electrifying audiences with his rousing techniques of change. His first bestseller, *Unlimited Power*, borrowed from the emerging science of neuro-linguistic programming, and he remains the best-known of present-day gurus.

Finally, although their simple messages do not require a full commentary, mention should be made of the following works: Elbert Hubbard's famous *A Message to Garcia* (1899), a short account of an act of military heroism that inspires the reader to "get the job done no matter what"; and Earl Nightingale's *The Strangest Secret* (1956), one of the bestselling voice recordings in history, which alludes to one of the great laws of success. Success scholars should certainly consider adding both to their library.

Fulfilling your potential

Chin-Ning Chu *Thick Face, Black Heart*
Jim Collins *Good to Great*
Angela Duckworth *Grit*
W. Timothy Gallwey *The Inner Game of Tennis*
Malcolm Gladwell *Outliers*
Baltasar Gracian *The Art of Worldly Wisdom*
Adam Grant *Give and Take*
Earl G. Graves *How to Succeed in Business without Being White*
Muriel James & Dorothy Jongeward *Born to Win*
Spencer Johnson *Who Moved My Cheese?*
Cheryl Richardson *Take Time for Your Life*
Sun Tzu *The Art of War*
John Whitmore *Coaching for Performance*

You need to be motivated to achieve success, but staying successful requires uncommon wisdom. These books uncover some of the factors and ideas that can help you achieve your potential.

Spencer Johnson's *Who Moved My Cheese?* highlights the need to cope with change and to generate it if you are to remain at the cutting edge, while Jim Collins reminds you through his study of great companies why it is not enough to be merely excellent, you must be the best in your field.

Personal coaching is a relatively new phenomenon that promises dramatic increases in productivity and well-being. Covered here are two of the seminal works in the field, Timothy Gallwey's *Inner Game of Tennis* and John Whitmore's *Coaching for Performance*. There is another outstanding title about work/life balance from life planner Cheryl Richardson.

When published in 1992, Chin-Ning Chu's *Thick Face, Black Heart* shook up the conventional western wisdom on how to achieve, and should be read by any serious success scholar. Likewise, the ancient *Art of War*, which despite its title is a work of philosophy, can provide the reader with a valuable win/win mindset for accomplishing serious goals. Both titles are a welcome alternative to the familiar diet of western success advice.

Prosperity

George S. Clason *The Richest Man in Babylon*
Russell H. Conwell *Acres of Diamonds*
Benjamin Franklin *The Way to Wealth*
John Paul Getty *How to Be Rich*
Napoleon Hill *Think and Grow Rich*
Robert Kiyosaki *Rich Dad, Poor Dad*
David S. Landes *The Wealth and Poverty of Nations*
Catherine Ponder *The Dynamic Laws of Prosperity*
Thomas J. Stanley *The Millionaire Mind*
Wallace D. Wattles *The Science of Getting Rich*

Prosperity and wealth titles have always been an important part of success literature. Benjamin Franklin knew the power of money to motivate back in 1758, when *The Way to Wealth* was first published in one of his almanacs. With a strong Puritan influence, the book preached thrift, hard work, and the idea that "time is money."

Far more recently, in his sweeping *The Wealth and Poverty of Nations*, David Landes lists similar attributes among those nations that have done well. Some countries, like some people, are born luckier than others in terms of resources, but those that have built wealth through their own devices rise to the top. John Paul Getty, for instance, was the son of a well-off oil businessman, but, as his autobiography reveals, he parlayed these merely good circumstances into a massive empire that left an important philanthropic legacy.

Thomas Stanley's *The Millionaire Mind* is a fascinating look into the habits and attitudes of hundreds of wealthy individuals, most of whom are self-made. Stanley concludes that the ability to spot opportunities, more than formal education, is a fundamental ingredient of financial success. Robert Kiyosaki's *Rich Dad, Poor Dad* points out that the difference between being rich and poor often boils down to whether someone makes the effort to develop some financial intelligence. On this theme, still going strong after over 70 years is George Clason's *The Richest Man in Babylon*, which has taught millions of people how to build a fortune through "paying yourself first."

A more spiritual approach to financial success is expressed in the writings of Wallace Wattles and Catherine Ponder, who picture the world as an essentially abundant place that rewards those who appreciate that fact. Influenced by New Thought teachings, these authors provide a calmer, perhaps more enriching road to wealth focused on "manifesting your good."

In a class of its own is Napoleon Hill's *Think and Grow Rich*, arguably the greatest success manual. The product of 20 years of research and a condensation of the monumental *Law of Success*, this book was first published in Depression-era America, yet its focus on fabulous wealth continues to inspire today's entrepreneurs. The mix of spiritual and practical ideas and Hill's excited and well-honed prose makes it an irresistible package.

Leadership and achievement

Warren Bennis *On Becoming a Leader*
Kenneth Blanchard & Spencer Johnson *The One Minute Manager*
Edward Bok *The Americanization of Edward Bok*
Warren Buffett (by Roger Lowenstein) *Buffett*
Andrew Carnegie *The Autobiography of Andrew Carnegie*
Henry Ford *My Life and Work*
Bill Gates (by Wallace & Erickson) *Hard Drive*
Steve Jobs (by Schlender & Tetzeli) *Becoming Steve Jobs*
Ray Kroc *Grinding It Out*
Abraham Lincoln (by Donald T. Phillips) *Lincoln on Leadership*
Nelson Mandela *Long Walk to Freedom*
J. W. Marriott Jr. *The Spirit to Serve*
Eleanor Roosevelt (by Robin Gerber) *Leadership the Eleanor Roosevelt Way*

Ernest Shackleton (by Margot Morrell & Stephanie Capparell)
   Shackleton's Way
Sam Walton *Made in America*

Leadership writing traditionally discusses particular people only in order to illustrate a theory. While the list above does include *On Becoming a Leader*, a valuable work by a major leadership theorist, it is more interesting and perhaps more valuable to look at the lives of actual leaders.

From the world of industry, *The Autobiography of Andrew Carnegie* has become a classic of personal achievement, charting a rise from poor Scottish boy to steel magnate to model philanthropist. Ford's *My Life and Work* is a richly enjoyable account of a comparatively late starter who changed the world by being both a great innovator and a master of organization. Less well known is Edward Bok's Pulitzer Prize-winning autobiography, which charts the remarkable progress of a Dutch immigrant boy who became one of America's leading editors and opinion leaders.

Leaping forward to the end of the twentieth century, Roger Lowenstein's biography of Warren Buffett offers a superb insight into one of history's great investors. Engrossing titles by Sam Walton and Bill Marriott expand the list of great contemporary business leaders.

Books that focus on what we can learn from the leadership experience of well-known figures are Donald T. Phillips' *Lincoln on Leadership*; Margot Morrell and Stephanie Capparell's *Shackleton's Way*, telling the gripping tale of the Antarctic *Endurance* expedition and its lessons for life in the business world; and Robin Gerber's analysis of the inspiring leadership of Eleanor Roosevelt.

Last but far from least, a book mostly written while its author was in prison is *Long Walk to Freedom*, Nelson Mandela's often painful story of a life diverted into a struggle to transform a whole nation—on the way creating perhaps the most admired leader of our time.

Notes on the text

The list of classics in this selection is not definitive, but I hope it is representative of the genre. While all of the books have been bestsellers, the main criterion for their inclusion was their impact and renown, or whether they filled a niche in terms of a particular subject or person. The books on Shackleton, Lincoln and Eleanor Roosevelt, for instance, may not be the original classic works relating to their subject, but are standout works of a comparatively new genre that attempts to extract the leadership lessons from the lives of the famous.

The leaders discussed are not specific markers for your own success—it is generally not a good idea to compare yourself to other people—but their stories illustrate a "way" of success that anyone can apply.

Two final notes:

❖ With each commentary there is a box referring you to similar works. Most of these are found elsewhere in this book, but, because there is significant crossover between the self-help and success fields, you will sometimes be referred to titles that appeared in *50 Self-Help Classics* (50SHC).
❖ Most commentaries will contain separate information on each author. The exceptions are those that have already presented facts from the author's life within the main body of the commentary.

So, onward to the classics. I hope you find as many usable ideas in these works as I have. What is provided here is only a taste of the literature (the main ideas, context, and impact of each title), which sits within a tradition of criticism and review; I have not provided book summaries as such. Scholars of success will want to feast on the real thing, so don't hesitate to acquire those titles that inspire you.

Reader bonus

The new chapters in this revised edition required some commentaries from the first edition to be taken out. The receive these for free, please send an email to tombutlerbowdon@gmail.com with 'Success' in the email subject.

50 Success
Classics

1867

Ragged Dick

"But Dick was too sensible not to know that there was something more than money needed to win a respectable position in the world. He felt that he was very ignorant. Of reading and writing he knew only the rudiments, and that, with a slight acquaintance with arithmetic, was all he did know of books. Dick knew he must study hard, and he dreaded it. He looked upon learning as attended with greater difficulties than it really possesses. But Dick had good pluck. He meant to learn, nevertheless, and resolved to buy a book with his first spare earnings."

"'I hope, my lad,' Mr Whitney said, 'you will prosper and rise in the world. You know in this free country poverty is no bar to a man's advancement.'"

In a nutshell

Whatever you do, you will be more successful if you do it with honesty, fairness, and to the best of your ability.

In a similar vein
Andrew Carnegie *The Autobiography of Andrew Carnegie* (p. 56)
Russell H. Conwell *Acres of Diamonds* (p. 80)
Benjamin Franklin *The Way to Wealth* (p. 104)
Orison Swett Marden *Pushing to the Front* (p. 242)
Samuel Smiles *Self-Help* (50SHC)

CHAPTER 1

Horatio Alger

The New York City of the mid-nineteenth century was an awful place for many of its inhabitants. Areas such as Five Points (the setting for the movie *Gangs of New York*) were dangerous and filthy, filled with abandoned or neglected children. Many slept outside at night, and most wore badly fitting, ragged clothes. During the day they hawked matches, sold newspapers, shined shoes, or picked pockets in order to get money to eat. The authorities did little to alleviate the situation, and in one celebrated incident a street urchin found naked was represented in a court case by the Society for the Prevention of Cruelty to Animals.

Horatio Alger, the chronicler of this world to a public who may have preferred not to know that it existed, was not himself a New Yorker, having been brought up in middle-class comfort in Massachusetts with a private school education followed by Harvard (see Rychard Fink's introduction to the 1962 edition).

Though he had had some writing published, *Ragged Dick, or Street Life in New York with the Boot-Blacks* was his first bestseller, setting the template for scores of poor-boy-makes-good novels that had a massive influence on young Americans (Groucho Marx and Ernest Hemingway were among those said to have devoured Alger's work). Here we will look at the outline of the story and Alger's significant place in the success literature.

The story

At a time when Central Park was still "a rough tract of land" lined with workers' huts, there was a bootblack known as Ragged Dick. With his mother dead and his father gone to sea, Dick spends his days shining boots for businessmen, his evenings (if he has some spare coins) watching cheap plays at the Old Bowery theater, and his nights in doorways wrapped up in newspapers. If he's flush he will stay at the Newsboys Lodging House for six cents a night and buy a meal at a café.

After an unexpected windfall, Dick rents a squalid room that to him seems impossibly luxurious. In return for tutelage, he lets another boy, the once well-cared-for and well-read Henry Fosdick, share his room. This two-person self-improvement society is perfect for both. Dick gets an "edoocation" and Fosdick a place out of the cold. Though they must live through a series of adventures, the boys find a way to succeed.

The tale is a page-turner, and the reader delights in Dick's joy at such simple things as a new suit of clothes, opening a bank account, and eating a piece of steak. As Alger makes clear, Dick, who by the end of the short book has become Dick Hunter Esq., is very likeable. He has pluck and wit to balance his earnest strivings to be "spectable" and, despite first-hand experience of the best rogues and swindlers the city has to offer, is a perennial optimist.

Following are some of Horatio Alger's lessons of success as learned by the young Dick.

Make your own luck

Dick's big break comes on a ferry crossing into Brooklyn. He sees a child fall over the side into the water and wastes no time before jumping in, somehow managing to pull the child to safety. The panicked father, who could not swim, is amazed to have his child alive and promises Dick any reward. Later, the man offers Dick a job in a counting house at $10 a week, many times his current earnings. A great stroke of luck? Not really, for Dick's selflessness was the cause of this good fortune, and his diligence in self-education every night meant that he could be hired without the slightest whiff of charity.

Luck happens to those who greatly increase the chances of its occurrence.

Whatever you do, do it to your utmost

Life seems to require that, even if we don't like what we are doing, we must do it to the best of our ability before we can move on to the next thing. Ragged Dick is only a bootblack, but he uses his "profession" to save money, meet a higher class of people, and generally better himself.

Become a reader

Dick meets the son of a wealthy man and shows him around the city for a day. Later, the boy's father tells Dick that "in this country poverty is no bar to achievement" and relates his own rise from apprentice printer to successful businessman. He notes that there was one thing he took away from the printing office "which I value more than money." When Dick asks what this was, the man replies:

"A taste for reading and study. During my leisure hours I improved myself by study, and acquired a large part of the knowledge which I now possess. Indeed, it was one of my books that first put me on the track of the invention, which I afterwards made. So you see, my lad, that my studious habits paid me in money, as well as in another way."

Be a saver, but be generous

When Dick receives an unexpected sum of $5, he opens a bank account. The amount that builds gives him a great source of security and pride, as he no longer has to live hand-to-mouth. While delighted that he is now a "capitalist," he is quick to help a friend in need. Fosdick, the boy with whom he shares his lodgings, wants to get an office job instead of shining shoes, so Dick purchases a suit of proper clothes for him. On another occasion he helps out a buddy whose mother is ill.

Never cheat, steal, or lie

Though temptations to do otherwise are often great, Dick has a personal code that "stealin' is mean." His sense of honor and fair play, which appears naive to "sophisticated" types, finally proves to be the source of his success. For someone who lives from day to day, his belief in "doing right" is remarkably farsighted. The character Mr. Whitney tells Dick: "Remember that your future position depends mainly upon yourself, and that it will be high or low as you choose to make it."

Honesty, which seems "old-fashioned" to the fast crowd, is the basis of all enduring success, since it brings with it knowledge of the self.

Don't drink or smoke

Long before medical evidence of its harm was available, Alger was calling smoking a "filthy habit" that gave no dignity to the smoker. Drinking, of course, was even worse. It was the enemy of frugality because you could blow your week's savings in a night on the grog, and the enemy of industry because the inevitable hangovers affected your working day.

The temperance movement seems archaic today, but scores of lives would be better without even a moderate intake of alcohol. To Alger it sapped drive, pickled the independent mind, and eroded good character.

Final comments

Despite being rattling good yarns that really can inspire, the common view of Horatio Alger's books is that they are quaint historical pieces with a simplistic message about striving and getting ahead. Yet success *can* be simple if you have the basic elements of personal character and aspiration, with some luck thrown in.

As Rychard Fink has noted, when *Ragged Dick* was written Herbert Spencer's writings on "the survival of the fittest" had some influence in America. Yet Alger's idea of success included a strong element of social responsibility or stewardship. You might make money, but ultimately it should be put back into society, as Andrew Carnegie did by funding public libraries. With his willingness to give to those in need, Alger makes Dick an example of compassionate capitalism.

Many of the villains in his books are rich boys who never had to make any effort to improve their character. Alger's main point is that we should strive for success not just to get a fortune, but to gain tenacity, discipline, frugality, and optimism—qualities that cannot be bought.

Horatio Alger

Born in 1832 in Revere, Massachusetts, at 14 Alger was sent to boarding school by his father, a strict Unitarian minister, followed by entry to Harvard University at 16. He enjoyed his time there, coming tenth in his class of 62 and becoming proficient in Greek, Latin, French, and Italian.

Forbidden to marry his college sweetheart, the heartbroken Alger defied his father by stating his intention to become a writer. He agreed to go to divinity school, but just before graduation escaped to Paris with some friends and enjoyed its liberal atmosphere. Back in America he was ordained and became a church minister in Massachusetts, but left for New York at the suggestion of William T. Adams, editor of Student and Schoolmate. *The weekly installments of* Ragged Dick *in this children's monthly were wildly popular, and a hardback version became a bestseller. Alger was the toast of New York and sat on various boards and committees for improving the lot of street children. He lived for a number of years at the Newsboys Lodging House and died in 1899.*

Alger's other books (over 100) include Strive and Succeed; Struggling Upward; Bound to Rise; *and* From Canal Boy to President, *about the life of assassinated President James Garfield.*

On Becoming a Leader

"Leaders have no interest in proving themselves, but an abiding interest in expressing themselves."

"What is true for leaders is, for better or worse, true for each of us. Only when we know what we're made of and what we want to make of it can we begin our lives—and we must do it despite an unwitting conspiracy of people and events against us."

In a nutshell

True leadership arises in the full expression of a person's unique potential.

In a similar vein

Abraham Lincoln (by Donald T. Phillips) *Lincoln on Leadership* (p. 230)

Eleanor Roosevelt (by Robin Gerber) *Leadership the Eleanor Roosevelt Way* (p. 272)

Ernest Shackleton (by Margot Morrell & Stephanie Capparell) *Shackleton's Way* (p. 290)

CHAPTER 2

Warren Bennis

Bennis was a major figure in the academic study of leadership, but also popularized the subject through bestsellers. In 1985 he co-authored *Leaders*, based on observation and interviews with 90 of America's leaders, ranging from astronaut Neil Armstrong to McDonald's founder Ray Kroc. The book's conclusion was that leadership is more crucial than we know, yet can be learned by anyone.

While *Leaders* is a business classic that analyzes the nature of leadership, *On Becoming a Leader* is more personal, asking how you can make leadership a habit of existence while around you the world becomes a blur of change. The second book is the product of more in-depth dialogue with a smaller number of people, 28 in all, including film director Sydney Pollack, feminist author Betty Friedan, and musician and A&M Records founder Herb Alpert.

What is a leader?

On Becoming a Leader provides many fine insights. Perhaps the key one, and the theme of the book, is this: True leaders are not interested in proving themselves, they want above all to be able to *express themselves fully*. Proving oneself implies a limited or static view of the self, whereas leaders, by continually seeking their fullest expression, must be willing to engage in periodic reinvention. For Bennis's leaders, life is not a competition but a flowering. Structured education and society often get in the way of leadership: "What we need to know gets lost in what we are told we should know." Real learning is the process of remembering what is important to you, and becoming a leader is therefore the act of becoming more and more your true self.

Leadership is an engagement with life itself, because it demands that your unique vision be accomplished, and that usually involves a whole life. When people protest that they can't lead, or don't want to lead,

19

they are usually thinking of management and giving speeches. But leadership is as varied as people, and the main question is not whether you will be burdened, but how you are challenged to escape mediocrity and conformity and really lead yourself.

According to Bennis, becoming a leader involves:

❖ Continuous learning and never-dying curiosity.
❖ A compelling vision: leaders first define their reality (what they believe is possible), then set about "managing their dream."
❖ Developing the ability to communicate that vision and inspire others to follow it.
❖ Tolerating uncertainty and taking on risk: a degree of daring.
❖ Personal integrity: self-knowledge, candor, maturity, welcoming criticism.
❖ Being a one-off, an original: "Leaders learn from others, but are not made by others."
❖ Reinvention: To create new things sometimes involves recreating yourself. You may be influenced by your genes and environment, but leaders take all their influences and create something unique.
❖ Taking time off to think and reflect, which brings answers and produces resolutions.
❖ Passion for the promises of life: a belief in the best, for yourself and others.
❖ Seeing success in small, everyday increments and joys, not waiting years for the Big Success to arrive.
❖ Using the context of your life rather than surrendering to it.

What does the last point mean? Bennis believes that late twentieth-century business life was mostly about managing rather than leading, with people and organizations focusing on small matters and short-term results. His message is: Stop being a product of your context, of your particular place and time.

You can see your context as the backdrop for your particular genius to develop, or you can let it enslave your mind. In many ways the path of a "driven" person is an easy one, since it does not require much thought. The leader's path is consciously taken, may be more challenging, but involves infinitely greater potential and satisfaction, not to mention better health. To lead, you have to make a declaration of independence against the estimation of others, the culture, the age. You have to decide to live in the world, but outside existing conceptions of it. Leaders do not merely do well by the terms of their culture, they create new contexts, new things, new ways of doing and being.

Some examples

Personal integrity, a compelling vision, and the ability to enjoy risk and uncertainty define leadership. Bennis uses the example of television writer/producer Norman Lear, who revolutionized US television by making shows such as *All in the Family* and *Cagney and Lacey*. For the first time, TV shows reflected real American people rather than cowboys, private eyes, and caricatured families. Lear saw a world that was waiting to be expressed, and expressed it. Not only did his shows break the mold, they were successful year after year.

In his assessment of American presidents, Bennis sees Johnson, Nixon, and Carter as driven men who projected their personal histories onto the country they ruled. Roosevelt, Truman, Eisenhower, and Kennedy, on the other hand, had the gift of personal reinvention and lived in the present to reshape the United States' future. Lincoln was perhaps the greatest president because he focused on what at the time seemed only remote possibilities: ending slavery and preserving the Union. His fits of deep personal depression were nothing put next to those mighty causes.

A world of leaders

Bennis's conviction is that we are in dire need of leaders. He wrote *On Becoming a Leader* when American economic leadership was being seriously challenged—we forget now, but in the late 1980s it did seem for a while that Japan was surpassing the US in production, wealth, and innovation.

Maybe the United States listened to Bennis and other leadership theorists, for the American economic resurgence was characterized by obsession with innovation and quality and the realization that firms get ahead by helping their employees reach their full potential. It took someone of the stature of Bennis to highlight the link between self-knowledge and business success, but this is now becoming accepted. The new type of leader is not satisfied with doing a job or running a company, but is compelled to find an outlet for their personal vision of the world. Now, the only way many companies can attract and keep the best people is by offering them more than merely money or prestige—they offer them the chance to make history. Consider, for instance, the motto of internet retailer Amazon.com: "Work hard, play hard, change the world."

Final comments

Bennis has probably done as much as anyone to shatter the myth of leaders as heroes, born not made. Above all, leadership is a choice and involves leading ourselves first.

We live in a democracy of leadership, in which everyone can lead in some way. As more people understand what leadership means and are taught to achieve their potential, it might be expected that competition will increase to ridiculous levels. However, competition is the result of everyone striving to win at the same thing, whereas personal visions are unique. To become a leader is to claim the power and assurance that come from being a one-off.

This commentary is based on the original edition of *On Becoming a Leader*. There is a new, updated and expanded edition that you may prefer to acquire.

Warren Bennis

Born in 1925, Bennis was the youngest infantry commander among the Allies to fight in Europe in the Second World War. Back in the United States at Antioch College, he found a mentor in Douglas McGregor, the ground-breaking management theorist, and was also influenced by Abraham Maslow. After studying group dynamics, he wrote about new organizational forms and coined the term "adhocracies" as the opposite of bureaucracies. He gained his PhD at Massachusetts Institute of Technology (MIT).

Bennis was president of the University of Cincinnati and executive vice-president at the State University of New York, and was on the faculty of MIT's Sloan School of Management, Harvard and Boston Universities, INSEAD, and the Indian Institute of Management in Calcutta. His other books include Organizing Genius *(1997),* Co-Leaders: The Power of Great Partnerships *(1999), the autobiographical* An Invented Life *(1993), and* Geeks and Geezers: How Era, Values, and Defining Moments Shape Leaders *(2002) with Robert J. Thomas. On* Becoming a Leader *has been published in 13 languages.*

Bennis was founder and Distinguished Professor of the Leadership Institute, Marshall School of Business, at the University of Southern California in Los Angeles. He died in 2014.

1947

How I Raised Myself from Failure to Success in Selling

"*I hope you will overlook and forgive me for using the personal pronoun 'I.' If there is anything in this book that sounds as though I am bragging about myself, I didn't intend it that way. Whatever bragging I've done was meant for what these ideas did for me, and what they will do for anyone who will apply them.*"

"*Talk about walking a mile to get a cigarette—when I started out to sell, I would gladly have walked from Chicago to New York to get a copy of this book, if it had been available.*" Dale Carnegie

In a nutshell

Every successful person knows how to sell what they offer. Enthusiasm and organization are the basic elements in selling.

In a similar vein

Dale Carnegie *How to Win Friends and Influence People* (50SHC)
Benjamin Franklin *Autobiography* (50SHC)
Les Giblin *How to Have Confidence and Power in Dealing with People* (p. 130)

CHAPTER 3

Frank Bettger

Frank Bettger had once been something of a baseball star, playing for the St. Louis Cardinals. An injury to his arm ended his sporting career, and with no particular skills he wound up cycling the streets of his home town, Philadelphia, collecting installments for a furniture company.

After two miserable years at this he tried his hand at selling life insurance and fared even worse, deciding that he was "never cut out to be a salesman." *How I Raised Myself from Failure to Success in Selling* is the account of what he learned to enable his transformation from struggler to the star of his firm. Though ostensibly about how to sell, it is in fact a classic personal success guide; though giving amusing insights into the life of an insurance agent in the 1930s and 1940s, it is in many ways quite timeless.

Confidence through speaking well

To overcome a desperate fear that clearly held him back from making sales, at the age of 29 Bettger inquired at his local YMCA whether there were any kind of speaking courses. Told that one was being taught at that very moment, he was introduced to the course leader, Dale Carnegie.

So began a long friendship with the author of *How to Win Friends and Influence People*. Bettger learned how to rid himself of the terror of saying a few words in front of an audience, and in time his problem became how to *stop* talking. Later, Carnegie would invite the young salesman to join him on a speaking tour across America.

Bettger had discovered the paradox that the best way of developing self-confidence quickly is through speaking to groups: once you have done it a few times, approaching someone important does not seem so horrifying, and thus you are able to enlarge your circle of contacts. As Bettger puts it, speaking publicly "gets you out of your shell." The ability to speak in front of other people heightens your general level of courage and is a cornerstone of a successful life. Do you know any achievers who are too frightened to speak in public?

The greatest selling secret

Bettger became so successful that he could have retired at age 40. What was it that vaulted him to the top rank of sales professionals? It may seem obvious, but if you don't have it you get nowhere: enthusiasm.

Once dropped from a baseball team for being too laid-back, Bettger decided he would prove a point to his former coach by doubling his level of enthusiasm in his new team. It worked so well that newspaper reporters nicknamed him "Pep" Bettger and he became the top player in the team, his income increasing by 700 percent. Later, when he wasn't doing well in insurance, he decided to apply the same level of enthusiasm to his work, again witnessing an astonishing difference in results.

The conventional wisdom is that you get enthusiastic when you achieve success at something—the feeling comes after the act. But Bettger discovered the truth of Harvard philosopher William James's observation that the act can create the feeling; that is, you can become excited about something simply by *acting* excited about it. Later in his book, Bettger presages today's cognitive science by suggesting that the practice of regular smiling creates a feeling of happiness and goodwill. Test this out for yourself, and remember that enthusiasm alone can transform your life and your earnings.

Getting organized

True to the maxim that success comes to those who simply show up, Bettger made a commitment to making at least four or five sales calls a day. In addition, he kept records of all his sales appointments.

With this disciplined approach he was able to review the results as a whole, working out the average amount of dollars that he made for each call, whether or not he sold a policy. Dedication to doing the legwork made his task of earning commissions seem much easier.

Another important factor in Bettger's success was that every Saturday morning he sat down and planned the week ahead. This not only made him more relaxed when he went into work on Monday morning; because he had thought about the people he was going to see, it also made the job more interesting. He notes that the famous effectiveness of the International Business Machines (IBM) sales force was due to their use of weekly planning sheets so that every hour of every day was accounted for. He concludes:

"Selling is the easiest job in the world if you work it hard—but the hardest job in the world if you try to work it easy."

Success may look fully formed when we behold it with the perspective of years, but those who have achieved it know that it arrived because they made every hour and every moment productive. We are often so fearful of whether or not we can achieve something that we cannot see that if it is broken down into smaller, daily steps it becomes much easier.

Organization and discipline are more important to success than are great amounts of energy. Bettger mentions one of the bestselling authors of his day, Mary Roberts Rinehart, who started writing novels late at night in response to family debt and the need to care for three children and a sick mother. When he met her, Bettger asked Mrs. Rinehart if the punishing schedule had worn her down. She replied, "On the contrary, my life took on a new zest." The unlikely fact that doing more gives you greater energy to achieve more is a timeless success secret.

Great ideas

Bettger's book is a compendium of everything he learned as a salesman. In its 35 chapters there are hundreds of great ideas. Here is a sample:

❖ The best salespeople do not "sell"—they find out what the other person wants, then help them find the best way to get it.
❖ When trying to sell something, talk mostly in terms of "you" and "your." This lets the other person know you are thinking mainly of their interests.
❖ Forget witty conversation—be a good listener instead.

- Invest in increasing your knowledge of your own industry. You can't afford not to.
- In contacts with clients, praise your competitors. It shows clients you are even-handed and won't hide anything from them.
- Use "witnesses" (i.e., satisfied clients) to sell your product to new clients. Then you can say, "Don't listen to me, listen to them."
- Use a magic question to keep yourself in the presence of a potential client. Ask them: "How did you happen to get into this business, Mr/s...?" The history of a person's career is always of the highest interest to them.
- Prepare for an audience of one as you would an audience of a hundred; i.e., prepare properly for every meeting.
- Be like Abraham Lincoln with his famous two-minute Gettysburg Address, and remember that the book of Genesis is only 442 words long—become a "master of brevity."
- When you greet someone, say their name.
- For 30 days, smile frequently and watch it transform your life.
- Don't ever engage another person in argument. Instead, ask questions whose answers are likely to bring them round to your viewpoint.

Final comments

To succeed as a salesperson, you require a level of self-discipline, determination, and courage that will serve you well in any other field. Though not the most respected of professions, sales has been the path out of mediocrity for many who had a truncated education. In Bettger's case, the psychological hurdles he had to overcome freed him from a sense of limitation.

Before you disregard this book, thinking "I am not a salesperson and have no interest in sales," perhaps you should widen your definition of selling. We all have to persuade others to buy into our ideas or agree to our suggestions, and you can do this with much greater effectiveness if you are willing to study a few easy techniques. Bettger's work is a great place to start.

Frank Bettger

Bettger was born in 1888 and grew up in Philadelphia. His father died without any life insurance, leaving Mrs. Bettger to cope with five small children, three of whom died in epidemics. Bettger's hero was another native of the city, Benjamin Franklin.

Bettger was persuaded to write How I Raised Myself from Failure to Success in Selling *by Dale Carnegie, who had earlier invited him to join a speaking tour of the United States to Junior Chambers of Commerce. Bettger's other bestseller was* How I Multiplied My Income and Happiness in Selling. *He died in 1981.*

1981

The One Minute Manager

"Everyone who worked with him felt secure. No one felt manipulated or threatened because everyone knew right from the start what he was doing and why."

"As he sat at his desk thinking, the new One Minute Manager realized what a fortunate individual he was. He had given himself the gift of getting greater results in less time."

In a nutshell

Clarity about goals saves a huge amount of energy that can be deployed productively in other areas.

In a similar vein
Warren Buffett (by Roger Lowenstein) *Buffett* (p. 48)
Ernest Shackleton (by Margot Morrell & Stephanie Capparell)
Shackleton's Way (p. 290)

CHAPTER 4

Kenneth Blanchard & Spencer Johnson

A young man searches all over the world for an example of a great manager. He wants to work for one and learn how to become one. But most of the workplaces he has seen do not provide any great inspiration. He meets hard-nosed managers who get things done but whom the staff do not much like, and pleasant managers who love their staff but do not pay enough attention to the bottom line.

Could there exist a manager who combines the best qualities of each? The young man hears about someone who seems to fit the bill, ironically in a nearby town. To his surprise, this manager agrees to see him right away and talk about how he manages his people. So begins the allegory of the one minute manager.

You are to be forgiven for being wary of a method of managing people that purports to take only one minute. Can it really work? Sales figures for *The One Minute Manager* suggest that:

❖ managers dream of spending less time on staff motivation and problems and will grasp at anything that suggests a way out; or
❖ there must actually be something to this style of management.

The way of the one minute manager
There are three secrets of or elements to one minute management:

❖ Agree on goals (no more than half a dozen) with staff members. Make sure that each goal is written on a separate piece of paper. This is "one minute goal setting." From this point on staff know exactly what is expected of them and will rarely come to the boss with problems—they know they are hired to solve them.
❖ Staff should reread the goals frequently as a means of ensuring that

31

performance matches expectations. They should also provide detailed records of progress for the managers. This is not so that the manager can breathe down their neck, but so that he or she can "catch them doing something right." This allows for "one minute praisings," which provide immediate and specific positive feedback on actions undertaken.

❖ If a person has the skills to do something right and it is not done right, the manager will provide a "one minute reprimand." This stern rebuke is of the action or behavior, not the person, and the manager will express consternation that it is not up to the staff member's usual high standards. After the reprimand, the manager reminds the person how much they are valued.

The second part of the story attempts to explain why one minute management works.

One minute goal setting works because "the number one motivator of people is feedback on results." We like to know how we are doing, and if we are doing well we feel good. The one minute manager has a plaque on the wall reading: "Take a minute—Look at your goals— Look at your performance—See if your behavior matches your goals." Simple but effective.

One minute praisings are also effective for motivational reasons. It is rare to find someone who knows how to do everything well from day one; you have to put some effort into training. "So the key to training someone to do a new task is, in the beginning, to catch them doing something approximately right until they can eventually learn to do it exactly right." Discipline doesn't work with people who are not secure in what they are doing, only encouragement does. Praise gets them moving in the right direction. Though it need take up very little time, praise is the fuel that can drive a whole enterprise.

One minute reprimands work because they are the fairest form of feedback for correcting below-par performance. Since goals have been set and expectations are so transparent, the person will usually see when the reprimand is fair. The manager is respected because he or she has "spoken the simple truth." As the reprimand is quick and focused on specific action (not the person themselves), there is less bad feeling; when the encounter is over it always ends on a good note and can be soon forgotten or even made light of.

Managing to lead

The very simplicity of one minute management will deem it suspect in some people's eyes, yet it is little more than the application of efficiency to workplace interpersonal relations. The philosophy of "taking very little time to get big results" comes from a nuts-and-bolts appreciation of human nature.

The story's one minute manager admits that management cannot always be performed in a minute. It is more a symbol of the idea that managing people can be much less complicated than we think. There's no need for endless sessions to discuss objectives and problems. Some time needs to be invested in establishing goals, but after that the contact between boss and subordinate can be minimal.

Consider some successful examples of this way of managing people. Investor Warren Buffett (see p. 48) employs business managers whose small number of objectives are so clear that he rarely needs to meet with them. They get on with the job and send him periodic reports. Antarctic explorer Sir Ernest Shackleton (see p. 290) was so respected by his crew members because they knew exactly what was expected of them; if they were reprimanded for anything, there was always a clear and rational reason. More recently, GE boss Jack Welch explained his management style as "kicks and hugs," which were meted out or given only according to strictly outlined, previously mapped-out goals. This did not create a climate of fear—if people did not measure up they could blame no one but themselves.

One further thought: The ideas in *The One Minute Manager* are not merely for the work environment, they can apply to many areas of personal relations. To be "tough and nice," for instance, should be the goal of any parent.

Final comments

After decades of weighty tomes on management science and organizational behavior, *The One Minute Manager* came as a breath of fresh air for managers. It may seem simplistic, but it was firmly based on the latest findings in behavioral psychology. Blanchard and Johnson's genius was to dress up this knowledge in the more attractive form of a story.

With today's flatter organizational structures and emphasis on working in teams, it could be argued that the book is less relevant. It seems to express an older, hierarchical, and sexist model of the workplace, "the boss and his subordinates." What is more, today we enjoy making the distinction between mere managers and leaders—while the latter inspires, the former simply manages.

Yet true leaders, as the examples above suggest, will find it difficult to get anywhere without some basic people management skills. They will seek to create relaxed workplaces in which people have all the time they need to pursue important goals. This sense of relaxed purpose arises because everyone knows exactly what their role is; there exist both transparency and clarity of purpose.

Kenneth Blanchard & Spencer Johnson

Blanchard has a BA from Cornell University in government and philosophy, an MA from Colgate University in sociology and counseling, and a PhD in administration and management. He is the co-author of a widely used academic text, Management of Organizational Behavior: Utilizing Human Resources, *and was professor of leadership and organizational behavior at the University of Massachusetts, Amherst. He also runs his own corporate training and development company.*

Johnson's biography is on page 194.

Over 750,000 copies of The One Minute Manager *are in print. Its success has spawned spinoff titles including* Leadership and the One Minute Manager, The One Minute Sales Person, *and* Putting the One Minute Manager to Work.

The Americanization of Edward Bok

"Eventually, then, Bok learned that the path that led to success was wide open: the competition was negligible. There was no jostling. In fact, travel on it was just a trifle lonely. One's fellow-travelers were excellent company, but they were few! It was one of Edward Bok's greatest surprises, but it was also one of his greatest stimulants. To go where others could not go, or were loath to go, where at least they were not, had a twang that savored of the freshest kind of adventure."

In a nutshell

Work for your own success, but ensure that your achievements lift up the wider community.

In a similar vein

Horatio Alger *Ragged Dick* (p. 12)
Andrew Carnegie *The Autobiography of Andrew Carnegie* (p. 56)
Orison Swett Marden *Pushing to the Front* (p. 242)
David J. Schwartz *The Magic of Thinking Big* (p. 278)

CHAPTER 5

Edward Bok

Edward Bok was six years old when, in 1870, his family arrived in
New York. They had been reasonably well off in the Netherlands
but had lost money in bad investments and now sought a new start.
Their story is typical of the millions who came to America at this time,
and the fact that one of their two sons rose to some prominence is not
particularly remarkable. What is more unusual is that the young Bok,
despite being thrown into school without a word of English, came to be
one of the opinion leaders of his day and a master of the language.

*The Americanization of Edward Bok: The Autobiography of a
Dutch Boy Fifty Years After* won the Pulitzer Prize for autobiography.
It is not the standard "how I made it" narration, but a reflection on the
migrant experience and to what extent the new country shapes a person. It is a success classic because, writing in the third person, the
author objectively attempts to identify what enabled him to become an
achiever. As with many migrants, he found that necessity was a great
motivator. If you have read your fill of the lives of the great industrialists, you may find Bok's account of his rise in the world of words
refreshing.

Making a mark

Mr. and Mrs. Bok did not adjust easily to their adopted country. Having
previously had servants, Bok's mother could not cope with the burdens
of running a household on a limited budget, and for a time his father
was unable to find good work. To earn money for the family, Edward's
first sign of entrepreneurial zeal was selling water and lemonade to people in Brooklyn's streetcars, and he later began cleaning the windows of
a bakery and serving behind the counter for 50 cents a week.

He began his journalistic career by going to parties and writing
accounts of them to sell to newspapers. At 13, Bok left school for a job

as an office boy at the Western Union Telegraph Company, where his father had obtained work as a translator. Concerned at his lack of education and eager to emulate the successful men of the day, he saved up for a biographical encyclopedia. This purchase became the basis of a letter-writing campaign to gain the autographs of famous people. Amazingly, he received correspondence from many of the powerbrokers of his time, including Presidents Garfield and Hayes and Generals Ulysses S. Grant and William Sherman. The letters became celebrated in the newspapers and consequently Bok met some of his correspondents, including Hayes, Grant, and Mrs. Abraham Lincoln. He also extended his autograph collecting to literary America, and in time met and struck up friendships with Oliver Wendell Holmes and Henry Longfellow.

This wealth of biographical information found an outlet when Bok noticed that the picture cards of famous people that came with packets of cigarettes were blank on the flip side. He contacted the maker and proposed providing information on the life of each person on the rear of the card. The maker agreed, and Bok co-opted journalists to help him write hundreds of potted biographies. The little business, more importantly, allowed him to develop his editorial skills.

Toward success

When Bok was 18 his father died, and to make extra money to support his mother he began producing theater programs and selling the advertising for them. His first chance at editing came with the production of the society organ *The Brooklyn Magazine*, which grew into a significant success.

By day he was still working at Western Union, which had been taken over by the famous financier Jay Gould. As part of his self-education Bok had learned stenography and began taking down Gould's correspondence. He also began playing the stock market by following Gould's moves. Though he did well this was not Bok's calling, and, resisting the advice of the great man, he left to pursue his dream of a career in publishing, with the publisher Henry Holt.

In his spare time, Bok saw an opportunity to create a syndicated press to sell weekly columns to newspapers across the country. The first columnist was the esteemed preacher and writer Henry Ward Beecher, who became a great mentor and friend. Then Bok expanded his business to create a "Woman's Page," syndicated to many newspapers. Bok also wrote a weekly "literary letter from New York," sold to 30 newspapers.

In his day job, Bok had now started working at the publisher Scribner's Sons, selling advertising in *Scribner's Magazine* and meeting the likes of Robert Louis Stevenson and Andrew Carnegie.

Whatever it takes

In a chapter titled "The Chances for Success," Bok addresses the conventional wisdom that the business world is a thrusting jungle, where everyone jostles for advantage and favoritism is rife. To his surprise he found that merit was the basis of getting ahead, and that instead of competition, hard work and determination won the day.

Most of the young men he had worked with could only complain about how little they were getting paid for the little work they did. Come five o'clock, it never ceased to amaze him how crowded were the elevators in his building! His own philosophy was that if he was given a piece of work to do, he would finish it that day even if it meant staying late.

In a society driven by merit, he was confounded by how little merit there was:

"He looked at the top, and instead of finding it overcrowded, he was surprised at the few who had reached there; the top fairly begged for more to climb its heights."

Because he had adopted the philosophy that a person "got in this world about what he worked for," he had achieved more by the age of 25 than many do in a whole career.

The work of a lifetime

In 1889, against the advice of his Scribner's colleagues and his mother, Bok took up the position of editor of the *Ladies' Home Journal*, a magazine with a circulation of around 440,000. He accepted the job not because he knew anything about women, but because he could see massive potential in women's readership and publications.

Bok wanted a more informal, uplifting feel to the magazine combined with high-quality articles. Given interesting new departments, hundreds of thousands of letters flooded into the magazine. Most were replied to if not printed, because Bok saw the enterprise not simply as a journal but as a "great clearing-house of information." This attention to the reader made subscribers incredibly loyal, and before too long circulation had doubled. After the new sections were in place, Bok raised the tone to include serialization of the novels of some of the finest writers of the day, such as Rudyard Kipling, and nonfiction by the likes of Jane Addams and Helen Keller. Totally new for a women's magazine was the inclusion of writing by US presidents, first Benjamin Harrison and later Bok's friend Theodore Roosevelt.

Why was the magazine so successful? Bok suggests that, in addition to catering to popular appeal with the usual sections on fashion and so on, he aimed, as he put it, "constantly to widen its scope and gradually lift its standard." He did not simply "give the people what they wanted"—the conventional recipe for commercial success—but tried to lead them to a slightly higher plane:

"The American public always wants something a little better than it asks for, and the successful man, in catering to it, is he who follows this golden rule."

In the longer term this created greater satisfaction and loyalty.

Bok used the *Ladies' Home Journal* not merely to improve the minds of its readers but also their living environments. Appalled at the low standard of houses for those who could not afford architects, he partnered with an architect to print ready-made home designs that could be used by builders. This was a great success, and the esteemed architect Stanford White stated that Edward Bok, an editor, had "more completely influenced American domestic architecture for the better than any man in his generation." Bok went further by printing color pictures of model house interiors to inspire the home decorator, and included in the magazine handsome prints of famous paintings that were put up in millions of homes. At about this time the *Journal* started selling a million copies an issue, a milestone for magazine publishing.

Bok also had the magazine raise public awareness of the growth of billboard advertising, cruelty to birds killed for their feathers, and the drying-up of Niagara Falls for the sake of power companies. He and owner Cyrus Curtis refused advertising from patent medicine manufacturers because there was no scientific basis for their concoctions, which helped build the case for US food and drug legislation. After editorials calling for greater sex education to prevent venereal disease, 75,000 readers canceled their subscriptions, but Curtis and Bok, believing it was the right thing to do, persevered.

After doing what he could to help the American war effort, Bok retired as editor of the *Journal*, 30 years after he had begun. On his departure it was selling two million copies an issue, "the most valuable piece of magazine property in the world." It had become a national institution.

In his retirement Bok wrote more books and became a philanthropist, his endowments including the $100,000 American Peace Award; the Harvard Advertising Awards; the Philadelphia Commission; and a chair in literature at Princeton University. The *Ladies' Home Journal* is still sold today.

Final comments

A Dutch immigrant with little education who came to influence a generation through the most prosaic of vehicles, a women's magazine, Bok's is a classic story of migrant success. The closest modern comparison for his achievements would be Oprah Winfrey, who at a time when daytime television was going further downmarket decided to promote books and reading. Like Bok, Winfrey did not give people what they wanted, but instead something a little higher. Such people do not just sell products, they are respected and loved.

Bok's early retirement (he was only 56) surprised everybody, but he was determined not to go to the grave working. He felt that this was the fate of too many American men, and he admitted that he remained "European" in putting quality of life first. While he considered that the greatest thing about his adopted country was its idealism, its failing was favoring quantity over quality. While one part of him always kept an eye on success through numbers, knowledge and art were what inspired him.

Bok's grandmother had given him the simple advice to "make the world a better and more beautiful place because you have been in it." With his emphasis on increasing the American people's store of knowledge and culture, Edward Bok certainly met his grandmother's measure of success.

The Magic of Believing

"Gradually I discovered that there is a golden thread that runs through all the teachings and makes them work for those who sincerely accept and apply them, and that thread can be named in a single word— belief. It is this same element or factor, belief, which causes people to be cured by mental healing, enables others to climb the ladder of success, and gets phenomenal results for all those who accept it."

"Undoubtedly, we become what we envisage."

In a nutshell

Every great thing starts with a thought and is powered into realization by a belief.

In a similar vein

James Allen *As a Man Thinketh* (50SHC)
Joseph Murphy *The Power of Your Subconscious Mind* (50SHC)
David J. Schwartz *The Magic of Thinking Big* (p. 278)
Florence Scovel Shinn *The Secret Door to Success* (p. 284)
Wallace D. Wattles *The Science of Getting Rich* (p. 320)

CHAPTER 6

Claude M. Bristol

C laude Bristol was a hard-headed journalist for several years, including stints as a police reporter and as church editor of a large city newspaper. In this post he met people from every denomination and sect and later read hundreds of books on psychology, religion, science, metaphysics, and ancient magic. Gradually, Bristol began to see the "golden thread" that runs through all religions and esoteric teachings: that belief itself has amazing powers.

Having spent years thinking about the power of thought, he had assumed that others knew something about it too. He was wrong. Strangely, he found that most people go through life without realizing the effect that strong belief can have on reaching their goals: they leave their desires vague and so they get vague outcomes.

When Bristol was a soldier in the First World War, there was a period in which he had no pay and couldn't even afford cigarettes. He made up his mind that when he got back to civilian life he would have a lot of money. In his mind this was a decision, not a wish. Barely a day had passed after his arrival back home when he was contacted by a banker who had seen a story about him in the local newspaper. He was offered a job, and though he started on a small salary, he constantly kept before him "a mental picture of wealth." In quiet moments or while on the telephone, he doodled dollar signs on bits of paper that crossed his desk. This definiteness of belief, he suggests, more than anything else paved the way for a highly successful career in investment banking and business.

Bristol had learned the truth of philosopher William James's statement, "Belief creates its verification in fact." Just as fearful thoughts set you up to experience the situation you can't stop thinking about (the biblical Job said, "What I feared most had come upon me"), optimistic thoughts and expecting the best inevitably form favorable circumstances.

Belief and destiny

Napoleon Bonaparte was given a star sapphire when he was a boy, accompanied by the prophecy that it would bring him good fortune and make him emperor of France. Napoleon accepted this as fact, and therefore to him at least his rise was inevitable.

Bristol tells the intriguing story of Opal Whiteley, the daughter of an Oregon logger, who believed herself to be the daughter of Henri d'Orleans, a Bourbon with a claim to be king of France. There was a diary purportedly written by her describing her royal parents, although most believed it to be a hoax. Nevertheless, when Opal was in her twenties she was spotted in India, being pulled along regally in a carriage belonging to the Maharaja of Udaipur; it turned out that she was living in the royal household. An Oregon newspaper man who had known Opal in her childhood remarked: "It was uncanny, almost supernatural, the manner in which circumstances suited themselves to her plans."

This brings us to *The Magic of Believing*'s strongest message: that virtually anything can be yours, and you can be anything, if you are able to develop a "knowing" about it that you don't ever need to question. Bristol says of Napoleon and Alexander the Great, "They became supermen because they had supernormal beliefs." Your belief about yourself and your place in the world is arguably the main determinant of success.

The subconscious servant

If you can understand the relationship between the conscious and the subconscious mind, Bristol says, you will get to the core of belief power. The subconscious continually works to express our deepest beliefs and desires. It is a faithful servant that renews, guides, and inspires, but to get the most from it requires great respect for and faith in what it can do. Because the subconscious operates in terms of imagery, it is vital that we feed it mental pictures of what we desire. It can then go to work in living up to the image placed before it, by giving us intuitions about what to do, where to go, who to meet.

Somehow the subconscious is connected to all other parts of our mind, and through the law of radiation and attraction it can attract events and people to us that will assist in making our dreams reality. However, it will only find ways to make the image real if that image is clear and convincing; hence the importance of the mental pictures of success that we feed it. The force of belief cannot really work in our favor until the belief becomes literally part of us, settled in the sub-conscious mind as a fact.

Projecting thought and belief

Bristol notes that all the great electrical scientists—Edison, Steinmetz, Tesla, Marconi—were interested in telepathy. It was not ridiculous to them that thoughts could move through the air, that thoughts alone could affect events if, like a good radio signal, they were strong and clear.

Bristol borrows from New Thought principles to suggest that there is intelligence in everything that exists in the universe and that we are all linked by a kind of universal mind. Jung had a similar idea with his "collective unconscious." The force of your belief represents a trans-mitter to the universe that enters the minds of other people and even inanimate objects. The more powerful your broadcast, the more likely that the world will pick it up and react accordingly. It was not impossi-ble, said astronomer Sir Arthur Eddington, that the physical laws of the universe could be made subject to human thought, and modern quan-tum physics does not rule it out either.

Bristol's explanation is that a person with a strong belief will exist at a certain vibration that seeks its like in the form of matter. Thus he reaches the startling conclusion that we do not achieve deeply felt goals by action alone, but are helped along depending on the quality and intensity of our belief that they will be achieved.

The power of suggestion

Charms, talismans, and good-luck pieces of any kind do not on their own bring good fortune, Bristol comments, it is the belief in their effi-cacy that is powerful. Why do people chant, repeat affirmations, bang drums, or count beads? Repetition is another way to implant a sugges-tion in our minds, the "white magic" that enables us to turn a wish into an expectation. By ritualizing it, by giving it structure, the idea changes from being a mere wish to being imminent reality. We give thanks for what is or is about to be. The "terrific force of thought repe-tition," Bristol says, first overcomes reason by acting on our emotions and then penetrates into the subconscious, where it is only a matter of time before the thought is enacted. This, of course, is the principle behind successful advertising and propaganda.

Bristol includes a warning about misuse of the mental technology associated with strong belief and suggestion: It is a power to be used constructively, not to achieve dominance. His book is dedicated to "independent thinkers of all times" who wish to use belief for creative, life-affirming ends. He talks a great deal about the power of belief to heal physically, for instance.

Final comments

Maxwell Maltz, author of *Psycho-Cybernetics* (see 50SHC), said, "The law of mind is the law of belief itself." By this he meant that belief, more than anything else, is what makes us tick. It is the great shaper of who we are.

Think of some of the great belief systems in history: Buddhism, Christianity, Islam, communism, capitalism. For good or ill, these systems of thought became beliefs that have shaped our world. Are the beliefs you have about yourself strong enough to change *your* world?

The Magic of Believing is repetitive and rambling, its references are dated, concrete tips for employing its ideas are few, and you may find yourself saying, "Get to the point." Some readers will also be turned off by the unscientific nature of the book, which contains little bibliographic foundation. Yet the strange thing about it is that it can reveal more on second, third, or fourth readings. Bristol knew, after all, that ancient esoteric writings were often purposely opaque to shield their secrets from the uninitiated or those who might abuse them. You may not love reading this book, but merely having it around could serve as a valuable reminder of the power of belief.

It may also be difficult to stomach some of the "mind stuff," as the author calls it. He himself was skeptical, but then realized that we all summon the magic of believing when we desperately want something to come into being. The pianist Liberace was said to have turned his life around after reading *The Magic of Believing*. And in a chapter called "Women and the science of belief," Bristol evokes the names of Marie Curie, Mary Baker Eddy (founder of Christian Science), Florence Nightingale, Harriet Beecher Stowe (author of *Uncle Tom's Cabin*), and actress Angela Lansbury as examples of people who drew on the power of believing to achieve great things. Lansbury told an interviewer, "When you've learned how to draw on your subconscious powers, there's really no limit to what you can accomplish." The mental powers of these women were tremendous, yet we can develop their same "belief intelligence" for our own lives.

Claude M. Bristol

Born in 1891, Bristol served as a soldier in the First World War in France and Germany. He worked on the army newspaper Stars and Stripes *until 1919.*

The Magic of Believing was written, Bristol says, for ex-servicemen and -women who would have to adjust to civilian life and try to prosper. It was published when he was in his fifties and followed the success of a booklet entitled TNT: It Rocks the Earth.

Bristol was a popular speaker to clubs, business organizations, and salespeople. He died in 1951.

Buffett

"On Wall Street his homespun manner made him a cult figure. Where finance was so forbiddingly complex, Buffett could explain it like a general-store clerk discussing the weather."

"Buffett's genius was largely a genius of character—of patience, discipline and rationality. These were common enough virtues, but they were rare in the heat of financial passions, and indispensable to anyone who would test his mettle in the stock market. In this sense, Buffett's character and career unfolded as a sort of public tutorial on investing and on American business. Buffett was aware of his role from the very beginning, and he nurtured a curious habit of chronicling his escapades even as he lived them."

In a nutshell

Genuinely successful investment requires both courage and character.

In a similar vein
George S. Clason *The Richest Man in Babylon* (p. 68)
Benjamin Franklin *The Way to Wealth* (p. 104)
John Paul Getty *How to Be Rich* (p. 124)
Robert Kiyosaki *Rich Dad, Poor Dad* (p. 208)

CHAPTER 7

Roger Lowenstein

Currently the fourth wealthiest person in the world, Warren Buffett is also arguably the greatest investor in history. In six decades, he has parlayed a stake of less than $100,000 into $73 billion. Shares in his company Berkshire Hathaway are now trading at over $262,000 *each*, and Buffett himself has hundreds of thousands of them—none of which he has ever sold.

His investing strategies have been written about extensively, but what broad lessons for success can we draw from the man himself? Lowenstein's biography *Buffett: The Making of an American Capitalist* was, prior to Alice Schroeder's, the first serious full-length portrait, and it is from this richly enjoyable book that we glean the following.

The seeds of a fortune

Omaha, Nebraska, was wilderness until the 1850s, but grew into a town once Abraham Lincoln designated it the eastern terminal of the Union Pacific Railroad. Boiling in summer and freezing in winter, it had a reputation as a cultural wasteland.

The Buffetts had been in Omaha for over a century when Warren Buffett was born in 1930, into modest circumstances. Buffett's father, Howard, had wanted to be a journalist but worked in a bank, which retrenched him in the Depression. The family had so little money that Warren's mother often skipped her dinner to give her husband a full portion. This period of lack apparently had a big effect on Warren. The second of three children and the only son, he was obsessed with numbers and facts and confessed very early on his desire to be rich. A favorite boyhood book was *One Thousand Ways to Make $1000*.

Howard Buffett eventually ran a successful stock brokerage and also achieved a surprise election to Congress in 1942 as a Republican. Young Warren hated living in Washington, but took pleasure in building up paper routes that, while he was still a teenager, were bringing in $175 a week (a regular adult wage); the $6,000 he saved was the foundation of his fortune.

He did well in school, coming 16th out of 374, and attended the Wharton School of Finance at the University of Pennsylvania. He applied to Harvard for further study, but was turned down. This proved to be a great blessing in disguise, because his second choice, Columbia, was the academic home of Benjamin Graham, the genius pioneer of stock market analysis.

Entering the fray

Until Graham, stock picking had basically been gambling, but the professor gave it a methodology that the young Buffett instantly "got." As Lowenstein puts it: "Investing without Graham would be like communism without Marx—the discipline would scarcely exist." Graham's method was the opposite of speculation: he looked for the underlying value of a stock and for discrepancies between this value and the stock price. If you bought a stock very cheaply, it could be virtually free of risk. The emphasis on research, analysis, and looking only to the facts of a business suited Buffett's personality perfectly; he could work alone.

Although Buffett's father warned him against entering the stock market, he started working in his father's brokerage. He also took a Dale Carnegie seminar in public speaking and at age 21 was giving a night course at the University of Omaha on investment principles—to fortysomething professionals. Later he went to work for Graham's investment fund in New York, but knew that he wanted to work for himself, with his own fund, and went back to Omaha.

Begun with his own capital and that of local Omahans, by the end of the third year Buffett's fledgling fund had doubled in value; after five years, when the Dow stock market index had risen 74 percent, the fund had increased by a remarkable 251 percent.

Before he was 35, Buffett was managing $22 million and had a personal net worth of $4 million. In the 1960s this was rich. Yet his life hardly changed at all. He continued to live in the same unimpressive house he had bought in the 1950s for $31,500, and asked his wife, Susie, to buy a better car than their VW because "it looked bad when he picked up visitors at the airport." His drab office accommodation was on the same street where he lived, and he worked in total secrecy.

Investing style

A large part of Buffett's success came from the fact that he did not think like the crowd. The key to being a good investor was to recognize the value of things when "everyone" knew that they weren't worth much. He never worried if the market price of a stock he had bought experienced a big drop, because it was obvious to him that the fundamentals would see it rise again.

Indeed, as the 1980s boom got under way, the shares that Buffett had bought dirt cheap during the Nixon years of stagflation began to rise. By 1983 he had entered the *Forbes* list of richest Americans and his "value investing" had begun to attract a great deal of attention. In an off-the-cuff talk, he said:

"I will tell you the secret of getting rich on Wall Street. [Pause] *Close the doors. You try to be greedy when others are fearful and you try to be very fearful when others are greedy."*

This contrarian approach took guts, but Buffett was unwilling to go the easier but less ethical route of unfriendly takeovers, greenmailing (holding firms to ransom by buying up their stock), or dealing in junk bonds. A good example is his acquisition of a portion of the *Washington Post*, the paper that had uncovered the Watergate scandal. The stock was selling as if the company was worth $100 million, but its assets were worth four times that. The political side of it appealed to Buffett, and he made a lifelong friendship in its president, Katharine Graham. In terms of return, Berkshire's initial $10 million investment in this company became $205 million at the time Lowenstein was writing, and in 2003 the stake was worth $1.3 billion.

Such a jump in value is not uncommon for one of Buffett's companies. As an investor he is a purist in his belief that the state of the economy or political worries should never affect your decisions about whether to buy a stock. Forecasting, he feels, is a waste of time—his job is to analyze a *company*, not an economy. When judging a company, Buffett cares less about its growth prospects or even size of profit; what he focuses on is the *return on investment*, or percentage profit on each dollar invested. "I'd rather have a $10 million business making 15 percent than a $100 million business making 5 percent," Buffett has said. "I have other places I can put the money."

Buffett is a risk taker in the sense that he has been willing to bet a quarter of Berkshire Hathaway on one stock, but not a gambler because he looks only for "sure-fire things." He imagines the stock market being like having a lifetime punch card on which you're only allowed 20 holes. With such a restricted choice, you would make sure that the stocks you did invest in were right.

What is most radical about Buffett is that once he chooses a stock, he hangs on to it. Selling a stock you have held for a long time, he says, is "like dumping your wife when she gets old." In short, he highlights the difference between the true investor and the trader. As Lowenstein puts it:

"Buffett had always craved, and had always felt enriched by, continuity: to work with the same people, to own the same stocks, to be in the same businesses. Hanging on was a metaphor for his life."

Some of his larger stakes have included See's Candy, the media companies Capital Cities and ABC, Disney, Gillette, Wells Fargo, Coca-Cola, Salomon Brothers, insurer GEICO, and reinsurer General Re. Notice that none of these is a technology stock. When the dot-com boom got into full swing, Buffett was accused of being "past it" because he never invested in technology companies. It was thought that Berkshire would be badly affected by only investing in "old-economy" stocks. Buffett protested that "he had never seen an electron" and stuck to the same investing formula he had always employed. His investing approach has now, of course, been validated.

Personal traits

In contrast to mutual fund supremos like Peter Lynch, Lowenstein observes, Buffett seems like something from another era. He has no computer in his office ("I am a computer," he once told an interviewer) or even a calculator, and he spends most of his time reading (annual reports, newspapers) or talking with business partners and old friends. His "one concession to modernity," Lowenstein notes, is a private jet dubbed *Indefensible*. Buffett acquired it only because he got tired of people asking him for stock tips when he was flying economy on commercial flights.

His favorite food is the cheeseburger, and he is famous for guzzling Cherry Cokes. Lowenstein says that Buffett's focus is so great that he either doesn't notice or doesn't have time for things that we normally associate with a well-rounded person. On a trip to Paris he wasn't the least interested in sightseeing, and he stays at his beachfront home in Laguna Beach in California for weeks on end without going near the water. He is continually amazed by the magic of compounding interest, and when his wife spent $15,000 on refurnishing their house, Buffett complained to a golfing partner, "Do you know how much that is if you compound it over twenty years?"

When his wife, Susie, decided to move to San Francisco to pursue her singing career, Buffett was devastated, but they never divorced, still went on vacations together, and she accompanied him to important gatherings. His girlfriend, Astrid Menks, who became his wife after Susie died in 2004, apparently functioned in this unusual situation as if it were totally normal. Buffett's great dislike is change, and as with the companies he invests in, the people around him are "for keeps."

His three children, now adults, remember him up in his study with greenback wallpaper ("the temple"), always reading. The rest of the family seem to have excused him from most normal fatherly activities, but he encourages his children to do what they love rather than chasing money. The chapter on the younger Buffetts' relationship with their famous father is fascinating reading.

Citizen Buffett

For a self-made billionaire, Buffett is unusually liberal. He quit the Omaha Rotary Club (of which his father had been president) because he thought it racist and elitist, and he also boycotted a local country club because it denied membership to Jews. Living in a predominantly white neighborhood, his household was also unusual in 1960s America in that he and Susie often entertained black Americans.

Lowenstein writes: "Unlike his isolationist and antigovernment father, Warren recognized a *need* for government." He does not rail against regulation and privately thinks that taxes for the rich should be *raised*. He feels that the energy people put into paying less tax diverts them from their real jobs in life. In one of his famous annual letters to investors, he wrote that the goal of investment is not to pay the least money to the government, but to come away with "the largest after-tax rate of compound." Knowing that you have to pay tax should make you more careful in the investments you make.

When Buffett is asked what needs to be done to reform the welfare system, he prefers to talk about "welfare for the rich." He dislikes stock options for executives because they are overgenerous at the expense of the shareholder. Many CEOs, with their hugely inflated compensation packages, are "wards of the corporate state"—not true capitalists, he feels, but bureaucrats. Buffett also warned of corporate excesses a couple of years before Enron and other supposed corporate giants fell.

Final comments

Although it needs updating to take account of Buffett's moves over the last 20 years, why is Lowenstein's portrait of the great investor still so enjoyable? If you know nothing about investment, the book can educate you while telling a compelling story of one of the great minds of our time, and this commentary can only provide the skeleton of that story. Get the book for the details.

Buffett is interesting because the way he lives and works is more akin to the style of an artist or philosopher: Berkshire Hathaway is his "canvas" and his relationship with his partners he sees as a sacred trust. Those who have invested with him tend to keep their shares for decades and consider themselves members of a "privileged tribe," Lowenstein notes.

Benjamin Graham said that one of the three important elements of a successful investor was "firmness of character." Buffett has this in spades, because his style of investment has required him to stick to his convictions. As Lowenstein correctly notes, Buffett is so attractive because his value investing goes hand in hand with ideas like loyalty, integrity, and keeping things for a long time. These seem out of step with our era, yet they prove their worth in their results.

Buffett has pledged to give away the bulk of his fortune and most of it is being given to the Bill and Melinda Gates Foundation. The disbursement will be the largest charitable donation in history. Gates and Buffett are long-term friends.

Roger Lowenstein

While himself the owner of Berkshire Hathaway stock, Lowenstein did not interview Buffett for the book, talking only with Buffett family, friends, and business associates. A former Wall Street Journal *reporter, Lowenstein is a director of the Sequoia Fund, set up in 1970 by Warren Buffett's friend Bill Ruane.*

His other best-known book is When Genius Failed, *on the rise and fall of the mutual fund Long-Term Capital Management.*

The Autobiography of Andrew Carnegie

"*No kind action is ever lost. Even to this day I occasionally meet men who I had forgotten, who recall some trifling attention I have been able to pay them, especially when in charge at Washington of government railways and telegraphs during the Civil War, when I could pass people within the lines—a father helped to reach a wounded or sick son at the front, or enabled to bring home his remains, or some similar service. I am indebted to these trifles for some of the happiest attentions and the most pleasing incidents of my life.*"

"*My advice to young men would be not only to concentrate their whole time and attention on the one business in life in which they engage, but to put every dollar of their capital into it . . . As for myself my decision was taken early. I would concentrate upon the manufacture of iron and steel and be master in that.*"

In a nutshell

Be voracious in your learning and ensure that others benefit from your intellectual and monetary wealth.

In a similar vein
Henry Ford *My Life and Work* (p. 98)
Benjamin Franklin *Autobiography* (50SHC)
John Paul Getty *How to Be Rich* (p. 124)

CHAPTER 8

Andrew Carnegie

Andrew Carnegie's grandfather had been the first to establish a small lending library in Carnegie's native Dunfermline, Scotland, at a time when there were no public libraries. As humble linen weavers his family was far from well off, but the love and respect for book knowledge made a permanent mark on young Andrew. Later, when he was rich, libraries were the obvious choice for his largesse and received massive endowments.

Though not very well educated himself, Carnegie appreciated the value of an open mind. Like Benjamin Franklin, he knew that "leaders are readers" and that wealth is created from deeper knowledge and better thinking. When his first donated library came to be built, he was asked for his coat of arms to put above the entrance. He didn't have one. Instead, he asked for a plaque portraying the sun and its rays and the words "Let there be light."

The Carnegie story in brief

Born in 1835, Carnegie enjoyed his childhood in the bosom of an extended family. His father moved the family to the United States when he was in his early teens, but Carnegie's accent and love of all things Scottish never left him.

In Pittsburgh he obtained employment as a telegraphist and a railway clerk and made his way up through the Pennsylvania Railroad Company. When the Civil War erupted, he was asked to take charge of US government railways and telegraphs, which he did with distinction. He was a Republican and opposed slavery, and this was his great opportunity to serve the cause.

In addition to his huge capacity for work and a way with people, Carnegie chose his vocation well. America's railroad system was in rapid expansion, and he comments that "a manufacturing concern such as ours could scarcely develop fast enough for the wants of the American people."

After selling the largest iron and steel works in the United States, he became the richest person in the world. He spent his retirement years at his beloved Skibo Castle in Scotland, and died in Lenox, Massachusetts, in 1919.

His will left over $100 million for building public libraries throughout the US and Britain and provided large gifts to universities. The peace-loving Carnegie was saddened by the outbreak of the First World War and also endowed institutions that would promote peace and research the causes of war.

Carnegie's tips for work and life success

Invest in yourself
Carnegie disliked speculation in stocks. He thought it a much better investment to choose an industry, learn everything about it, and invest in your own business:

"I believe the true road to preeminent success in any line is to make yourself master in that line. I have no faith in the policy of scattering one's resources, and in my experience I have rarely if ever met a man who achieved prominence in money-making . . . who was interested in many concerns."

This is the power of focus, of sacrificing what you might gain by broadening in order to gain a smaller but well-defined market.

...but spread the risk
Because of his great success at so young an age, Carnegie developed the reputation of being fearless and reckless in business. This image, he says, could not have been further from the truth. In fact, he never risked his own capital or that of his partners to any great degree: "When I did big things, some large corporation like the Pennsylvania Railroad Company was behind me and the responsible party."

You don't have to risk everything to think and act big. Carnegie's lesson is to get another party to carry the risk and use its reputation to assist your enterprise.

Success comes from openness and treating people well

Carnegie sought to create transparency in the management of all his industrial plants. He kept them very well ordered and clean and welcomed government inspectors. He always sought good relations with his labor force and generally gave employees what they wanted, within reason. The famous Homestead plant strike in which several men died occurred while he was away in Scotland, and it is unlikely that it would have happened if he had been there.

He made many of his staff rich. Plant manager Charles Schwab was the first person in American to be paid $1 million a year. In Napoleon Hill's *Think and Grow Rich*, Hill notes that this huge sum was not for Schwab's technical expertise but for his superb ability to motivate. Like all great successes, Carnegie was a student of human nature and knew that effectively channeling a work force's energies was the mark of a true leader. He noted: "I did not understand steam machinery, but I tried to understand that much more complicated mechanism—man."

Be master of your mood

"A sunny disposition is worth more than fortune. Young people should know that it can be cultivated; that the mind like the body can be moved from the shade into sunshine."

Read those three lines again. Carnegie's simple statement encapsulates hundreds of self-help and success books.

Public speaking is just speaking

Carnegie had two rules for speaking:

1 Talk *to* people, not *at* them.
2 Be yourself, don't try to be an "orator."

Remember Carnegie's advice and you won't have to take any expensive courses. It should be added that in order to "be yourself" you have to have spent time working out who you are and what you stand for. Oration suggests stating the world as you would like it to be. Speaking comes from the heart, which is always true.

Enlarge your circle

Carnegie's friends included Judge Mellon, Matthew Arnold, James Blaine, William Gladstone, President Harrison, Mark Twain, and Herbert Spencer. These relationships were not cultivated so that he could name-drop, but so that he could learn directly from their unique knowledge and experience. Always seek out interesting people.

Seek knowledge and value, not money alone

One evening in 1868, aged 33, Carnegie wrote a memorandum to himself while living at the St. Nicholas Hotel, New York. He began the memo with "Thirty three and an income of $50,000 per annum!" and then stated that he could organize his business affairs so as to bring in the same sum annually, while spending the surplus on "benevolent purposes." Getting more philosophical, he wrote of his intention to retire at 35 and henceforth devote his life to reading and study. Of course he did no such thing, but in these words you have the seeds of his later philanthropy. Knowledge gained from reading and study represented real value; a good life was one that truly opened the mind. Money alone was worthless.

Travel to broaden your mind

Carnegie loved travel, particularly when it had an element of adventure, and urged others to see more of the world. His book *An American Four-in-Hand in Britain* chronicled a journey on horse and cart the length of the country. In his travels he tried to learn deeply about the cultures he encountered, for example while in China he read Confucius and in India the thoughts of Buddha and Zoroaster. Such respect for all religions was characteristic of Carnegie's open-mindedness and also of his belief that seeing new places gives people a greater appreciation of the whole.

Final comments

In its modest tone, the book reminds the reader of Benjamin Franklin's autobiography, and like Franklin's it amazes in the story of what a person from very average beginnings can achieve in one lifetime. You almost tire of the detail on those who helped him and became his mentors, and although single-minded, a driven and at times ruthless man, Carnegie was always eager to repay favors and share his success. He speaks with great fondness of his childhood and was devastated when his mother and brother, both of whom had been instrumental in his success, died of typhoid fever, but his late and happy marriage gave him a fresh lease on life.

Carnegie's massive endowment of libraries was one of history's great acts, and his name is now more closely identified with the money he gave away than the money he made. His story suggests that the amassing of wealth by a single individual, if that person has high motives, is one of the best ways to change the world for the better.

1992

Thick Face, Black Heart

"One of the results of reading this book will be the shattering of your traditional concepts of ruthlessness. Thick Face, Black Heart is not about ruthlessness. You will learn that by adapting and adopting a form of non-destructive ruthlessness, you will gain the freedom necessary to achieve effective execution of your life's tasks."

"The first superficial exposure to Thick Face, Black Heart is often shocking and repellent because it can serve the criminal as easily as the saint."

In a nutshell

Reclaim the "killer instinct" as a natural part of who you are.

In a similar vein
Baltasar Gracian *The Art of Worldly Wisdom* (p. 144)
Thomas J. Stanley *The Millionaire Mind* (p. 296)
Sun Tzu *The Art of War* (p. 308)

CHAPTER 9

Chin-Ning Chu

I n 1949, as Mao's communist army closed in on Shanghai, a family boarded what was to be the last commercial flight out of China. Chin-Ning Chu, only three years old, had been born into a world of affluence, but when she and her family landed in Taiwan they would have to start all over again.

In her early twenties she moved again, this time to the United States. Two books accompanied her: Sun Tzu's famous *The Art of War* and a more obscure tome by Lee Zhong Wu, *Thick Black Theory*. There was something in this latter book that Chu knew was important. Published in 1911, she describes it as a "frank discussion of the uses of ruthlessness and hypocrisy" that was such a challenge to the powerful that it was quickly banned. The book would become an important source for Chin-Ning Chu's unique philosophy of life and business, expressed in *Thick Face, Black Heart: The Asian Path to Thriving, Winning and Succeeding.*

Thick face

What does the "thick face" part of the title mean? Chu simply combined the Asian concept of face (i.e., saving face) and the western concept of a thick skin to make "thick face," meaning a self-image that allows us to brush off criticism. She observes that if you are willing to have people not like you, you will go far.

Chu notes that "the world has a tendency to accept our own judgment of ourselves." If you exude self-confidence, people will naturally want to let you succeed. Self-doubt creates a perception of incompetence. The example given is of Colonel Oliver North and the Iran-Contra affair. Because he never doubted that his actions were those of a patriot and not a criminal, the public and the courts eventually believed him. "A man less convinced of his own righteousness would have been

63

severely punished for his crimes and ostracized by the public."

What you believe about yourself, the world will believe about you.

Black heart

While the concept of thick face relates to how others see you, the idea of black heart is about achieving your ends.

The black-hearted person may seem as if they lack compassion; however, compassion can be shortsighted. If a boss cannot bring himself to make a few employees redundant, Chu says, he may witness the collapse of the whole business. Sometimes, to keep to your goals and achieve a result that is better overall, you have to be perceived as "bad."

Appreciate that everyone has a killer instinct, and that sometimes we must draw on it. There is a direct correlation, Chu writes, between willingness to use your killer instinct and your success in life.

There are degrees of "thick face, black heartedness." Some will do anything to achieve a result, not caring about the effect on others. This is the black heart of con men and the wicked, who eventually understand that most of their failures are due to their own character defects. The higher level of black heart is reached when you are not driven by your shortcomings or emotions, taking action that is driven by your true spirit.

"Contrary to common understanding, a good man's actions are not always gentle. They may be ruthless, cold and dispassionate."

Chu notes that the best surgeons are those who concentrate on the task at hand, minimizing pain for the patient. They are cruel to be kind. This is the "way of the warrior."

Darkness and light

Acknowledge that all human beings are a combination of darkness and light. The universe is full of opposites requiring an "other" to exist. To have the necessary drive to live life to the full, you must appreciate and utilize all aspects of your character. If you like to present yourself as sugar-coated, you will lose out on any opportunities that may require you to seem sour or hardened.

If you are a naturally negative thinker, make the most of it and don't try to adopt false positivity. Don't fall into the trap, Chu says, of thinking that you must change yourself before you will have success. You can succeed just the way you are.

The problem with "virtue" is that it can lead to stern or even violent righteousness. If someone considers themselves virtuous, they have laid the ground for a witch-hunt of people they consider to be lacking in virtue. The thick face, black heart practitioner knows that virtue is a construct; what matters is whether a person has the courage to express their full personality in their life and their work.

Deception without deceit

In the West people have drummed into them the concepts of good and evil, black and white. But the reality, which most Asian people accept, is that there are shades of gray.

You need to learn that you can be good at the art of deception without being deceitful. You must also appreciate that sometimes, to achieve something great and worthy, it is difficult not to bring an element of deception into your actions.

The book highlights Abraham Lincoln (see also p. 230), who in his slow ascent to power followed the majority opinion about segregation and slavery. He knew that if he had not, he would not have gained power. However, with a solid electoral victory behind him he made the famous Gettysburg Address, proclaiming that "all men are created equal."

Dharma

The word *dharma* comes from Sanskrit and means "to support, uphold and nourish." It is the natural law that makes the world hang together in its divine coherence.

At the personal level, *dharma* is the duty that is yours to fulfill in your lifetime. You cannot be a soldier and refuse to fight; you cannot be a doctor and refuse to operate. If you are a writer, you can't work in a bank. Once you commit yourself to your duty, the universe has a way of protecting you and freeing you from other worries.

Adharma is going against your purpose in life, which only gives you and the world misery. Chu looks at the former leaders of the Philippines and Pakistan, Corazon Aquino and Benazir Bhutto. Aquino adopted the patriarchal style of her martyred husband, Bhutto the hard-line style of her father. Neither approach was right for the times in which they governed, and both women ultimately failed. They did not create their own political style, forgetting the dharmic lesson to "be yourself."

Yielding

One of Chu's main points is that to survive and thrive "amid the cunning and the ruthless," you have to acquire the ability to yield. A thick face, black heart person will not always hit back if struck. They may just accept the blow if it means that by appearing to yield it will help them to achieve their ends. Gandhi's powerful nonviolence is a good example.

In the Asian world, Chu says, "heroes are not judged for their prowess in hunting and shooting tigers, but rather for their strength and ability to endure the humiliation of being pigs."

Ditch pride and preciousness if you want to succeed.

Wealth

The Chinese character for wealth is composed of two symbols: a seashell, an ancient symbol of trade, and a symbol that literally translated means "brilliance," but implies the uniqueness that each of us has in terms of a talent or ability. Wealth therefore comes from selling what is unique about you (in terms of a product or just you as a person). Although money itself is a mystery, whatever best expresses your brilliance will inevitably lead you to wealth. It will free you from poverty and give you a mindset that attracts abundance.

Final comments

With its strange title and compelling mixture of spirituality and ruthlessness, *Thick Face, Black Heart* was always going to stand out. Its publication was not so much a breath of fresh air but a quake that shook up much of the conventional thinking about personal success. Many American success authors had dabbled in eastern wisdom and incorporated it into their books, but Chin-Ning Chu grew up with Chinese culture and only later imbibed western influences.

Only some of the broad ideas of *Thick Face, Black Heart* can be conveyed here. Read it for the inspiring stories of leadership and endurance and for the author's anecdotes of business and personal life in America and Asia.

Some will find the book distasteful. When the author retells being betrayed by an associate, you may wonder whether she attracted these events to herself by her own "black heart" and self-confessed arrogance. Possibly, but the overwhelming effect of the book is positive. Many people decide that to get ahead in life it is easiest to go by others' rules. This does work for a time, but the result will be a rather shriveled-up person. The philosophy of *Thick Face, Black Heart* allows you to reclaim the dark power inside and wed it to utter conviction about the person you are and the work that is right for you to do.

Chin-Ning Chu

Born in 1947 in Tienjin, China, Chu was brought up a Catholic but was also immersed in Buddhist, Taoist, and Confucian teachings. She grew up in Taiwan but moved to the United States in 1969.

A respected commentator on US–China and US–North Korea relations, Chu was president of Asian Marketing Consultants and chairperson of the Strategic Learning Institute, an educational firm.

Her other books include The Asian Mind Game, The Secrets of the Rainmaker, The Working Woman's Art of War, The Bridge to the Pacific Century, *and* Do Less, Achieve More.

After a battle with cancer, Chu died in Taiwan in 2009.

The Richest Man in Babylon

"In old Babylon there once lived a very rich man named Arkad. Far and wide he was famed for his great wealth. Also he was famed for his liberality. He was generous in his charities. He was generous with his family. He was liberal in his own expenses. But nevertheless each year his wealth increased more rapidly than he spent it."

In a nutshell

The principles of wealth building are free to all, but only a minority use them to their advantage.

In a similar vein

Warren Buffett (by Roger Lowenstein) *Buffett* (p. 48)
Benjamin Franklin *The Way to Wealth* (p. 104)
Robert Kiyosaki *Rich Dad, Poor Dad* (p. 208)
Thomas J. Stanley *The Millionaire Mind* (p. 296)

CHAPTER 10

George S. Clason

Babylon was once the richest city in the world, known for its lavish houses, palaces, and huge city walls. It created fertile farmland where once there had been desert through the use of irrigation. But as George Clason notes in a historical sketch at the end of *The Richest Man in Babylon*, it was also the cradle of modern finance: money as the means of exchange, tradable property titles, promissory notes, and all forms of lending and borrowing were highly developed. Its prosperity continued for centuries because its inhabitants were allowed to make money freely. Even slaves, if they could earn a bit on the side, could eventually buy their way to freedom.

Babylon's success inspired Clason to write a series of fables that would demonstrate the unchanging principles of finance and wealth building. They became very popular and were distributed by banks, insurance companies, and other employers to teach the benefits of saving and hard work. "The Richest Man in Babylon" was one of these stories, and they were later collected into the inspirational classic we know today.

Escaping mediocrity

In the book's first story, two friends—a chariot builder and a musician—reflect on where their working lives have taken them. Though pleased to have wives and young families, they struggle to make ends meet and wonder if there could be another way.

The conversation turns to a man they grew up with, now considered to be the richest man in Babylon. His name is Arkad, and they resolve to go to see their old friend and seek his advice. They ask Arkad how fate has come to make him rich. He immediately rebukes them for assuming that "fate" has contributed anything to his success, telling them that they have only remained poor "because you have either failed to learn the laws that govern the building of wealth, or else you do not observe them."

While still a boy, Arkad had noticed that wealth, if it did not actually create happiness, certainly enhanced the quality of life. It made it possible to furnish a house well, wear good clothing, build temples for the gods, sail the seas, or eat exotic food from distant lands. He resolved that his lot would not be that of the poor man, but that he would make himself "a guest at the banquet of good things."

Yet with no inheritance due to him, he realized that he would have to put effort and study into the ways of wealth. He started a job as a scribe, laboring long and hard writing laws and other things on clay tablets. One day, in return for a particularly difficult task on which he had to work through the night, Arkad asked the client, a money lender, if he would teach him some of the secrets of money.

Paying yourself first

The man agreed, and in the morning revealed this principle: "A part of all you earn must be yours to keep." Arkad felt a little short-changed at this, since he felt that it was obvious—wasn't *all* you earned yours to keep? Living expenses quickly eat up whatever you earn, the money lender observed, which means that you become a slave to your work and earn merely to survive. However, by putting aside at least 10 percent of your earnings and marking that off as "not for expenditure," over time this amount builds and starts earning money for you, without you having to do any work. It matters little how much you start with, as long as you observe the rule to pay yourself first out of whatever you earn. You will soon not even notice the absence of this small amount.

After some setbacks, Arkad's savings grew to a satisfying amount. This pleased the old money lender, to the extent that he asked the young man to run part of his large estate. Later he shared in its profits. The lesson: Those who know the laws of money seek each other out. While many pay lip service to financial principles, the principles never work for them because they don't take *action*.

Yet the money lender's advice is not that of a penny pincher. He counsels Arkad to enjoy life and not strain to save too much, as long as he is continually increasing his pot of saved money.

Wisdom or gold?

If you had a choice of gold or wisdom, which would you choose? We catch up with the rich man Arkad later in the book, when his son Nomasir has grown up and is ready to inherit his father's fortune. However, the father first wants his son to go out into the world and learn how to make money on his own.

He is given three bags of gold as a head start, plus a clay tablet with "the five laws of gold" engraved on it. Not surprisingly, Nomasir pays little attention to the tablet. His first use of the money is to bet most of it on a horse-racing scam (he loses most of that), followed by purchasing a shop with someone he doesn't know well (it folds). As his situation grows desperate, he remembers the clay tablet and its five laws. In brief, they are:

1. Money comes to those who save.
2. Money multiplies for those who invest it.
3. Money stays with the person who entrusts it to wise people.
4. Money is lost when invested in things with which you are not familiar.
5. Money is lost at a fast rate by pursuing get-rich-quick schemes.

Realizing that he has violated these laws, Nomasir learns them by heart. He goes on to earn money and invest it wisely. Ten years later he returns to his father, who has laid on a feast. He places on the table three bags of gold: one is to repay the money his father had originally given him, but the other two, he says, are for the wisdom on the tablets. He says to those gathered:

> *"Without wisdom, gold is quickly lost by those who have it, but with wisdom, gold can be secured by those who have it not."*

Someone who does not know the laws may enjoy windfalls, but they are likely to lose the money just as quickly. The five laws not only help you build wealth, but if you follow them they protect you from losing what you have built.

Living within your means

One of the important messages of the book, particularly for our age of high debt, is that as well as "paying yourself first," *at the same time* you should pay off your debts. Thus, 10 percent to yourself, 20 percent to your debtors on a pro rata basis, and the rest to live on. Many people are put off saving because they think first about the weight of their debts. But as soon as you see the growth of your unspent cache of money, it will motivate you to add to it. "Touch not the one tenth that is fattening the purse."

In an amusing twist, the book follows the discovery of five clay tablets by an archaeologist working in Mesopotamia (the area where Babylon was located). They are sent to a professor for translation, and something strange happens. The professor and his wife apply the laws of the 2,000-year-old tablets to their own lives, and their financial situation is turned around. The professor observes in a letter: "Who would believe there could be such a difference in results between following a financial plan and just drifting along?"

Although it seems obvious, the richest man in Babylon got that way because he lived within his means. In time, anyone who can live on 80 or 90 percent of their income can become rich.

Final comments

As with most fiction of an instructive kind, the prose in *The Richest Man in Babylon* will not win any awards. However, its little stories have inspired many readers toward responsible fortunes, including Robert Kiyosaki (see *Rich Dad, Poor Dad*).

The book's "cures for a lean purse" include not gambling and owning your own home (because it reduces the cost of living and increases your enjoyment of life). Most importantly, it teaches you why you must become someone who draws dividends from investments instead of merely earning money from labor—letting money be your slave rather than vice versa. Even if you are older, it is not too late to make the transition. If you seek your betterment you will be rewarded.

The Richest Man in Babylon belongs to that group of titles within the success literature dealing with saving, investing, and financial propriety, in which setting goals, a strong work ethic, and an optimistic attitude are all important. But how do you reconcile these ideas with those of the more spiritual prosperity authors such as Catherine Ponder and Wallace Wattles? Both financial knowledge *and* a strong awareness of abundance are necessary if you are to accrue wealth in a satisfying, sustainable way. Everyone knows that the greedy and miserly, even those who have great wealth, are not happy. Equally, while "trusting in God as the source of your supply" may bring you unexpected gains, it pays to increase your knowledge of the earthly world's financial ways and laws. With both faith and knowledge you can create fortunes that will last, and the wisdom you have attained on the journey can be used to help others.

George S. Clason

Born in Louisiana, Missouri, in 1874, George Samuel Clason attended the University of Nebraska and served in the US Army in the Spanish–American War.

He began a long career in publishing, founding the Clason Map Company of Denver, Colorado, which produced the first road atlas of the United States and Canada. In 1926 Clason published the first of a number of pamphlets on the secrets of financial success. They were later put together as The Richest Man in Babylon, *which has sold over one and half million copies.*

Clason died in California in 1957.

2001

Good to Great

"No matter how dramatic the end result, the good-to-great transformations never happened in one fell swoop. There was no single defining action, no grand program, no one killer innovation, no solitary lucky break, no miracle moment. Rather, the process resembled relentlessly pushing a giant heavy flywheel in one direction, turn upon turn, building momentum until a point of breakthrough, and beyond."

In a nutshell

Don't be satisfied with being merely good or excellent. Discover what it takes to be great.

In a similar vein
Steve Jobs (by Schlender & Tetzeli) *Becoming Steve Jobs* (p. 186)
David S. Landes *The Wealth and Poverty of Nations* (p. 222)
J. W. Marriott Jr. *The Spirit to Serve* (p. 248)
Sam Walton *Made in America* (p. 314)

CHAPTER 11
Jim Collins

Most great companies enjoyed years of obscurity before their results compelled the world to look at them. In fact, they seemed just like any other company until a certain "transition point" saw them leave the pack behind.

The leaps into greatness did not occur through revolution. Contrary to popular opinion, these firms did not get in expensive new CEOs to turn things around. (That is the mark of a mediocre company.) And although the remarkable results of great companies sometimes make it appear as if their success happened quickly, the leap only happened after years of effort, what Collins calls "pushing against the flywheel."

The US drugstore chain Walgreens is an old company that for four decades followed the general market in its performance. Then, in 1975, the company left the average and began its remarkable success. From 1975 to 2000 it outperformed the stock market by 15 times. It also outperformed the technology star Intel by two times, the much-lauded General Electric by five times, and the famed Coca-Cola by eight times.

What accounts for a sudden and sustained rise out of mediocrity? Jim Collins began a five-year research effort to find out. Of the list of 11 great companies he came up with, whose inclusion in *Good to Great: Why Some Companies Make the Leap... And Others Don't* was based on superior performance for at least 15 years, Collins says, "a dowdier group would be hard to find." It included Fannie Mae (a mortgage finance house), Gillette (razors), Kimberly-Clark (diapers, paper towels), Kroger (discount supermarkets), Nucor (steelmaker), Philip Morris (cigarettes, chocolate, coffee), and Pitney Bowes (back-office equipment). For each of these Collins found a comparison company that had remained merely good (e.g., Eckerd for Walgreens).

What themes did he draw from the research?

A certain kind of leadership
Collins was not really interested in leadership when he began the study. He wanted to get away from the "great leader" complex of many

businesses, where it is thought that bringing in a dynamic leader will transform everything. He did in fact discover that leadership is extremely important, but the *type* of leader that makes for greatness was the surprise. Great-company leaders are an unusual blend of ambition and humility, "more like Lincoln and Socrates than Patton or Caesar." Collins describes Darwin Smith, head of Kimberly-Clark, as having an "awkward shyness and lack of pretense . . . coupled with a fierce, even stoic, resolve toward life."

Such leaders do not seem outwardly ambitious, because they channel their drive and determination into securing the long-term success of their company. They are reluctant to talk about themselves, instead pointing to the great people who have made their contribution and forever counting their blessings (despite the evidence of hard work, Collins was surprised how many mentioned the word "luck" in their personal and corporate successes). These leaders also share a passion for the products their firm creates, however commonplace. For instance, people at Gillette, mainly because it excited them, sank $200 million into developing the Mach 3 razor, which became a great success.

Because they put their firm first, these "level 5" leaders, as Collins calls them, ensure that whoever succeeds them is likely to be just as effective, if not more. In contrast, executives of the comparison companies wanted their personal record to stand out, the more so if they picked weaker successors. Level 5 leaders intentionally keep a low profile, "ordinary people quietly producing extraordinary results." Making fortunes through selling their shares to takeover artists or leveraged buyouts, it is hardly worth saying, is unthinkable. They are in it for the future greatness of the company, even well beyond their tenure. Many kept offices in the building long after retirement.

The right people

Conventional wisdom has it that if you want to start and build a great company, you develop the concept to perfection and then hire the best people you can find. Collins and his team, though, found that when the executives of good-to-great firms began their corporate transformations, they worked seemingly in reverse: "They *first* got the right people on the bus (and the wrong people off the bus) and *then* figured out where to drive it."

The benefits of this approach? If you have the right people from the beginning, they will be able to adapt to any changes in direction or strategy. You will not have to motivate them because they share the desire to achieve greatness and therefore are already motivated. Interestingly, the great companies pay no more than the merely good; remuneration is *not* a big factor in motivating people when they have something larger than money to aim for.

Finally, great companies have cultures that are "rigorous but not ruthless." Rigor means that everyone knows the standards they and the firm must live up to. If they are not met, they know they must go. Ruthlessness, on the other hand, is a characteristic of merely good companies. With little thought, they will hack off whole divisions through restructuring and sack thousands of workers through top-down decisions. Such a climate of fear is inherently unproductive and demotivating, whereas great companies have an *esprit de corps* that challenges everyone to be at their best. They know, as Collins puts it, that "great vision without great people is irrelevant."

Brutal honesty

Great companies are set apart by their reliance on the *facts* in making their decisions. They do not rely on management fads or heroic dreams of greatness to achieve their goals, instead engaging in continual self-assessment.

Collins found that charismatic leaders can often get in the way of a company's success, because the staff start to refer only to "what the CEO will think" instead of data being the basis for decisions. The best companies want the truth to be heard, whoever speaks it. They have a culture of questioning and openness uncorrupted by obsequiousness.

Collins quotes Winston Churchill: "I . . . had no need for cheering dreams. *Facts* are better than dreams." Churchill was also famous for his attitude of "never surrender." Great companies also have this combination of believing that they will prevail in the end, while being willing to face up to the difficult reality.

A reason for being

Great companies have a single idea or focus that guides everything they do. Such concepts may take many years to refine, but once in place can generate enormous success because they are so differentiated. Walgreens has as its self-defining concept the best, most conveniently located drugstores, with high profit per customer visit. Wells Fargo didn't try to beat Citicorp or Bank of America to be the biggest global American bank. Instead, it focused on being a very profitable bank with a focus on the western United States.

Collins has a three-circle model to test for greatness. The first circle is awareness of what you can be the best in the world at. This involves a realistic appreciation of your abilities; it is *not* about letting your ego run wild. Neither will it involve simply what you are competent at; what you have been doing for years may not be what you can be great at. The second circle is what drives your economic engine; that is, where exactly your profit comes from in the most abundance. The third circle is passion: very simply, doing only what you are deeply passionate about. If you can find something that you really can be best in the world at, that you love doing, and that makes you money, you have the beginnings of a great enterprise. If you have any two out of three, you are likely to be merely successful, not great.

The book is worth getting for the chapter describing the model alone, as you can apply it to your life as much as to the organization where you work. What is it exactly that you stand for? Can you sum it up in a few words? If not, your current efforts are likely to be scattered and lacking energy, just like the "merely good" companies.

Using technology wisely

Technology is never the basis for becoming great, Collins says, management is.

Technology was rarely mentioned as a major factor for success by executives in the great companies. It was never a case of "This technology will make the company," more like "We could use this to take us further with what we are doing." Without an opportunity-spotting culture in place, other companies chose technology for technology's sake, but the exceptional companies only invested in cutting-edge ways of doing things when it matched up with their larger vision.

Collins's assessment is that "technology by itself is never a primary cause of either greatness or decline." The wise use of technology, however, *is* part of great-company culture.

Final comments

Good to Great was researched at the height of the "new-economy" mania. Collins says of these years: "We entered a remarkable moment in history when the whole idea of trying to build a great company seemed quaint and outdated." Having a "culture of discipline," one of the key characteristics of great companies that he identifies, did indeed seem old-fashioned. It turned out that these firms had not become great through being in the right industry at the right time, but had identified their unique strengths and worked relentlessly to capitalize on them.

This conclusion is remarkably similar to that reached by David Landes in *The Wealth and Poverty of Nations*, who found that while geography and natural resources (chance) certainly affected the development of countries, what made them prosperous was their culture of effort and enterprise.

Before *Good to Great*, Collins wrote the celebrated *Built to Last*, about visionary, iconic companies that have stood the test of time. As the recipe book for hoisting yourself to an initial stage of greatness, *Good to Great* is actually the "prequel," Collins says. The value of *Built to Last* is that it can show you how to stay great.

Collins says that he doesn't think of his work as necessarily about companies or business. The principles of *Good to Great* can apply to any sort of organization, and he explicitly says that you can apply them to your *life*. You may be surprised how inspirational these books are; the excitement is in the knowledge that success can be measured and its lessons applied methodically. With both books you will have a well-researched foundation for success that puts results before charisma.

Jim Collins

Born in 1958, Collins has maths and MBA degrees from Stanford University. He heads a "management laboratory" in Boulder, Colorado, which studies enduring great companies. He was on the faculty of the Stanford University Graduate School of Business and previously held positions with McKinsey and Hewlett-Packard.

His other books include Great by Choice *(2011),* How the Mighty Fall *(2009), and* Good to Great and the Social Sectors *(2005).*

Acres of Diamonds

"Al Hafed heard all about diamonds that night, and went to bed a poor man. He wanted a whole mine of diamonds. Early next day, he eagerly besought the priest and asked him where diamonds could be found."

"Greatness consists in doing great deeds with little means—in the accomplishment of vast purposes. It consists in the private ranks of life—in helping one's fellows, benefiting one's neighborhood, in blessing one's own city and state."

In a nutshell

Whatever you desire is probably close at hand, if you are willing to open your eyes and your mind.

In a similar vein
Horatio Alger *Ragged Dick* (p. 12)
Napoleon Hill *Think and Grow Rich* (p. 174)
Wallace D. Wattles *The Science of Getting Rich* (p. 320)

CHAPTER 12
Russell H. Conwell

Russell Conwell once went on a trip along the Tigris River, in present-day Iraq, using a guide hired in Baghdad who was to take him out to the Persian Gulf. These river guides were like barbers in that they liked to talk, but the story this one told, Conwell insists, is easily verified.

There was a man, Al Hafed, who lived on the banks of the River Indus who had a nice farm with orchards and gardens, excess cash, a beautiful wife and children. He was "wealthy because he was contented." Then an old priest visited him and one night related how the world was made, including the formation of all the rocks, the earth, the precious metals and stones. He told the farmer that if he had a few diamonds he could have not merely one farm, but many. The farmer listened. Suddenly, he wasn't that happy with what he had thus far acquired in life.

He sold up and went traveling in search of diamonds, across Persia, Palestine, and into Europe. A couple of years later, what money he had was gone and he was wandering around in rags. When a large wave came in from the sea, he was happily swept under by it.

The man who had bought the farmer's land was another story. One day, watering his animals in the stream that ran through the property, he noticed a glint in the watery sands. It was a diamond. In fact, it was one of the richest diamond finds in history: the mines of Golconda would yield not just one or two but acres of diamonds.

Open your mind

In this tiny book, which is actually a transcript of a hugely popular lecture that he gave, Conwell relates similar true-life stories about the folly of going off to find your fortune when it is in your own backyard or staring you in the face. He suggests that most people are "pygmies of their possible selves," because they are not willing to accept, or it did not occur to them, that they have great untouched powers: "Families do not credit their own folks with abilities they attribute to other

81

persons. Towns and cities are cursed because their own people talk them down."

Conwell's message is that we shouldn't fall into the trap of thinking that all the great people and businesses are somewhere else. Consider that Henry Ford started designing and building his car on his own farm and built the famous Ford factories in the area where he had grown up. There was nothing special about Dearborn, Michigan—he made it special, without ever leaving his own backyard. Great investor Warren Buffett decided against moving his family to Wall Street. He stayed in Omaha, Nebraska, and made his billions there.

The discovery of true service

Conwell's other theme is that great service is basic to prosperity.

He tells of the financier John Jacob Astor the elder, who suddenly had to go into partnership in a millinery store because the owners could not keep up their mortgage payments. What did he do to get this business on its feet? He would go into the park and quietly watch the women strolling along, particularly the most confident and elegant, and take careful note of the hats they were sporting. Back in the store, he had these hats copied exactly. The result was that the store never made a hat or bonnet that a lady didn't like, and it boomed. Left behind was the idea that "We make hats and try to sell them," to be replaced by "What women want, we sell."

From such basic service erupts great success, in this case a store that even in the nineteenth century made $17 million. You may think you have already considered it, but ask again: What do people *want*?

The problem with most people, Conwell says, is that their wealth is "too near." You need to develop an open mind to spot the obvious. This will never happen if you are continually speeding off to the next opportunity, looking for a greener pasture. Genuine service is simple, but it may only occur to you what this is when your mind has been quieted. Without finding some quiet time to yourself you will not be able to see the wood for the trees. Leave time for meditation and contemplation, and answers will come.

Another way to start is by thinking about what *you* need. Chances are that if you need something, others will too. The woman who invented the snap button, first used in gloves, made her fortune this way. Conwell emphasizes: "It is the open-mindedness to little things that brings human success." The greatest minds think in simple terms, and the greatest people, Conwell says, are always straightforward.

You can't succeed if you have no interest in people and their needs. In Conwell's words, you must make yourself *necessary* to the world. What all great people have in common is that they make themselves a "medium" for good: they make the best products and provide them to the largest number. This, not taking money at a till, is service.

Final comments

Acres of Diamonds might seem to be from another era, but Conwell was one of the original American motivational speakers and his talk can still inspire. It costs next to nothing to buy, can be read in about half an hour, and every so often you may like to be reminded of its two lessons, which are so simple but so useful to remember:

❖ There's no need to look beyond yourself and your immediate circumstances to find the seeds of your fortune.
❖ Service is the key to success. Don't just sell things, find out what people really want. This requires greater than normal thought and observation.

Russell H. Conwell

Russell Herman Conwell was born in Worthington, Massachusetts, in 1843. He attended Yale College and in 1862, not yet 20, he raised a company of volunteer soldiers and fought on the Yankee side in the Civil War as a commissioned captain.

After the war Conwell studied at Albany Law School and practiced law, but later went to work as a reporter for the Boston Evening Traveller. *He traveled around the world for another journal, the* American Traveller, *and was 27 when he journeyed down the Tigris river. His wife died when he was still in his twenties.*

In his third career, in 1882 Conwell was invited to become pastor of a newly built Baptist church in Philadelphia. He would serve in this role for 43 years, also becoming a popular lecturer on the Lyceum and other circuits and writing a number of books. Easily his most popular lecture was "Acres of Diamonds," which he gave over 5,000 times and earned him, it is said, a million dollars. With the money he founded Temple University in Philadelphia. He died in 1925.

The 7 Habits of Highly Effective People

"It's incredibly easy to get caught up in an activity trap, in the busy-ness of life, to work harder and harder at climbing the ladder of success only to discover it's leaning against the wrong wall. It is possible to be busy—very busy—without being very effective."

"In the last analysis, what we are communicates far more eloquently than anything we say or do. We all know it. There are people we trust absolutely because we know their character. Whether they're eloquent or not, whether they have the human relations techniques or not, we trust them, and we work successfully with them."

In a nutshell

The first step on the road to success is good character. The second is openness to new perspectives. The third is ensuring that daily action is shaped by higher aims, with the knowledge that you always reap what you sow.

In a similar vein

Warren Bennis *On Becoming a Leader* (p. 18)
Muriel James & Dorothy Jongeward *Born to Win* (p. 180)
J. W. Marriott Jr. *The Spirit to Serve* (p. 248)
John Whitmore *Coaching for Performance* (p. 326)

CHAPTER 13

Stephen R. Covey

I mportant both as a self-help and a success work, *The 7 Habits of Highly Effective People* is the only book included in both *50 Self-Help Classics* and this volume. *50 Self-Help Classics* outlined the seven habits and the impact of the book, while this commentary goes beyond the habits themselves to explore Covey's idea of a successful person.

The 7 Habits of Highly Effective People is a masterful synthesis of higher-quality ideas in the success literature, placed on a methodological framework. It is self-help because it is the book you want to read when you feel like you are merely skating on the surface of life and are not being driven by values, and it is a work about success because it reminds you that real success is built on integrity and timeless principles. With this foundation, the sky is the limit to create and achieve, and to do so in good conscience.

Covey's successful person

We seek direction from people who we perceive have integrity. In its concern with integrating principles and action, *The 7 Habits of Highly Effective People* is therefore more of a leadership work than a motivational book.

Integrity means having a changeless core inside. This allows for an ability to cope with large amounts of change where others may be thrown off course. A person of character or integrity stays true to their values, desiring to be a better listener, to love unconditionally, and to seek to understand—in short, to be a successful *person* before anything else. Western society makes us want to have much; it is less concerned with our state of being, whether we are the person we believe we should be. Covey's message is that before we can begin to do, we must appreciate and refine who we *are*. His idea of a successful person is someone who:

❖ Makes and keeps commitments and honors promises.
❖ Admits mistakes quickly and openly.
❖ Appreciates the gap between stimulus and response. That is, you rarely *have* to do anything. If you do something, it is out of choice.
❖ Understands that time is precious and that success is simply being yourself but in an organized way.
❖ Is willing to do things that others cannot be bothered to do in order to achieve a higher aim.

It was a revelation for Covey when he discovered a statement made by the former secretary general of the United Nations, Dag Hammarskjöld, "that it is more noble to give yourself to one person completely than to labor diligently for the salvation of the masses." This resonated with him because in his work as a business consultant he had frequently come across organizations that had been rendered ineffective by the differing views of those at the top.

Covey had experienced this himself in trying to work with someone who had a totally different administrative style, and their differences were affecting the organization. Choking back fear, Covey decided to suggest a meeting and resolve the differences. As it turned out, the other man wanted to do this as much as he did. They solved the fundamental problem the organization was facing, instead of continuing to work busily away on separate projects. Covey's point is that we grow into successful, independent people by having the courage to address root problems instead of chasing after things that are "out there":

"Creating the unity necessary to run an effective business or a family or a marriage requires great personal strength and courage. No amount of technical administrative skill in laboring for the masses can make up for lack of nobility of personal character in developing relationships. It is at a very essential, one-on-one level, that we live the primary laws of love and life."

This point that success can best be developed through courage in daily personal interactions is one that is also made throughout Muriel James and Dorothy Jongeward's *Born to Win*. These small acts can be the making of a person, more than flashy public victories.

Through showing the way to reflect objectively on your own attitudes, Covey helps to prevent you imposing your way of seeing the world on others. Until you can understand others' ways of seeing, through really listening to them, you cannot be truly successful.

Seeing afresh

Covey explains that personal growth is often the result not of doing something new, but of seeing the same things in a new light. We all have mental maps of our world that we mistake for the actual territory. By clinging on to old maps we fail to see the true lie of the land and get lost. At this point, to regain our way we are likely to adopt external techniques or fixes, but without internal change this will not get us very far. We need to change our paradigms, the basic ways we have of seeing the world. Scientific paradigms, such as the Ptolemaic understanding that the universe revolved around the Earth, are replaced by new paradigms based on contradictory evidence.

New paradigms change everything. For example, you may have always believed that the best way to exist is to "go with the flow" and react as well as you can to external events; your "map" does not include the possibility of proactively shaping your experience through living according to goals. But if you decided to change your paradigm, the same territory you walk over every day would suddenly become a new landscape because, from a different perspective, you would be seeing it for the first time.

Covey quotes Albert Einstein: "The significant problems we face cannot be solved at the same level of thinking we were at when we created them." While smaller changes in our lives can be effected through alterations in attitude and behavior, the larger issues can only be addressed by a transformation of the self. To think in a totally different way we must become a different person, which does not happen easily. This is why Covey's basic unit of change is the habit, because what we do or think about all the time makes us who we are and becomes the lens through which we see things.

Another way of seeing paradigms is the concept of "life scripts," a blueprint for behavior that helps us to interpret the world and governs what we do in it. Most people accept life scripts from the environment (family, society) into which they have grown, but Covey reminds us that there is always the opportunity to write a new script—a space for making decisions based on truth. We all have this window of free will, but the genuinely successful seek to open it further. Anwar Sadat, the Egyptian leader who initiated the first Middle East peace accords, observed that a person who could not change "the very fabric of his thought" would not be capable of changing reality; only those continually willing to see things from new perspectives can have regular access to the truth.

Twice-creating success

When you build a house, Covey notes, you must have blueprints and plans before the earth is broken. The carpenter's rule is "measure twice, cut once." In business, you cannot drift along and hope to make money. Each product or service must be clearly thought out, with detailed plans for marketing, staffing, and resource allocation. This is the stage of "first creation." Most business failures result from under-capitalization, lack of research into the market, or having no business plan—all deficiencies in first creation.

The same is true for your life. "Overnight" success is usually the result of years of planning, practice, learning, and visualization of the desired result. You may have good fortune through other routes, but it is not likely to be enduring. No one ever drifts into meaningful success.

Singer John Lennon famously said, "Life is what happens to you while you are making other plans." Surely it is unwise to think about shaping your own life to the extent that Covey suggests? His argument is not that you can prevent life's inevitable surprises, simply that purpose shapes destiny. The paradox is that having some idea of where you want to end up (Covey gets you to imagine what people will say about you when you die; a surprisingly valuable exercise) actually allows more spontaneity in your life because you are more relaxed about where you are heading. There is less existential angst. You can either be shaped by the thoughts and intentions of other people, and call this "life," or you can adopt the law of twice creation to ensure that what manifests as life has been brought into being by *you*.

Final comments

The 7 Habits of Highly Effective People, more than most works in the success field, is a book of ideas. It heralded a new era for the genre in its shift back to the notion of building an unchanging core of personal principles, where before the emphasis had been more on manipulation of behavior to achieve certain ends.

Though this aspect is little discussed, it is undeniable that *The 7 Habits of Highly Effective People* foreshadowed many of the elements that make up the discipline of personal coaching, including the pursuit of "win/win situations;" empathic listening in order to have people solve their own problems; self-care and renewal to sustain productivity; goals to guide performance; and maintaining a work/life balance. While he never uses the term "coaching," the book includes many examples and anecdotes from Covey's experience as a father and his realization that "borrowing strength builds weakness;" that is, using your position as a parent or manager is a weak way of getting things done. You improve the world around you not by forcing solutions on it but by drawing out better outcomes from those involved.

It is ironic that *The 7 Habits of Highly Effective People*, though one of the most challenging success books to apply and implement, has also been the genre's bestseller in modern times. The book is a hit even in China, where amid the rapacious growth of a newly capitalistic economy people still have a hunger for success based on integrity. If there is only one message that you take from it, be it that you always reap what you sow, whether as a person, a business, or a nation. There are no shortcuts to fulfillment or lasting achievement.

Stephen R. Covey

Born in 1932, Covey had a Harvard MBA and spent most of his career at Utah's Brigham Young University, where he was a professor of organizational behavior and business management.

In 1984 he founded the Covey Leadership Center, which 13 years later merged with the Franklin Quest company to form Franklin Covey, a company selling learning and performance tools.

Covey's other books include Principle-Centered Leadership, First Things First, The 7 Habits of Highly Effective Families, *and* Living the 7 Habits.

Covey had several honorary doctorates and was voted one of Time *magazine's 25 most influential Americans. He lived in Utah and died in 2009, aged 79.*

2016

Grit

"The ability to quickly climb the learning curve of any skill is obviously a very good thing, and, like it or not, some of us are better at it than others . . . So why, then, is it such a bad thing to favor 'naturals' over 'strivers'? What's the downside of television shows like America's Got Talent, The X Factor, *and* Child Genius? *Why shouldn't we separate children as young as seven or eight into two groups: those few children who are 'gifted and talented' and the many, many more who aren't? . . . In my view, the biggest reason a preoccupation with talent can be harmful is simple: By shining our spotlight on talent, we risk leaving everything else in the shadows. We inadvertently send the message that these other factors—including grit—don't matter as much as they really do."*

In a nutshell

People believe that natural ability and intelligence are the tickets to success, but they are only helpful. In real life, it is focus and perseverance that are decisive.

In a similar vein
Malcolm Gladwell *Outliers* (p. 136)
Adam Grant *Give and Take* (p. 150)
Darren Hardy *The Compound Effect* (p. 166)
Gary Keller *The One Thing* (p. 198)

CHAPTER 14

Angela Duckworth

Angela Duckworth gave up a high-flying career in New York at management consultancy McKinsey to teach seventh-grade students mathematics. She noted how some students picked things up very quickly, but was surprised that the talented were not necessarily the ones who finished the year at the top. There was another group of less talented students who put in the effort and came out equally well or better. "I grew less and less convinced that talent was destiny," she recalls, "and more and more intrigued by the returns generated by effort."

She left teaching to study the psychology of achievement and as a graduate student was awarded a MacArthur Fellowship, known as the "genius grant." For Duckworth, whose Chinese-American father had repeatedly told his children, "You're no genius," there was a sweet irony in the award. Though she had passed through some top colleges and had now carved out a great research career in psychology, she hadn't even got into the gifted and talented program at her school. The award seemed proof of what she had spent years demonstrating in her psychology research: that "grit" matters more than talent.

Grit: The Power of Passion and Perseverance tells the story of her research, showing that the virtue can be cultivated to the extent that success largely becomes a matter of our own creation.

Some people keep going

When Duckworth began her research into the psychology of success, she didn't doubt that the most successful people had, along with other attributes, huge natural talent and luck. However, what stood out from the interviews she was doing with achievers was another attribute. Everyone knows people who have loads of talent, but for some reason never see it fulfilled because they drop out early when things aren't going well. What her successful people all shared was the ability to pick themselves up after failure. Many were far from talented at the beginning (the writer whose prose people laughed at, the athlete who wasn't very poised), but they *just never gave up*. "For most, there was no realistic expectation of ever catching up to their ambitions," Duckworth writes, but they enjoyed the chase and were obsessed with getting better. Their passion and perseverance could be summed up in one word: grit.

Yet how on earth would you measure such an old-fashioned notion as grit? One of Duckworth's mentors in college was the psychologist Jerry Kagan, who in the 1950s had been asked by West Point, the top military academy, to find out the type of recruit who would make it through the tough early training, known as "Beast Barracks," or "Beast," and who would drop out. Using Freudian techniques, Kagan failed to discover anything conclusive. In subsequent decades other psychologists looked at the issue of attrition, but no one came up with a good answer. West Point admitted people based on their "Whole Candidate Score," a number based on leadership potential, school grades, and sporting success. The higher the score, the more West Point thought the recruit would be likely to succeed in its tough environment. But the score wasn't actually a good predictor of who would make it through Beast Barracks. What seemed to matter more was something West Point psychologist Mike Matthews called "rising to the occasion"—which by definition can only be seen and measured in the moment, on the ground, in the harsh physical and emotional situations that recruits face every day.

Duckworth started thinking of statements relating to levels of passion and perseverance (such as "I finish whatever I begin") on which people could rank themselves. Her "Grit Scale" was first taken by 1,218 West Point cadets in the July 2004 intake. Duckworth quickly found that her Grit Scores did not match up at all to the Whole Candidate Scores that West Point used. Of the 71 cadets who dropped out of Beast that year, for instance, there were plenty of highly talented people according to West Point's measures. The Grit Scores, on the other hand, were incredibly accurate at predicting who would make it through and who would not. SAT scores, leadership ability, and athletic prowess were poor predictors.

After West Point, Duckworth was keen to try out her grit testing in the tough world of sales, and she got employees of a vacation time-share company to do the test. Half a year later, over half the sales-people had left—and her Grit Scale had been an almost perfect predictor of who would stay on and who would leave. She concluded that traits that psychological testing normally looks for—extroversion, emotional stability, conscientiousness—were not nearly as effective as grit in identifying job retention.

Duckworth obtained similarly clear results when researchers asked her to test levels of grit among Chicago high school students. The ones who graduated generally tested high on her scale of grit. She also did research among children who were competing in the Scripps National Spelling Bee. Among the contestants there was a surprisingly large range of natural verbal ability, but the children who went furthest in the competition were simply those who put in the most solitary practice hours (which most did not find pleasurable) and attended the most spelling bees. In other words, "just showing up" was, as folk wisdom suggests, important to success—but so was the dull task of memorizing the spelling of thousands of obscure words, when you could have been playing outside or watching television.

Guts and curiosity, not intelligence

When the reasons for a person's triumph can't be clearly identified, we tend to leap to the conclusion that their success is a "gift." We love to venerate the talented, or those we think of as natural geniuses in a particular domain, but the more we do so, the less we notice all the other factors that go into success.

Duckworth refers to a study of competitive swimmers by sociologist Dan Chambliss entitled "The Mundanity of Excellence," which showed that astonishing success is nearly always the result of a daily grind over many years. It seems we prefer "mystery to mundanity," and she quotes Nietzsche: "With everything perfect, we do not ask how it came to be . . . we rejoice in the present fact as though it came out of the ground by magic."

Francis Galton wrote one of the first expositions of why people succeed or fail, *Hereditary Genius* (1869), which put success down to a combination of ability, zeal, and capacity for hard work. Galton's friend Charles Darwin read the book and wrote in reply: "For I have always maintained that, excepting fools, men did not differ much in intellect, only in zeal and hard work; and I still think this is an *eminently* important difference." Darwin admitted he didn't have the kind of quick intelligence he observed in some people, he wasn't good at following abstract thought, and he had a poor memory. His talent was rather "in noticing things which easily escape attention, and in observing them carefully." Love for natural science and curiosity powered him. He kept thinking about the same questions and didn't give up on them. This combination of extreme interest and determination personifies grit, Duckworth says.

McKinsey is famous for hiring "the best and the brightest," but sometimes hiring on intelligence alone, Duckworth suggests, creates an organization of smug, narcissistic people who are out for their own gain instead of shared goals. The collapsed energy firm Enron also hired for sheer brainpower. Such a focus on intelligence leads to a failure to see other equally or more important traits that create an organization made for the long term. It leads to a dog-eat-dog environment of high rapacity and low integrity.

A theory of achievement

Duckworth's adviser in graduate school was the psychologist Martin Seligman. He told her she had plenty of data, but no real *theory* of the psychology of achievement. It wasn't enough to say that talent was overrated as the main factor for success, she had to work out *how* talent, effort, skill, and achievement fitted together. Duckworth duly arrived at a theory, which she represented by a two-part equation:

1. Talent x *effort* = skill
2. Skill x *effort* = achievement

Take two people, Duckworth says. The first is very talented, but only moderately hardworking. The second is only moderately talented, but works very hard. Within a set amount of time, both are likely to arrive at a similar level of skill. However, over time the hard worker acquires a key advantage, because she is consistently employing her acquired skill in combination with effort, and getting constant feedback on what needs improving. In putting in fewer hours, the more talented person is not getting this vital feedback and so their skills are not developing further. The striver moves further and further ahead, because their skill is like a built edifice that can't be destroyed.

Thus, in Duckworth's theory, the separation of talent and skill is key: the crucial point is that more effort makes skill even more productive. She admits that her equation doesn't take account of luck, or environmental factors like having a good teacher or parent. What it aims to show is that effort matters *twice*, first when applied to talent, and second when driving skill acquisition.

Rock-like commitment

Grit is not only about intensity of effort or working hard, Duckworth told a young entrepreneur, it means staying true to *one thing* despite all the difficulties that arise. Plenty of people have a passion for something, but a characteristic of those with high levels of grit is remaining passionate *over a long period of time*. It is not uncommon to meet chefs who love cooking now as much as they did when they were 13, or mathematicians who have been working on the same problem for decades. "Enthusiasm is common," Duckworth writes. "Endurance is rare."

We need a goal or passion that is strong enough to propel us on long and winding journeys to get us to our destination and to give our everyday tasks structure and meaning. Such a big mission (or what psychologists call an "ultimate concern") can involve small and medium goals that serve the main one. Duckworth notes that some people state a big goal, like wanting to be a doctor, but they aren't able to identify the small or medium goals that will enable them to get there. This amounts to fantasizing, which makes them feel good now, but has long-term costs. With gritty people, Duckworth notes, virtually everything they do, every minute they spend, serves their ultimate goal. Their whole life is shaped around the "ultimate concern."

It is possible to be a gritty villain, Duckworth admits, but there are more gritty heroes who wish to be of service. Behind all the remarkable people she has interviewed for her work, she found one thing: "the intention to contribute to the well-being of others." They love what they do, it is of deep personal interest, and they are often fiercely protective of their work and their routines. And they know that if they do their job exceptionally well, it can have a big impact on the world. This combination of self-directed and other-directed motives means, Duckworth says, that "you can want to be a top dog and, at the same time, be driven to help others."

Grit and practice

Although gritty people spend much longer than others on a task because they are so committed to getting better and seeing it through, this doesn't mean that spending a long time on something will make you good at it on its own. Rather, what matters is *continuous improvement*, or what the Japanese call *kaizen*.

It is not just length of practice that is relevant, but *better* practice—expertise researcher Anders Ericsson calls this "deliberate practice." It involves intense mental work that is meaningful but not always fun. Duckworth told some school students she worked with that trying to do things they can't yet do, failing, and learning what they need to do differently is exactly the way experts practice. If you're frustrated or feel like you don't want to go on, it doesn't mean you will never be good at something. It just means you need deliberate practice, involving a clear goal that stretches you; immediate feedback; and repeating the task after taking into account the feedback, usually on your own and in the same time and place each day. If nothing else, success means a willingness to fail and to fully accept the demands of practice. In short, to say: "That was hard! It was great!"

Final comments

Although some people discover their passion in a great moment, as when television chef Julia Child had her first mouthful of sole *meunière* in a French restaurant, in fact Duckworth found that most of the achievers she interviewed tried several different things before settling on their life's goal or purpose. Indeed, Child was in her forties by the time she discovered cooking.

What passion does is make us determined to succeed in what we love, which leads to us being grittier and more committed. The gritty are also happier, Duckworth contends, because their grit leads them to push themselves to fulfill their potential, which makes them feel good. A journalist who interviewed Duckworth said: "You know, I absolutely love what I do, too. It's amazing to me how many people I know who're well into their forties and haven't committed to anything. They don't know what they're missing."

A shortcut to grit would seem to be a contradiction in terms, but Duckworth advises finding a gritty company, team, or culture and making yourself part of it. A great team or organization can do half the work for you: because you want to fit in, it makes you lift your game. It is smart to put yourself in environments or situations that you know will test you; they encourage you to rise to the occasion.

Angela Duckworth

Born in 1970, Duckworth has a degree in neurobiology from Harvard and an MSc in neuroscience (the neurology of dyslexia) from Oxford University, which she attended on a Marshall Scholarship. In 2006 she was awarded a PhD in psychology from the University of Pennsylvania and is currently professor of psychology at UPenn.

While at Harvard she started a free summer educational enrichment program for children, an experience that led her to pursue a career as a teacher in San Francisco and Philadelphia. Prior to writing Grit *she gave a TED talk on the subject, which has been viewed nine million times.*

My Life and Work

"*From the beginning I could never work up much interest in the labor of farming. I wanted to have something to do with machinery. My father was not entirely in sympathy with my bent toward mechanics. He thought I ought to be a farmer. When I left school at seventeen and became an apprentice in the machine shop of the Drydock Engine Works I was all but given up for lost.*"

"*Good will is one of the few really important assets of life. A determined man can win almost anything that he goes after, but unless, in his getting, he gains good will he has not profited much.*"

In a nutshell

Continually refine your thinking power. Imagine something the world would really need. Make it cheaply as possible and sell it at the lowest price.

In a similar vein
Andrew Carnegie *The Autobiography of Andrew Carnegie* (p. 56)
Steve Jobs (by Schlender & Tetzeli) *Becoming Steve Jobs* (p. 186)
Ray Kroc *Grinding It Out* (p. 214)
Sam Walton *Made in America* (p. 314)

CHAPTER 15

Henry Ford

My *Life and Work* takes us inside the mind of a person who managed to change the world, yet who lived in relative obscurity for the first 40 years of his life. This was a long time to develop skills, both personal and mechanical, that laid the foundation for a massive enterprise.

Ford was that rare person, an inventor who went on to mass-produce his own invention. If you ever feel disheartened because you have an idea for a product or service for which you have been told there is no market, remember Ford's comment that "there never is for new articles." He saw fear as the result of dependence on other people and circumstances, and in every area of his life, from the avoidance of debt to the work ethic that he held sacred, Ford was an expression of what Emerson called "self-reliance."

The vision

Described by his mother as a born mechanic, the greatest moment in Ford's childhood was seeing a road engine, a steam vehicle used to haul farm machinery. It was the first vehicle he had seen not pulled by horses.

Always tinkering, by age 15 he could fix almost any watch and seriously considered becoming a watch manufacturer. But the idea of the "horseless carriage" was too great and, without the support of his father, Ford began to build one in the workshop he had constructed on the family farm.

At 17 he began work as an apprentice machinist, qualifying before time, and rose through the ranks. In his spare time he worked on a gasoline engine and dreamed of building a "universal car" that could transport people cheaply and reliably.

In his twenties he was inspired by a brief meeting with the inventor Thomas Edison; despite virtually everyone at the time saying that electricity was the future, Edison told him to stick at his engine.

Ford's employer offered him a major promotion on condition that he gave up his private obsession. His reaction? "I had to choose between my job and my automobile. I chose the automobile, or rather I gave up the job—there was really nothing in the way of choice. For already I knew that the car was bound to be a success. I quit my job on August 15, 1899, and went into the automobile business."

...and the reality

Without personal funds, Ford joined up with a group of investors to form the Detroit Automobile Company. He quickly found that they were more interested in quick profits than engineering a better machine and, after only a year and 20 cars, he resigned.

Four years later, the 40-year-old began the Ford Motor Company. It was capitalized at $100,000, and this time Ford owned a quarter of the stock. Over 1,700 cars were built in the first year of operation, and the Model A gained a reputation for reliability. The second year, giving in to pressure from business associates, Ford brought out three models and raised prices. The company sold fewer vehicles. He realized that he had to have ownership in order to have full control and, using income generated from sales, brought his holdings up over 50 percent, later increased to 100 percent.

In 1908–9 the firm sold over 10,000 cars, and again there was pressure to expand the range. Ford went in exactly the opposite direction. One morning in 1909 he announced that the company would now sell only one model: the Model T. What's more, it would be available in only one color. "Any customer can have a car painted any color that he wants so long as it is black," were his now famous words.

Success

While many believed that the car's low price would bring the firm's collapse, Ford himself expected the market to expand dramatically. It did. He started building the largest factory in the world, Highland Park, and production capacity leaped from 6,000 to 35,000 cars, while the number of staff merely doubled.

By the early 1920s the company employed 50,000 people and was turning out 4,000 cars a day. In 1921 alone, 5 million cars were produced. By the end of the decade, 15 million Model Ts would be run off the assembly line. This was the miracle of mass production.

Universal demand

The first automobiles were considered a "rich man's toy," sold on the basis of pleasure and status. Fords were advertised for their utility. Many people could justify the cost if it was used for travel to work or to carry the family around. The cars were also sold on the basis of simplicity of use, which gave rise to the saying: "Anyone can drive a Ford."

It was price, though, that really made the Model T universal. In 1909–10 it had cost $950. Ten years later, it was selling for $355. How was this possible? Ford abhorred the idea of trying to get the highest price for the car. Instead, his strategy was to base prices on the cost of manufacture. If his factories could be made more and more efficient, the consumer would win. Like Sam Walton with his Wal-Mart stores, Ford discovered that he could make more profits from selling greater numbers of the product at a lower price, than selling fewer at a higher price. If you manage to sell a high-quality product cheaply via low-cost methods, "you will be meeting a demand which is so large that it may be called universal," Ford wrote.

Work and wages

As America's assembly lines grew in number, the prevailing wisdom became that repetitive work numbed the body and spirit. Earning a way-above-average $6 a day, Ford workers were less concerned. Henry Ford believed that high wages increased the stability of the work force and helped the men to concentrate, knowing that their families were taken care of. It also allowed them to be consumers, not just for Ford cars but for other goods and services that kept the economy buoyant.

Ford's hiring methods were unusual. The firm wanted to know little more about prospective workers than their name, age, marital status, and whether they were willing to work. Not speaking English and having a criminal record were not a problem. It did not hire "experts" because they usually only knew what could *not* be done; Ford preferred "fools who would rush in" to tackle problems with an open mind.

Blind people, deaf and dumb people, those with only one leg or arm—all were employed by Ford at the same wage as the able-bodied. He wrote:

"I think that if an industrial institution is to fill its whole role, it ought to be possible for a cross-section of its employees to show about the same proportions as a cross-section of a society in general. We always have with us the maimed and the halt."

Such an enlightened philosophy is taken for granted now, but it wasn't in the 1920s.

The ideal of service

In the early days of the car industry, Ford points out, there was no after-sales service. Car makers were totally focused on selling rather than building a relationship with customers, and it was considered good business to charge a lot for spare parts because the owner had no choice but to buy them.

Ford believed that the sale of a car was merely the beginning of a relationship with a buyer. He built his cars to last, but also made sure that parts were transferable across models, cheap, and easy to install. This ideal of service might have seemed crazy to other manufacturers, but the trust it built up among the public was priceless.

His early experience with investors demonstrated that the principle of "return on the dollar" often sabotaged the creation of an enterprise that would grow into something substantial. Businesses were not cash cows; they should offer something that made lives better, and if they achieved this, good returns would naturally flow.

Final comments

A major figure of the twentieth century, Ford combined two traits often seen in the super-successful person: an original, far-reaching vision that carries with it the potential to change the world; and an obsessive attention to detail that can drive people mad.

Ford's dark side included spying on managers and belief in conspiracy theories about Jewish bankers taking over America. He has also been ridiculed for the famous saying that "history is bunk." This was his shorthand for the belief that education should not be about remembering facts, but about teaching people how to think better. Despite how well he paid, Ford could not help noticing that most people chose jobs that enabled them not to have to think, while his admiration of Edison was based on the inventor's ability to "think things through."

His achievements are of course inspiring, but what message did Ford mean us to take from *My Life and Work*? Some comments late in the book about the concept of "use" perhaps provide the key. He counsels against worrying too much about savings and investments as we normally think of them. He says:

"You are not 'saving' when you prevent yourself from becoming more productive. You are really taking away from your ultimate capital; you are taking away the value of one of nature's investments."

Refining your ability to think should be your investment priority; it always provides the best returns.

1758

The Way to Wealth

"Many a one, for the sake of finery on the back, have gone with a hungry belly, and half starved their families; silks and satins, scarlet and velvets, *as Poor Richard says,* put out the kitchen fire. *These are not the necessaries of life; they can scarcely be called the conveniences, and yet only because they look pretty, how many want to have them. The artificial wants of mankind thus become more numerous than the natural."*

"You may think perhaps that a little tea, or a little punch now and then, diet a little more costly, clothes a little finer, and a little entertainment now and then, can be no great Matter; but remember what Poor Richard says . . . beware of little expenses; a small leak will sink a great ship . . . *and moreover,* fools make Feasts, and wise men eat them.*"*

In a nutshell

Diligence and frugality build character as they create wealth.

In a similar vein
Horatio Alger *Ragged Dick* (p. 12)
Warren Buffett (by Roger Lowenstein) *Buffett* (p. 48)
Benjamin Franklin *Autobiography* (50SHC)
Samuel Smiles *Self-Help* (50SHC)
Thomas J. Stanley *The Millionaire Mind* (p. 296)

CHAPTER 16

Benjamin Franklin

Peple associate Benjamin Franklin with statesmanship and being a drafter of the American Declaration of Independence, but his bread-and-butter work for many years was as a publisher, specifically of almanacs.

The meat of an almanac is the calendar, and to liven up the pages Franklin hit on the idea of filling up the blank spaces with inspiring quotes and aphorisms. Though some were borrowed, others he invented, and they became a platform for his homespun philosophy of frugality and hard work, but more valuably tips on "procuring wealth."

Called *Poor Richard's Almanack* (Franklin's *nom de plume* was Richard Saunders), these bestselling volumes came out every year for a quarter of a century.

Listening to Father Abraham

What was later called *The Way to Wealth* was actually the preface to the 1758 almanac. It was a handy way of putting Franklin's maxims on the benefits of thrift into one place, but it became hugely popular and was translated into many languages.

What made it enjoyable and enduring was Franklin's use of a storytelling device by which Richard Saunders happens to overhear an old man, Father Abraham, lecturing a small crowd in a town square waiting for a public auction to begin.

The men gathered there voice the time-honored complaint that "times are tough," but the wise elder tries to knock some sense into them—quoting heavily from *Poor Richard's Almanack*. This naturally delights the author, who admits that while his writings have brought some "solid pudding," critical acclaim has eluded him. Now he has the even greater prize of witnessing his maxims become common currency. With this set piece, Franklin achieves the double benefit (the great marketer that he was) of advertising his own product and giving it greater credibility.

Spouting the familiar refrain of the small businessperson, one of the crowd suggests that they can't prosper with such a heavy tax burden. The old man replies:

"The taxes are indeed very heavy, and if those laid on by the government were the only ones we had to pay, we might more easily discharge them; but we have many others, and much more grievous to some of us. We are taxed twice as much by our idleness, three times as much by our pride, and four times as much by our folly, and from these taxes the commissioners cannot ease or deliver us by allowing an abatement."

He reminds them of a saying in the 1733 *Poor Richard's Almanack* that "God helps them that help themselves."

Hard work and independence

Remember that this was pre-revolutionary America, still tied by the apron strings to England. The ethic of strident independence and personal responsibility that we now associate with the United States and writers like Emerson had yet to grow to maturity. Franklin scholars suggest that his early writings reflect a world being born with new virtues—principally economic ones. In the new land, thrift and industry were more likely than anything else to bring success. With weaker social structures, not class or position but money was security.

It was Franklin who said, "time is money." Father Abraham quotes Poor Richard's warning: "Dost thou love life, then do not squander time, for that's the stuff life is made of." This is the famous Protestant work ethic in action; instead of merely working enough to eat and survive, building up wealth is a sign of God's grace. Franklin was not very religious, but he recognized that the secret of a better life is the personal development to be gained from working hard. It is not so much what you gain financially, but the self-worth and self-discovery that come from pushing yourself. In slothfulness you learn nothing. Wake up late and you seem to be chasing the day; rise early and you feel in control. "Early to bed, and early to rise, makes a man healthy, wealthy and wise."

To counter the common penchant for instant gratification, Father Abraham again throws a quote from the almanac at his listeners, namely "Constant dropping wears away stones, and by diligence and patience the mouse ate in two the cable."

With such an image, it is easy to grasp *The Way to Wealth*'s message of the virtue of persistence.

The joy of frugality

Franklin knew that people were motivated by the prospect of being rich, but that being frugal was not an especially exciting idea. His solution was to develop witty slogans that conveyed the dignity of the saver, such as "Plough deep, while sluggards sleep, and you shall have corn to sell and to keep" and "At the working man's house hunger looks in, but dares not enter."

People are always hoping for a windfall, because it lets them off the hook of being careful about their daily expenses. One modern-day heir to Franklin is Thomas Stanley, who in his books *The Millionaire Next Door* and *The Millionaire Mind* reveals that the wealthy generally do not play the lottery; they know that over a long time what you save in keeping living expenses to a minimum can, if invested, add up to a fortune. Franklin expresses this fact as "A fat kitchen makes a lean will" and "Beware of little expenses; a small leak will sink a great ship."

When people do receive an inheritance or some gain for which they have not had to work, they imagine a life of leisure. As Poor Richard puts it, "A child and a fool . . . imagine twenty shillings and twenty years can never be spent." Those who cannot appreciate time have the most money problems.

The debtor's prison

Franklin's point is that those with money are more free and independent than their neighbors. The way to wealth lies first in eliminating debt, which lightens the spirit and makes you more confident and therefore more productive. "Tis hard for an empty bag to stand upright," Poor Richard says.

Yet Father Abraham, toward the end of his speech, adds a note of moderation. Lest we all become misers, he is reminded that work and savings "may all be blasted without the blessing of heaven." Don't be uncharitable to those who really need it, because the one thing worse than being a prisoner of debt is being a prisoner of your conscience.

Although it requires hard work and discipline that you alone can muster, prosperity is still a gift in which others can share.

Final comments

As the old man's harangue draws to a close, the market opens and those in the crowd promptly forget everything they have heard, "buying extravagantly."

While the path to wealth is clearly marked, few are willing to adapt themselves to the modest discipline that the journey requires. Instead, we choose the shinier track of debt-driven consumption, which we find further along is covered in vines and thorns.

It has been argued that Franklin did not follow his own model of frugality and industry, and it is true that he is better known for his risk taking and dashing achievements. *The Way to Wealth* may thus seem to be solely for humble folk in hard times, a quaint little essay of only historical value. But consider that Warren Buffett, the most successful investor the world has known, enjoys quoting its maxims and lives according to its tenets of industry, frugality, and debt aversion. Success does often require big risks and vision, but for the details of your working life and control of expenses, it is worth remembering the words of Father Abraham.

Benjamin Franklin

Born in 1706, Franklin was the son of a chandler and the youngest of 17 children. His early working life was as an apprentice to his brother, who produced one of America's first newspapers. In Philadelphia he set up his own printing shop and by his late twenties was publishing the highly successful Poor Richard's Almanacks. *By his early forties he was wealthy enough to retire. He pursued civic improvements such as founding a library and starting a fire department, and his experiments with electricity resulted in the invention of the lightning rod.*

Franklin was a major figure in the Pennsylvania Assembly, which led to his role as negotiator between Britain and colonial America, and he served on a committee that drafted the Declaration of Independence. He was later ambassador to France. Franklin's Autobiography *was unfinished at his death in 1790, but is a personal development classic.*

The Inner Game of Tennis

"The player of the inner game comes to value the art of relaxed concentration above all other skills; he discovers a true basis for self-confidence; and he learns that the secret to winning any game lies in not trying too hard. He aims at the kind of spontaneous performance which occurs only when the mind is calm and seems at one with the body, which finds its own surprising ways to surpass its own limits again and again."

In a nutshell

Your body is smarter than you think: trust it to achieve the goals you have set.

In a similar vein
Mihaly Csikszentmihalyi *Flow* (50SHC)
Cheryl Richardson *Take Time for Your Life* (p. 260)
John Whitmore *Coaching for Performance* (p. 326)

CHAPTER 17

W. Timothy Gallwey

When Gallwey wrote *The Inner Game of Tennis* in the 1970s, there were not many books on the mental side of sports. It was thought that relentless practice of physical skills, combined with sheer willpower, made the best players.

Gallwey's experience as a tennis player and a coach, however, was that willpower and positive thinking were not reliable bases for a great game. You cannot force your brain and body to achieve results. He discovered that there is a much easier route to performance, which involves letting the intelligence of the body and the unconscious mind express what it knows. *The Inner Game of Tennis* combined Gallwey's background in education with his tennis experience to create a truly original work that became a surprise bestseller. With its emphasis on equality between teacher and learner, it was also the seminal work in the personal coaching field.

A new way to play

The conventional way of the tennis coach is to criticize every detail of your game and give you a hundred instructions about what to remember when you step on to the court. But this is not the way the body likes to play. As a tennis pro, Gallwey found that asking players simply to watch him take shots was more effective than issuing instructions, because you learn more effectively by letting your unconscious mind absorb images of good play. His conclusion was that "conscious trying—directed by the conscious mind—often produces negative results."

You know this instinctively by the fact that when you are playing at your best you are not thinking in a technical way about your shots—you are a fluid unity of mind, body, court, and racket. You are, to use Mihaly Csikszentmihalyi's famous term, in a state of "flow." On a good day, it all seems easy.

If this ability to master "the art of effortless concentration" is the basis of the inner game, how do you go about it? Can it be created at will?

The two selves

As a player and trainer, Gallwey noticed that most people who have had tennis lessons know the correct way to make a shot. The problem is acting on what you know. Once you have the skills, your mental game is the problem. You sabotage your play by putting yourself down after a bad shot, worrying about the consequences of losing, or coming to terrible conclusions about your abilities.

Gallwey's discovery was that when someone goes out on to the court, two people are playing: Self 1, the instructing, motivating, calculating coach; and Self 2, the one who actually goes out and plays. The first self is the "teller," the part of you that shouts, "C'mon!" to put more intensity into your game, while the second self is the "doer," playing with a storehouse of memories of every shot ever played. Without the badgering of Self 1, Self 2 could play brilliantly. The further Self 1 takes matters into its own hands, forcing instructions to "improve" play, the worse the play actually gets.

Quiet the mind

Gallwey's experience as a tennis coach underwent a transformation. He moved from being a technical instructor of "good" shots to simply being a quiet model of good play. Instead of criticizing or complimenting his students he would just ask them to watch him over and over, then let their mind and body unconsciously replicate his actions. By discouraging judgments from either student or coach, the player's ability was revealed and their potential could be realized. Students would "discover" their shots rather than "manufacture" them.

Gallwey quotes the Zen master D. T. Suzuki: "Man is a thinking reed but his great works are done when he is not calculating and thinking." Uncluttered with words or instructions, a still mind makes for the best performance. An unquiet mind starts to judge. We like to say, "That was a terrible shot," when in fact it was a shot—not good or bad—and we have tagged meaning on to it. Once you have given an emotional meaning to an event, you are less able to be fully aware of the next moment because you are caught up in emotion. You will not be able to see your play clearly, only through the mists of fury or despond. If you can notice what is happening without too much judgment you will naturally maintain concentration and seize opportunities. If you keep judging yourself negatively, it will add up to a negative statement about your whole self—it becomes a self-fulfilling prophecy.

Paradoxically, success comes when you temporarily withhold judgments of success or failure but notice what *is*. Without such distortions, you can be calmly effective. To play at your best, you must live every second in the present. This is concentration. The easy way to concentration is through noticing all the details of the game: the way the ball spins, the sound it is making when it hits the racket, the way your arm is moving to take a shot, your breathing. While on the surface this may seem a bit dreamy, it is in fact the opposite, because the moment you really notice things you are not worrying about what will happen next or hitting yourself for the point you missed—all your energies are focused on this moment, this point. The burst of energy, creativity, and resolve that comes from existing in the moment is what the writer Eckhart Tolle calls "the power of now."

Larger rewards

The Inner Game of Tennis is interesting because it asks what success is. For Gallwey, it turned out that winning games was less important than overcoming his nervousness on court. Playing to the best of his abilities without sabotaging his game with poor thinking—this was victory.

People who look only for measurable success, Gallwey says, can have a one-dimensional existence. It is possible to go through life being so focused on external achievement that you forget to appreciate the wonders of nature, neglect to love those closest to you, and never stop to reflect on your broader life purpose. You need to make a distinction between a compulsion to succeed for the sake of winning and a desire for success that will enrich your life and those of others. As Gallwey puts it:

"Winning is overcoming obstacles to reach a goal, but the value in winning is only as great as the value of the goal reached."

In other words, the purpose of success is not necessarily the achievement of a goal, but the self-knowledge that you gain in striving toward it.

The Inner Game of Tennis is very much influenced by eastern teachings, particularly Zen Buddhism. Gallwey's premise is that through not being attached to the fruits of victory (i.e., winning the trophy), you paradoxically become free to play the game for itself in a more relaxed and powerful state of mind. Through nonattachment, winning is more likely.

Tennis, or any other sport, is simply the medium through which you learn more significant elements such as concentration, Gallwey says. Working on your inner game is worth doing, because if you can improve your concentration or be more relaxed under pressure, these skills are obviously going to benefit every area of your life, not merely the one you trained your mind for. In his 1970s language, Gallwey describes this as "unfreakability."

Final comments
The Inner Game of Tennis laid the foundation for today's personal coaching industry. It put forward ideas that are now commonplace in coaching, such as trusting people to come up with their own solutions; asking questions instead of instructing; visualizing successful outcomes; and appreciating the value of each moment.

Its ideas were important to the emerging field of sports psychology, and the corporate world also latched on to it. Gallwey's comment that "almost every human activity involves both the outer and the inner game" explains its wide impact. The book helped to pave the way for today's view that work should be a means of self-expression in addition to being merely a way to make money, and has contributed to the realization that "relaxed concentration," not fierce self-punishment, more effectively leads you to true success.

There is a surprising amount of information in this slim book, much of it not touched on here. Spanning human nature, the way the brain and body work, and the meaning of competition and success, *The Inner Game of Tennis* can be enjoyed even if you have little interest in sport.

W. Timothy Gallwey

Born in 1938 in San Francisco, Gallwey won the boys' division of the US National Hardcourt Championships at 15 and while at Harvard University, where he majored in English literature, captained the tennis team. He served as an officer in the US Navy, and as an educationalist helped to found a liberal arts college.

During a break from his career in education, Gallwey took up the post of tennis pro at a club in Seaside, California. What he had learned while practicing yoga he applied to coaching, with remarkable results. Though not warmly received by professional coaches, The Inner Game of Tennis *became a surprise bestseller. Gallwey became a corporate trainer, teaching inner game principles to Apple, Coca-Cola, and others.*

His other books include The Inner Game of Golf, Inner Skiing, The Inner Game of Music, The Inner Game of Work, *and* The Inner Game of Stress.

1992

Hard Drive: Bill Gates and the Making of the Microsoft Empire

"Gates was immediately hooked. Whenever he had free time, he would run over to the Upper School to get more experience on the system. But Gates was not the only computer-crazed kid at Lakeside. He found he had to compete for time on the computer with a handful of others who were similarly drawn to the room as if by a powerful gravitational force. Among them was a soft-spoken, Upper School student by the name of Paul Allen, who was two years older than Gates."

"Seven years later, the two classmates would form Microsoft, the most successful startup company in the history of American business."

In a nutshell

In your field of work, see what can be achieved by "setting the standard."

In a similar vein
Malcolm Gladwell *Outliers* (p. 136)
Brent Schlender & Rick Tetzeli *Becoming Steve Jobs* (p. 186)

CHAPTER 18

James Wallace & Jim Erickson

B ill Gates is today best known for being the richest man in the world, thanks to the astounding success of the company he co-founded. But what do we really know of Gates the person, and what was the secret of Microsoft's success?

There are now many Gates biographies, but *Hard Drive*, written by two Seattle journalists, still gives the best insights into the early years of Microsoft and what it was like to work under its CEO. If you have even a mild interest in the computing world, entrepreneurship, and wealth creation, this is a fantastic read, better than many novels. If you are about to start a business, it may expand your thinking of what you should aim for.

At another level, if you use a Microsoft operating system or application, it is fascinating to learn of the long road that was traveled before these products seemed easy to use. Although this was a company that grew incredibly fast, it was still almost 15 years before Windows became a household name.

Hard Drive was written in 1992 and covers only Microsoft's first 15 or so years, but these were the most interesting from a success perspective.

Seeing the future, and acting

It is well known that Gates started Microsoft with friend Paul Allen when he was only 19, after dropping out of Harvard. However, by that time he was already an expert programmer, having spent the previous few years working on a primitive computer at school. When still in his final year, he was offered a job at $165 a week (with

Allen) to debug the computer system of a defense contractor. His school, the enlightened, expensive Lakeside in Seattle, allowed him to take a whole semester off to do the job.

Gates and Allen had talked about starting their own software company for years, and shared a vision that almost everybody would someday have their own personal computer (this was in the age when computers filled whole rooms and were so expensive, only corporations and the military had them). If this happened, why should *they* not be the ones who provided the software?

Gates's parents, however, expected him to go to college, and when he duly arrived at Harvard his intention was to find people who were smarter than he was. Disappointed, he spent a lot of time playing poker in addition to doing some math courses, but it was still a fruitful period. Wallace and Erickson note:

> *"At Harvard, Gates read business books like other male students read* Playboy. *He wanted to know everything he could about running a company, from managing people to marketing products."*

When Allen saw an article in *Popular Electronics* about a new "personal computer" that was being made by a company called MITS in New Mexico, he and Gates realized they had to make their move. The pair flew south and convinced the hardware firm that they could write a program that would actually make the "Altair" computer usable by enthusiasts. Relocating to Albuquerque, in a great hurry they tailored a version of the BASIC programming language for the Altair. Gates put everything into the new business, taking only a few days off during its first two years. However, it soon became obvious to the public that the real value in the computer was its software, and Gates and Allen were eager to sell their program to other firms. Eventually they were able to wiggle out of the contract they had made with MITS and became free to sell versions of BASIC to other companies. Amazingly, these included big names such as General Electric and National Cash Register. The tiny outfit began to make real money.

Later, after Microsoft had relocated to Seattle to be nearer Gates's parents, he confessed to a fellow programmer his two ambitions: "to design software that would make a computer easy enough for his mother to use and to build a company bigger than his dad's law firm."

By 1981, having made an agreement with industry Goliath IBM, Microsoft had already overtaken the revenues of that law firm.

Above all, a business

Potential clients coming to Microsoft's headquarters frequently thought Gates was the scruffy office boy. At 25 he still looked 17, and often wore a pizza-stained T-shirt he had slept in the night before. Yet once the youthful CEO started talking, Wallace and Erickson note, clients forgot his age. Clearly a master not only of the technical stuff but of the business of the computer industry, he even wrote his own contracts, taking clauses from corporate law textbooks.

In his zeal for customers Gates went for market share first, often quoting too low for the work involved and imposing ridiculous time-frames on his programmers. Yet his ethos of "satisfy the customer first, profits second" meant that the company raced ahead of its competitors. In the early days, Wallace and Erickson note, "Gates sustained Microsoft through tireless salesmanship," making cold calls and haranguing potential buyers until they relented. In an echo of Michael Gerber's advice of "work *on* your business, not in it," Gates, although an excellent programmer, was always slightly more inspired by the *business* of Microsoft and where it could go than by the actual products themselves.

He was always an intense communicator, willing to tear a person to pieces on some intellectual, business, or programming point. Yet he was also able to listen and change his mind in a hurry if the facts pointed that way. Microsoft hired people in his image: very high IQ, passionate, and willing to work around the clock. When a deadline loomed, the whole company would be forced into a frenzy, "pulling all-nighters" to meet deadlines. Gates's habit of making it onto planes just before the gates closed was symbolic of a larger outlook of taking things to the edge. It was at this edge, he once noted, "where you most often find high performance."

Windows of wealth

Microsoft's informal company motto was "We set the standard." Not just an empty morale booster, it reflected the prizes that would go to the firm that established proprietary industry standards for systems and applications. And by designing software "easy enough for [Gates's] mother to use," the company would find a universal audience for its products.

In the famous Windows operating system, the two visions came together. However, there was a long and rocky path to this fulfillment:

❖ The initial version took 30 of the company's best programmers two years to create and test, involving 80 work years. Hundreds of screaming fits preceded the launch date.

❖ Once released, it was a commercial and critical flop. An improved version still did not set the world alight.

❖ Windows 3.0, released in 1990, finally delivered on the system's initial promise, selling three million copies in its first year alone.

❖ Even including the many elements lifted from Apple's "graphical user interface," Windows was seven years in the making.

Today, Windows and Microsoft Office applications such as Word and Excel still power many of the world's computers and continue to rake in money for the company.

Windows may have revolutionized personal computing, but marketing played a vital part in its establishment as an industry standard. For this job, Microsoft hired Rowland Hanson, previously head of marketing for Neutrogena. In the cosmetics industry branding was everything, and Hanson felt that in the computer industry too, having good software was only half the battle. To be really successful, Microsoft had to have its name connected with its products. People had to want not just programs, but *Microsoft* programs. Hanson's goal, the authors note, was "to make Microsoft the Sara Lee of the software industry."

After the success of its third version, Windows did indeed become a famous brand with an equally famous logo. It has been an astonishing cash cow for Microsoft. By "setting the standard," even if many people considered that standard not to be the industry best, Microsoft found (to IBM's chagrin) that the real money was in the "soul" of a machine—its software—rather than bits of metal and molded plastic.

Final comments

Was there something special about Gates himself that enabled Microsoft to emerge No. 1 in the software industry, or was it just a case of good timing, along with a basic amount of brainpower and work, as Malcolm Gladwell suggests in *Outliers*?

What really set Gates apart was the boldness of his vision—"A computer on every desk, and Microsoft software in every computer"—and his brilliance as a businessman. While it is hard to believe now, many very intelligent people in the early 1980s thought personal computing would not amount to much and that business applications were the real growth area. In betting their young lives on the former, Gates and Allen reaped the benefits, although luck certainly played its part. For instance, in its hurry to put a personal computer on the market, IBM had to use other companies' software and create a machine out of nonproprietary parts. This gave Microsoft a huge opportunity, as the ubiquity of IBM "clones" meant that the software, rather than the machines themselves, became what was valuable. And yet, it could also be said that if Gates and Allen had not had the vision in the first place, they may not have made so much of the opportunity. This is a key success principle worth reiterating: Without some kind of vision of what you want to achieve, it is unlikely you will notice the specific opportunities that can make it happen.

As well as being a great read, *Hard Drive* highlights the benefits of working in a "star" company. In business strategy terms, this is one that doubles in size every year or so because it is the clear leader of its fast-growing category. Most of the early employees of Microsoft became multimillionaires or billionaires once stock options were introduced. Charles Simonyi, for instance, who oversaw the development of Microsoft Word and Excel, once spent $25 million on a two-week holiday on the Russian space station. Thousands of other employees hit a bonanza just by working in the right company at the right time. They had to be brainy to get their foot in the door and then work very hard, but their experience shows that if you are not one to start a business on your own, picking the right employer is often half the task in becoming successful.

James Wallace & Jim Erickson

Wallace and Erickson wrote Hard Drive *while working as investigative reporters for the* Seattle Post-Intelligencer. *Wallace was a senior journalist for the newspaper, specializing in technology and aviation, and followed* Hard Drive *with a sequel,* Overdrive: Bill Gates and the Race to Control Cyberspace *(1997).*

Erickson moved to Hong Kong in 1997 and became business and technology editor for Time *magazine. He is currently managing editor of Alizila, a website devoted to news on the Alibaba company.*

How to Be Rich

"After all, 'richness' is at least as much a matter of character, of philosophy, outlook and attitude, as it is of money. The 'millionaire mentality' is not—and in this day and age, cannot be—merely an accumulative mentality. The able, ambitious man who strives for success must understand that the term 'rich' has infinite shades of meaning. In order to justify himself and his wealth, he must know how to be rich in virtually every positive sense of the term."

"To be truly rich, regardless of his fortune or lack of it, a man must live by his own values. If those values are not personally meaningful, then no amount of money gained can hide the emptiness of life without them."

In a nutshell

Live by your own values; be your own person.

In a similar vein
Warren Buffett (by Roger Lowenstein) *Buffett* (p. 48)
Andrew Carnegie *The Autobiography of Andrew Carnegie* (p. 56)
Thomas J. Stanley *The Millionaire Mind* (p. 296)

CHAPTER 19

John Paul Getty

*H*ow to Be Rich is essentially a series of articles that Getty was commissioned to write by *Playboy* magazine. His intention was to explain himself and why he was a businessman, and secondly to get behind the myths of what it was like to have great wealth. Hence the title of the book: not how to *get* rich, but how to *be* rich.

Wildcatter to mogul

John Paul Getty's father, George Getty, had grown up poor on an Ohio farm, but later managed to get through law school supported by his wife. He became a successful Minneapolis attorney and did well in the Oklahoma oil rush.

John Paul was born into this relative prosperity in 1892, an only child. He writes fondly of a teenage apprenticeship as a roustabout in the oil fields, then very much a dusty frontier place of rough men, "where gambling halls were viewed as the ultimate in civic improvements." In utter contrast, he then spent two years at Oxford University before returning to the States.

He had planned to enter the US diplomatic service, but at 22 went into business on his own as a wildcatter (an independent oil driller and speculator) and got lucky with some oil leases. He was a millionaire by age 24. Deciding to "retire," he enjoyed himself for a couple of years, but his parents were not pleased, his father telling him that he had a duty to build and operate businesses that created wealth and a better life for people.

The oil rush had shifted to California and Getty decided to invest in new oil leases near Los Angeles. His business rapidly expanded over the next few years, but his father's death in 1930 was a setback. It was said that Getty Sr. left John Paul $15 million. In fact it was $500,000.

During the Depression of the 1930s, Getty came up with the idea of an integrated oil company spanning exploration, refining, and retail marketing. He bought up oil stocks, which were now very cheap, purchased the Pierre Hotel in New York at a bargain price, and began a difficult 15-year takeover of the Tidewater Oil Company, then one of California's largest. After the Second World War Getty Oil gambled $12 million on oil concessions in Saudi Arabia. Though it took a further four years and $18 million for the wells to produce, by then the world had become aware of the vast reserves in the area, and the gamble paid off handsomely.

In 1957, *Fortune* magazine named Getty the richest man in America, with an estimated worth of $1 billion. He would from then on receive an average of 3,000 letters a week from strangers requesting money.

JPG's tips on success in business and in life

Beat your own path

How to Be Rich was written at the zenith of large-company capitalism, when the species "organization man" evolved to make the most of his small place in the corporate machinery. Getty describes this person as "dedicated to serving the complex rituals of memorandums and buck-passing." In contrast, Getty's "office" in his early years in the oil fields was the front seat of a battered Model T Ford.

Most executives, Getty observed, would rather become "boot-lickers" to those above them than risk rocking the boat. This was actually counterproductive, because the only real security in the workplace was reserved for those who demonstrated that they could add value. Successful businesspeople, he believed, were usually rebels of some description whose wealth was built on rejection of the status quo. For example, Getty does not mention his purchase of oil stock at low prices after the Wall Street crash as a boast, but to demonstrate that the businessperson who does not follow the pack often "reaps fantastic rewards."

Be open-minded

Getty had invited an outspoken socialist to a dinner party at his Sutton Place mansion just outside London. Another guest, a fellow American, was appalled. Getty did not apologize; in fact, he felt he was honoring the great American tradition of encouraging dissent. Hearing views different to your own, he believed, "adds spice, spirit, and an invigorating quality to life."

Writing at the beginning of the 1960s, he correctly forecast that the "vanished dissenters" would soon reappear, and knew that the economic future would be brighter because of it. Getty's moral was that wealth was only ever generated by open minds, because only such intellectual openness enables us to see opportunities that others do not. The alternative was a society "lulled into a perilous somnolence," unable to tell the difference between spin and truth, prey to lobbyists and propagandists. Despite appearances, like many of the truly rich Getty was something of a radical.

Enrich your life with art

Getty humbly saw himself as a patron of the arts on a scale at least equaling the Medicis of Renaissance Florence and is amusing when discussing the average American's lack of cultural knowledge. He called art "the finest investment," not merely because it more than held its own financially, but because of the pleasure of living with beautiful things. In return for enriching the world, the wealth creator has a duty to support those who live for their art. Yet he also saw business itself in creative terms, noting that those at the top are "creative artists" instead of simply "artisans of business."

On collecting itself, Getty dissolves the myth that it is a rarefied pastime for the rich, mentioning several acquaintances in regular jobs who had built up excellent collections. Anyone with enough money can pay top dollar at Sotheby's, but the true collector is a scholar who appreciates the background of each piece bought. As Getty rather poetically puts it:

"To me, they are vital embodiments of their creators. They mirror the hopes and frustrations of those who created them—and the times and places in which they were created."

What could be more fascinating or enriching?

Get the facts, then act

In a chapter titled "Business Blunders and Booby Traps," Getty says that many mistakes in business and in life result from a failure to distinguish between fact and opinion or hearsay.

He once commissioned a geologist to report on the potential of an oil lease. The report said that there was little chance of finding oil, so

Getty sold the lease. It later turned out to be part of the huge Yale oil pool. Yet Getty did not blame the expert, only himself for accepting his view without question and not getting another opinion.

Businesspeople frequently accept as fact what they have heard or read without doing their own investigation or study. This is not so bad on its own, but when the results will affect a whole enterprise and the livelihoods of workers, it is an important point. If you *have* made a decision that is based on facts, stick to it. Have the courage of your convictions. The relaxed businessperson, Getty says, is always much more effective, and if you have done your homework your resolve will be less likely to be sabotaged by worry.

Final comments

Getty notes that of the tens of thousands of Americans who take their lives each year, a significant number are classed as "economic suicides." His point is that many scramble for and achieve financial success, but when they get it they find that it lacks meaning. People need to believe that their efforts are increasing value and enriching the world in some way, that they are engaged in real creative effort and not simply status seeking.

Getty himself gained a reputation as a miser because he famously put a payphone in the hall of his Sutton Place mansion. (Guests had been using the regular phones to make transatlantic calls.) Yet with the passage of time, we can see that if it were not for the man's dedication to eliminating waste and maximizing resources, millions of people today would not be enjoying what he left. He is now, after all, more famous as an art collector and philanthropist. The collection he created is one of the world's best—as anyone who has been to the Getty Museum at Malibu, California, will attest.

Getty was a great believer in the free enterprise system, but was not the arch-capitalist that many people think. He never complained about high wages, taking the Henry Ford view that a work force that was not well paid would not buy the products you were trying to sell. As for unions, he respected their desire to better the lot of the worker and considered them a legitimate part of a productive economy.

A millionaire had to accept everything with good humor, Getty realized. When he was named "richest man in the world," he had a hard time explaining to journalists that he did not sit on mountains of

cash; nearly all his wealth was tied up in infrastructure and operations, and he was working 16–18 hours a day to keep it all going. He
admits that his marriages suffered and fell apart as the result of his
dedication to work, and there were books he had wanted to read and
didn't have the time for—but on the whole, he reflected, he had led an
exciting and rewarding life.

1956

How to Have Confidence and Power in Dealing with People

"Various scientific studies have proven that if you learn how to deal with other people, you will have gone about 85 percent of the way down the road to success in any business, occupation, or profession, and about 99 percent of the way down the road to personal happiness."

"Human relations is the science of dealing with people in such a way that our egos and their egos remain intact. And this is the only method of getting along with people that ever brings any real success or any real satisfaction."

In a nutshell

Everyone hungers for appreciation and acceptance. If you can genuinely provide these you will have the key to human influence.

In a similar vein

CHAPTER 20

Les Giblin

For every person who loses their job because they have failed to do it effectively, another two get the sack because they cannot deal properly with other people. In the opening pages of his 1950s classic, Les Giblin says:

"If you will stop and think a minute, the chances are that you will say that the people you know who are the most successful, and enjoy life the most, are those who 'have a way' with other people."

But how do they acquire this "way"?

He suggests that people with top-rated interpersonal skills have a much better understanding of human nature; they don't think of human nature in terms of "good" or "bad" or how they would like it to be, but *as it is*. Naturally, this understanding of what drives people provides greater insight into why they act the way they do, allowing greater ease and power in communication.

Recognizing the divine spark

Influence is an art, Giblin says, that stems from knowledge of the sensitivity of the ego. He mentions the case of a man who strangled a woman who fell asleep while he was talking to her, and a boy who robbed a bank to prove his manliness after having been teased for years about his buckteeth. The more wounded the ego, the greater the extremes a person will go to in order to defend it.

Yet the ego has also been described as a "divine spark" that gives us the belief that we can do great things. We take for granted our own value and dignity, and any approach to dealing with people must take this into account. Just as the body needs food, a person needs this sense of self-worth to be frequently affirmed; a rich person needs compliments as much as one who is downtrodden.

When respect is not given, the ego may enlarge to make up for the attempt to shrink it; this is why loud-mouthed and dominating people are usually found to have low levels of self-esteem. But how do you deal with such people? If you enter into a fierce exchange with them you may "win the argument but lose the sale." Giblin says that fighting fire with fire will only inflame the other person. On the premise that "a hungry dog is a mean dog," the only way to influence a troublemaker is to feed their ego, by finding something—even something small—with which you can genuinely compliment them. Though we are often told to appeal to a person's reason to convince them of something, in truth reason is not a great persuader.

Giblin relates the story of General Oglethorpe, who had no success with his logical arguments in persuading King George to fund a new colony in America—until he pointed out that none of the colonies had yet borne the king's name. Thus the state of Georgia was born, fully financed, from insight into the cravings of the ego. If you want to get someone to do something for you, always think of a personal reason why they would be willing to do it, something that will affirm their identity. "Men and women who have the most influence with other people are men and women who *believe* other people are important," Giblin says.

How to convince

Giblin refers to three Yale psychologists who found through a series of tests on people that the best way to get ideas accepted is to *calmly present the facts*, with no threats or attempts to force the argument. People like to make up their own mind. He refers to other researchers from New York University who spent hundreds of hours eavesdropping on salesmen at work and also watched debates at the United Nations to see who won and why. Their conclusion was that the UN professionals were less successful in getting their point across because they tried to beat down their opposition through argument. The fundamental mistake made in trying to convince another person of something, the researchers found, is to attack them (their ego). This may force a victory of sorts, but not one in which the other person comes to see things the way you do. Giblin says:

"Tell a man that his ideas are stupid, and he will defend them all the more . . . Use threats, or scare tactics, and he simply closes his mind against your ideas, regardless of how good they may be."

Giblin's "Six tested rules for winning arguments" include No. 5: "Speak through third persons." People won't necessarily listen to *your* argument for something, but they will listen to impartial third parties. This is why a lawyer produces witnesses to convince a jury and why customer testimonials are employed to sell a product. Use common or expert opinion as a low-pressure means of getting people to think your way.

No. 6 is "Let the other person save face." Giblin notes that often people would change their mind to your way of thinking except for one thing: they have already committed to their position and can't or won't back down. But the "skillful persuader" is always able to find a loophole through which the other person can crawl gracefully, rescuing them from their own argument.

Drawing forth friendliness

Studies of successful individuals reveal a common denominator: skill in using words. They are good at small talk and engaging people in conversation. Less successful people are afraid of saying something stupid, so are less inclined to pipe up. Giblin mentions the English author John Ruskin, who said that he wrote well only when he was not trying to write well. The same applies to conversation. To be good it must be relaxed, and to be relaxed there must be a fair amount of idle banter. Even Shakespeare wasn't afraid to be trite.

A game show host has the ability to make people feel at ease because of his light-hearted chitchat, yet nobody thinks him a fool—he has an uncommon skill. He gets people talking by asking them about the one thing he knows they are truly interested in: themselves. We say to "strike up" conversation, because you must start small, with a spark, but it can lead to a bonfire of ideas and amusement. Don't be afraid of small talk; if nothing else, it is a way to find out interesting information. "Nuggets and gems in conversation come only after you have dug a lot of low-grade ore," Giblin remarks.

One further tip on conversation: Because anything that threatens self-esteem is dangerous, you should never be sarcastic. Giblin points to research showing that people do not like to be made fun of, even by close friends, but will never mention it because it would make them sound like a bad sport.

How to motivate others

The best way to get a job done is not to ask someone to do something for you, Giblin says, it is to ask them to help you think about how to do it. This makes them feel appreciated for their brain, not just their brawn, and they will be motivated to demonstrate their intelligence. Winston Churchill, Giblin reports, said: "I have found that the best way to get another to *acquire* a virtue, is to *impute* it to him." Let a person know you think they can do something, and they will.

Final comments

At first glance, this book is a good example of the shallow personality technique manuals that we associate with the 1950s and 1960s. In fact, it is more like Carnegie's *How to Win Friends and Influence People* in its insistence on genuinely valuing the importance of other people and recognizing the centrality of people skills to success.

It may seem the sort of book that only a salesperson would buy, but this assumption could deprive you of tips and ideas that could turn out to be vital to your success. Most of its references are dated, but the book endures because people do not change. To be a scholar of success you have to be a student of human nature, and *How to Have Confidence and Power in Dealing with People* is highly valuable as a guide to people *as they are*.

Les Giblin

Giblin was born in Iowa in 1912. Through his "human relationship clinics" and other seminars, he has worked to improve interpersonal skills in many of America's largest companies and hundreds of sales and marketing clubs. He is a former top salesman and was Salesman of the Year in 1965.

His other books include the bestselling Skill with People. How to Have Confidence and Power in Dealing with People *has sold over half a million copies.*

2008

Outliers

"We are so caught up in the myths of the best and brightest and the self-made that we think outliers spring naturally from the earth. We look at the young Bill Gates and marvel that our world allowed that thirteen-year-old to become a fabulously successful entrepreneur. But that's the wrong lesson. Our world only allowed one thirteen-year-old unlimited access to a time-sharing terminal in 1968. If a million teenagers had been given the same opportunity, how many more Microsofts would we have today? To build a better world we need to replace the patchwork of lucky breaks and arbitrary advantages that today determine success—the fortunate birth dates and the happy accidents of history—with a society that provides opportunities for all."

"Everything we have learned says that success follows a predictable course. It is not the brightest who succeed . . . Nor is success simply the sum of the decisions and efforts we make on our own behalf. It is, rather, a gift. Outliers are those who have been given opportunities—and who have had the strength and presence of mind to seize them."

In a nutshell

People attribute their achievements to themselves, but much of their success can be traced to their circumstances and making the most of lucky opportunities.

In a similar vein

Angela Duckworth *Grit* (p. 90)
James Wallace & Jim Erickson *Hard Drive* (p. 116)
Adam Grant *Give and Take* (p. 150)
Ray Kroc *Grinding It Out* (p. 214)

CHAPTER 21

Malcolm Gladwell

From Samuel Smiles to Tony Robbins, the personal development world has revolved around the belief that achievers are not the product of their environments, but rather became great by transcending their circumstances in the creation of something new. Malcolm Gladwell was suspicious of this notion of the "self-made" person, and with *Outliers: The Story of Success* he set about providing evidence for an alternative view that emphasizes background, genes, time, and place as the determinants of success. A person is no more than the tip of an iceberg of culture, family, and nation, therefore casting someone as their own noble and great creation is misleading.

"We pretend that success is exclusively a matter of individual merit," says Gladwell, but "things are not that simple." *Outliers* is about the

"people who were given a special opportunity to work really hard and seized it, and who happened to come of age at a time when that extraordinary effort was rewarded by the rest of society. Their success was not just of their own making. It was a product of the world in which they grew up."

There is no mystery to success—even to how we explain the existence of super-achievers, or what Gladwell calls "outliers"—other than seizing the opportunities provided.

Whether you agree with his ideas or not (see the critique below), *Outliers* is an important book in the success literature because it is a genuine attempt at a *theory* of success. If success is ever to become a discipline like, say, management or psychology, much more research needs to be done at both the conceptual level (what success is and its causes) and the scientific level (what ideas or strategies have been proven to work, empirically). Gladwell's book is a real contribution to that end, written with his usual panache and fascinating examples.

I timed my birth perfectly

One of the paragons of success in our age is Bill Gates, founder of Microsoft. But Gladwell asks the question: How much of Gates's success was down to him, and how much of it was lucky birth timing and having family who supported his love of computing?

Born in 1955, Gates was lucky to come of age at the dawn of the personal computer era. As a teenager, he had access to a primitive Teletype computer at his private school, Lakeside, in Seattle, which made basic programming possible for a novice with a lot of time on his hands. When computers were extremely expensive, this kind of access was highly unusual. Gates was also very lucky to have lived near the University of Washington, which had a computer that was booked solid all the time—except between 3 A.M. and 6 A.M. In the middle of the night, Gates would rouse himself and steal away from the family home, taking over the university's computer to program when no one else was around. Finally, he was highly fortunate to have been at a school that let him and his friend Paul Allen take a whole term off to work on a commercial programming project. Gates told Gladwell, "I had a better exposure to software development at a young age than I think anyone did in that period of time, and all because of an incredibly lucky series of events."

For Gladwell, Gates's story is a perfect illustration of the fact that people who seem exceptionally gifted at what they do in fact turn out to have been given exceptional opportunities. More than that, they took advantage of those opportunities at just the time and place when the payoff for seizing them was great. It turns out that Gates was the perfect age to be on the ground floor of the personal computer revolution, in the sense that he was too young to have got caught up working for a large player like IBM (and been simply an employee), but just old enough to be out of school and ready to build something new (which he did, dropping out of Harvard to co-found Microsoft in 1975 with Allen).

The heroic Gates myth makes him out to be a one-in-a-billion kind of guy, but in Gladwell's mind this thinking is wrong. Gates simply had unusual access to a powerful computer and the brains to make the most of it. Gladwell writes:

"If a million teenagers had been given the same opportunity, how many more Microsofts would we have today? To build a better world we need to replace the patchwork of lucky breaks and arbitrary advantages that today determine success—the fortunate birth dates and the happy accidents of history—with a society that provides opportunities for all."

The crucial facts around Gates's success were environmental: a fine school near a good university, loving and supportive parents, lucky birth timing. He had a high IQ, but if he had been born in a poor country or come of age in, say, the Great Depression, the opportunities just would not have existed to make the mark that he did.

Disguised blessings

What constitutes "fortunate" circumstances, though, is in the eye of the beholder.

Gladwell observes that growing up relatively poor, and as part of a minority, can often be an advantage. In analyzing the fortunes of New York's immigrant Jewish community, he finds that socio-economic status was not a disadvantage, in that it made parents all the more determined for their children to succeed in mainstream professions like medicine and law and to get their family out of the low-status, low-paying garment trade.

In the 1950s, young Jewish lawyers were turned away from Establishment firms for not being Anglo-Saxon and Protestant, so had to build their own companies. Driven to succeed, men like Joe Flom did so by being willing to take on work that traditional firms found distasteful, such as corporate takeovers and divorce. When, years later, the corporate takeover boom happened, Flom and colleagues were well placed to take advantage of it, and many fortunes were made. Gladwell notes that the lawyers didn't "triumph over adversity." No, "what started out as adversity ended up being an opportunity." When one route was closed off, it forced them to take another way, which proved to be the seed of their success.

People are fond of saying that they got a head start in life, but sometimes it may be just as beneficial to begin without one. Furthermore, their advantage reduces the longer the race. It is natural for parents to want to give their children a head start, and natural for us to bemoan or be thankful about whether we ourselves received one, but in no case should we be fooled into thinking that an initial advantage is *decisive*. Success is more complex than that; it is not, as motivational books suggest, about "overcoming obstacles" in any heroic sense, but simply about seeing restrictions as pointers to move in another, even more fruitful direction.

Brains, work, or opportunity: What matters most?

Gladwell attempts to dismantle the belief that intelligence is decisive in success. He draws on research to show that IQ matters only up to a point. Beyond a higher than average IQ of 120, say, having additional points on the scale "doesn't seem to translate into any measurable real-world advantage." You just have to be smart *enough*, and beyond this point it is "traits of personality and character," as the intelligence researcher Arthur Jensen put it, that make all the difference. British psychologist Liam Hudson observed: "A mature scientist with an adult IQ of 130 is as likely to win a Nobel Prize as is one whose IQ is 180." At age 20, two scientists may not have been even when it came to figuring out some mathematical problem, for instance, but once into their full careers the scientist with the lower IQ can easily have made up for the deficiency in sheer brainpower in other areas: greater knowledge, more systematic research skills, better ability to make connections in ideas, or the social smarts to get ahead in the workplace.

The intelligence pioneer Lewis Terman tracked children with high intelligence into adulthood. He found that it was not the difference between them in intelligence that was the important factor in real-life success, but family background. The most successful came from reasonably well-to-do homes "filled with books," and half had fathers with a college degree at a time when higher education was much less common. The group who had not done so well came from "the wrong side of the tracks." What upper-middle-class kids get that others don't, Gladwell says, is "concerted cultivation" by their parents. This adds greatly to their self-confidence and gives them, he notes, a sense of entitlement.

If being reasonably, but not unusually, smart and having a supportive background are significant, they are not enough on their own, however. The crucial decider in who becomes a star in their chosen field is incredible skill built up through thousands of hours of practice or activity in that area. Here Gladwell discusses the famous "ten-thousand-hour rule," which says that to get really good at anything requires at least 10,000 hours of deliberate practice. Obviously, the younger you are when you become extremely good at something, the more opportunities will arise to build on that. It may seem like someone is a *wunderkind* born with a remarkable talent, but the truth is more prosaic.

For instance, between 1957, when John Lennon and Paul McCartney started jamming together, and 1964, when they toured America, the Beatles had played on stage around 1,200 times. That time included their residency in Hamburg, an intense period when they sometimes performed two or three times a day. Gladwell describes Hamburg as a "crucible" for the group that set them apart, making them incredibly tight as musicians while allowing them to experiment, far from home, with new songs and gauge the audience's reaction. Indeed, Gladwell notes that nearly every success story in his book "involves someone or some group working harder than their peers . . . Working really hard is what successful people do." Although 10,000 hours may be "the magic number of greatness," as Gladwell puts it, it is instructive that the Beatles only got to go to Hamburg through their manager's chance meeting with a German impresario. Success is never down to a single thing, but is rather a combination of talent, work, luck, and environment.

Critique and final comments

Gladwell is right to elevate background, cultural legacy, and the times as key shapers of success or failure in life. When he says, "Successful people don't do it alone. Where they come from matters. They're products of particular places and environments," he is right—to an extent. Our genes, quality of upbringing, educational opportunities, and the country we are born in are all extremely important, but is life really that deterministic? Gladwell's argument takes no account of *personal transformation*, which by its nature can never be predicted. It is one thing to have in place "a predictable and powerful set of circumstances and opportunities," but this is usually only half of the story. The other half is a person's decision to answer a great call or challenge that will take them to a higher level. As not everyone is willing to stir the waters of a settled life, not everyone will take this leap. Just as it is difficult to predict how someone will react in an emergency or in time of war, so it is impossible to foresee how a mature adult will respond to alluring but difficult opportunities, even relatively late in life.

The only thing we can be certain of when it comes to people is that they will continually surprise us. The ultimate outcome of a person's life will hinge on unpredicted personal revolutions that push them in some new direction. These inflection points make the difference between, for instance, a man who is fading into obscurity as a retired sales executive, and one who in his 50s mortgages his home to finance a risky rollout of a restaurant chain (McDonald's) that inspires him like nothing else has before. No one (perhaps not even Ray Kroc himself) could have predicted such an internal revolution. Yes, the combination of heritage and luck is "critical to making [the successful person] who they are," as Gladwell has it, but never does it account for *what* they do. As many people effectively become someone else during their lifetime, it is possible for "where we came from" to be both important and irrelevant at the same time.

In *Zero to One*, venture capitalist Peter Thiel took aim at the "smart" thinking on success, voiced by everyone from Gladwell to Warren Buffett to Bill Gates, that it is largely down to being lucky enough to be born in the right place at the right time, with good parents and helpful genes: winning the lottery of life. This philosophy means that we too easily dismiss, Thiel says, what may be unusual about successful people, such as the serial entrepreneur who finds value where others don't look. Thiel recalls the words of Ralph Waldo Emerson: "Shallow men believe in luck, believe in circumstances . . . Strong men believe in cause and effect."

Thiel argues that you can't understand Gladwell's book without understanding that he is a Baby Boomer (born in 1963), part of a generation for whom every year saw a natural improvement in living standards, and on whom chance shone brightly. Gladwell set out to make a critique of the self-made businessperson, but in Thiel's mind *Outliers* is more a reflection of Gladwell's generation, which by fortunate circumstances of postwar prosperity was allowed to elevate chance (as long as you stayed within the law, you would end up okay) above planning. Today's generations, Thiel says, have to be much more focused. To succeed they can't just rely on going to

142

college to get ahead, or on a natural progression of good jobs; they have to become really great at one thing, and stay ahead of changes in the economy or society. This requires deep thought, ingenuity, and creativity.

It is fashionable to believe that luck and randomness rule, but if you look closely at the achievements of very successful people, you find that their "good fortune" was the result of self-developed habits like grit and guts, thinking far into the future when no one else was bothered, and having the desire to transcend their circumstances and even their personality.

Malcolm Gladwell

Gladwell was born in 1963 in Britain. His father was an English mathematics professor and his mother a Jamaican-born psychotherapist. Growing up in Ontario, he attended the University of Toronto, from where he graduated in 1984 with a degree in history.

For almost a decade Gladwell worked at the Washington Post, *as first a science writer and then its New York City bureau chief. Since 1996 he has been with the* New Yorker, *writing regular feature articles.* Time *magazine named him one of its "100 Most Influential People."*

Gladwell's other books include The Tipping Point: How Little Things Can Make a Big Difference *(2000),* Blink: The Power of Thinking without Thinking *(2005; see* 50 Psychology Classics), *and* David and Goliath: Underdogs, Misfits, and the Art of Battling Giants *(2013).*

1647

The Art of Worldly Wisdom

"21 The art of success
*Good fortune has its rules, and to the wise not everything depends
upon chance . . . the real philosopher has only one plan of action:
virtue and prudence; for the only good and bad fortune lie in
prudence or rashness."*

"65 Elevated taste . . .
*You can judge the height of someone's talent by what he aspires to. Only
a great thing can satisfy a great talent."*

In a nutshell

Make distinctions; look for subtlety and nuance. Success requires fine
observation of human nature and refinement of the self.

In a similar vein
Chin-Ning Chu *Thick Face, Black Heart* (p. 62)
Sun Tzu *The Art of War* (p. 308)

144

CHAPTER 22

Baltasar Gracian

*T*he *Art of Worldly Wisdom* should be read by every contemporary success scholar. You may be familiar with Machiavelli's *The Prince*, but Gracian's relatively obscure work is much more applicable to succeeding in everyday life, is richer philosophically, and is overall much more enjoyable. Unlike *The Prince*, it does not ask you to build your success on the bodies of other people; rather, eminence and influence are to be achieved through observation and personal refinement.

First translated into English as *The Courtier's Manual: Oracle and the Art of Prudence*, this work of a Spanish Jesuit priest has been quietly influential among those who know for the last 300 years. It was imitated by Le Rochefoucauld, whose *Maxims* (1665) followed Gracian's style of succinct character analysis, and the English essayist Joseph Addison considered the work of great value. Friedrich Nietzsche wrote, "Europe has never produced anything finer or more complicated in matters of moral subtlety." Arthur Schopenhauer translated it into German and thought of it as "a companion for life."

Christopher Maurer's excellent translation and introduction to the work have revived interest in Gracian and are used here.

Becoming substantial

Once a popular girl's name in the English-speaking world, Prudence is now old-fashioned. Yet in most dictionaries to be prudent means to be shrewd, wise, discerning, and penetrating. Its Latin root, *prudentia*, means foresight.

Without these qualities, is it likely we would ever succeed? Gracian compels each of us to become "a person of substance." Of the 300 aphorisms that comprise his book, consider no. 75:

"A person of substance. *If you are one, you will take no pleasure in those who aren't. Unhappy is the eminence that isn't founded on substance . . . Only the truth can give you a true reputation, and only substance is profitable. One act of deceit calls for many others, and soon the whole ghastly construction, which is founded in the air, comes tumbling down."*

Every era will have its gold rushes, booms, and bandwagons, but Gracian's statement that "only substance is profitable" should be remembered. In the success literature Benjamin Franklin expounded the notion, and Stephen Covey made it the foundation of *The 7 Habits of Highly Effective People*.

Patience and success

Aphorism no. 55 is: "Know how to wait":

"Stroll through the open spaces of time to the center of opportunity. Wise hesitation ripens success and brings secrets to maturity. The crutch of Time can do more than the steely club of Hercules . . . Fortune gives larger rewards to those who wait."

This is obvious enough, but the way Gracian says it reconnects you with the power of waiting for the right moment. Though it involves self-discipline, the payoff is watching your stakes slowly rise.

The famous and brilliant are attractive, but the very heights they climb make them susceptible to falls. What people love irrationally, Gracian says, they can also end up hating with the same passion. As he says elsewhere:

"Be excessive in your perfection but moderate about showing it. The brighter the torch, the more it consumes itself and the less it lasts. To win true esteem, make yourself scarce."

Are you a person who knows how to wait, or are you a bright torch? Is what you are doing with your life something that will endure? In aphorism no. 57 Gracian writes:

"Thoughtful people are safer. Do something well, and that is quick enough. What is done immediately is undone just as fast, but what must

last an eternity takes that long to do. Only perfection is noticed, and only success endures . . . So with metals: the most precious of them takes longest to be refined, and weighs most."

Mastering yourself and knowing your talents

Without self-mastery you can never master others, says Gracian. The essence of power is self-knowledge, and a major part of this is emotional intelligence. At all times seek to be a civilized person, avoiding the vulgarity of uncontrolled passion:

"52 Never lose your composure. Prudence tries never to lose control. This shows a real person, with a true heart, for magnanimity is slow to give in to emotion. The passions are the humors of the mind, and the least excess sickens our judgement. If the disease spreads to the mouth, your reputation will be in danger. Master yourself thoroughly and no one will criticize you for being perturbed, either when things are at their best or at their worst. All will admire your superiority."

Gracian's philosophy is about finding the "edge" that will separate you from the pack. While able in his roles as chaplain, confessor, and administrator, he knew that he had no special talent in them. He realized that his true role was as a scientist of success and character, and he sought out the scholarly, the cultured, and the powerful in order to reduce their knowledge, and his own observations, to a valuable essence. This was not an obvious job description in his time and place, and indeed the church tried to stop him publishing his writings.

Almost speaking to himself, one of Gracian's aphorisms is "Know your best quality, your outstanding gift." Discovering your area of superiority is a central task in life; without this effort you will waste your time imitating others.

Communicating

As a writer, Padre Gracian was perhaps biased about the power of good writing. However, he understood that if you could communicate with finesse your standing would be greatly enhanced. The successful person is always a master convincer, whether it be in writing or in person. In the 14th aphorism, Gracian observes:

"The wrong manner turns everything sour, even justice and reason. The right one makes up for everything: it turns a 'no' golden, sweetens truth, and makes old age look pretty. The 'how' of things is very important, and a pleasant manner captures the attention of others . . . Speak and act well and you will get out of any difficult situation."

The Art of Worldly Wisdom apparently has some popularity among spin doctors for its insights into how to present things well, yet such people should not gloss over the fact that Gracian counseled never to exaggerate. And for the chatterer, he offered the view that whether something is good or bad, its announcement will benefit from brevity. Making things only as long as they need to be induces a trust that the windbag and the wordy never gain.

Final comments

These are only a handful of Gracian's 300 epigrams. If you would like to do more than scratch the surface, get the book. Christopher Maurer's translation is very accessible for everyday use, and contains some fascinating insights into Gracian's personal life.

The Spain in which the priest lived was in long-term political decline and much less stable than it had been. Some of the aphorisms seem to come from a position of fear, and *The Art of Worldly Wisdom* may seem very cynical in places. Overall, though, the book is timeless in its attempt to expose the truth about human action and motivation, "the way people are, rather than the way they would like to be or appear."

Gracian's message is that good people do not disadvantage themselves because they are good, but because of their rosy naïveté. Your task is to spread further what goodness you have while working *within* the world.

Although the church did not like him publishing such a worldly and political work, Gracian's manual, in its emphasis on reason and the intellect, is very Jesuitical. For a man of the cloth it is perhaps surprising that there are few hard and fast moral rules in the book, only—as Maurer notes—"the conviction that to reach perfection one must adapt to circumstance." Rigidity of mind can win some battles, but only the mutable and mindful are enduringly successful.

Baltasar Gracian

Born in 1601 in Belmonte, a village in the Spanish region of Aragon, in his teens Gracian lived in Toledo and Zaragoza, studying philosophy and letters. He entered the Jesuit order at age 18 and remained in it for the rest of his life. At various times he was chaplain, professor, administrator, and confessor (personal priest) to aristocrats, and was rector and vice-rector of several Jesuit colleges.

His earlier works include treatises on the ideal qualities of political leaders, El héroe *(1637) and* El politico *(1640). However, his literary masterpiece is considered to be* El criticón, *"The Master Critic" (1651–57). A satirical novel that contrasts primitive life with "civilization," when the third volume was published without the permission of the Jesuit order, Gracian was removed from his post in Zaragoza and exiled to a small country town. He died there in 1658.*

Christopher Maurer is a professor of Spanish at Boston University. He has also translated the works of Spanish poet Federico García Lorca and is an authority on Renaissance and Baroque Spanish poetry.

Give and Take

"If we create networks with the sole intention of getting something, we won't succeed. We can't pursue the benefits of networks; the benefits ensue from investments in meaningful activities and relationships."

"This is what I find most magnetic about successful givers: they get to the top without cutting others down, finding ways of expanding the pie that benefit themselves and the people around them. Whereas success is zero-sum in a group of takers, in groups of givers, it may be true that the whole is greater than the sum of the parts."

"Every time we interact with another person at work, we have a choice to make: do we try to claim as much value as we can, or contribute value without worrying about what we receive in return?"

In a nutshell

Being a giver in the workplace can have immediate costs, but opens you up to greater long-term benefits.

In a similar vein

Warren Bennis *On Becoming a Leader* (p. 18)
Angela Duckworth *Grit* (p. 90)
Malcolm Gladwell *Outliers* (p. 136)
Donald T. Phillips *Lincoln on Leadership* (p. 230)

CHAPTER 23

Adam Grant

Being generous with our time, knowledge, skills, and money makes us feel good and has many positive effects. Yet we also worry that in being "good," we will watch more rapacious people move ahead more quickly, and we will somehow be penalized for our generosity.

Adam Grant set out to test this assumption. He is an organizational psychologist and became the youngest tenured professor at the Wharton School. He spent a decade looking at the concept of "reciprocity" (the extent to which people give or take) in the workplace, studying organizations from Google to the US Air Force. Reciprocity studies cut across psychology, sociology, and anthropology, and *Give and Take: Why Helping Others Drives Our Success* is an elegant summation of the research of recent years, including Grant's own. It is also a compelling guide to personal and career success, showing how people who are continually looking for ways in which they can contribute tend to have higher satisfaction and achievement levels. This is not at all obvious in the short term, but becomes evident in the long run. "Successful givers are every bit as ambitious as takers and matchers," Grant argues. "They simply have a different way of pursuing their goals."

Giver, taker, or matcher?

We know that success depends on hard work, talent, and luck, but there is a fourth element, Grant says: how we interact with others. Research has identified three basic "styles of reciprocity" in the workplace: giving, taking, and matching.

Takers believe they live in a competitive world and put their own interests first. They are on a mission to prove their competence and know they must continually promote themselves to keep ahead of the pack. For takers, generosity of spirit may be a nice idea, but it's for losers. If you do not put your own interests first, no one else will. Takers are not caricature-like mean people, and in fact many will give of their time and resources. Yet they will always give *strategically*, having weighed the likely gains of their actions.

At the other extreme are *givers*, whose focus is on what others may need from them. A giver will offer their expertise, connections, or resources because they see others having a need for them, regardless of the cost to themselves. Of course, "giving without keeping score" is the basis of good marriages and relationships, and most people are like this when it comes to those they love. But in the workplace it is not the norm. At work, most people are what Grant calls *matchers*, seeking a fair return for whatever they put out.

Which style is the most or least successful? An array of studies has given us the answer: In their efforts to help others regardless of the cost to themselves, givers (from medical students to engineers to salespeople) are often rated at the *bottom* by their peers. For instance, engineers rated the giving types among them as being low on technical skill and ability to meet deadlines, and in a study that Grant did of salespeople, givers had sales revenue that was two and a half times less than that of their peers: "They were so concerned about what was best for their customers," he notes, "that they weren't willing to sell aggressively."

If the givers end up at the bottom, then who is at the top: takers or matchers? Surprisingly, it is the givers, again. While engineers with the lowest productivity may be givers, as already noted, those with the *highest* productivity are givers, too. Across other fields and professions the same holds up: givers tend to be found at the bottom *and* the top, with the takers and matchers in the middle.

The giver advantage

How exactly can givers come out on top? Grant provides an interpretation of Abraham Lincoln's career to show how.

So many times did Lincoln put others ahead of himself that he was 51 years old when he finally became US president. In the shorter term he had jeopardized his career several times by giving his votes to others in congressional elections, but in the long run his generosity and lack of ego won him many admirers—among both the voting public and his competitors for office—and these traits propelled him to the presidency.

Grant's point is that the timeframes for success for givers are longer than for the other reciprocity styles. Goodwill, trust, and relationships take many years to achieve. As one entrepreneur said to Grant, "Being a giver is not good for a 100-yard dash, but it's valuable in a marathon." Grant puts it another way: the giver advantage *grows over time*. However, in the connected internet age, he ventures, perhaps givers don't have to wait so long for success, since their giving is more visible to more people, and goodwill can be built in a shorter time. Early in the book he refers to a study of Belgian medical students, the givers among whom did not get good grades. Later on he tells the full story: while the giving students did poorly early on, the study also found that with each year of their degree these students caught up to their peers, and by the end were surpassing them.

The accepted pattern of success is that you succeed first, then you give something back. However, perhaps this should be replaced by a new model: giving first without conditions sets you up for success later on. After all, Grant notes, rich countries today are largely based on services; 80 percent of Americans, for instance, work in service jobs. When you look for a doctor, lawyer, real estate agent, plumber, or teacher, you will choose them based on whether you think they have your best interests at heart and not whether you think they are trying to get something out of you.

Grant references the work of Shalom Schwartz, known for his research into the values and guiding principles that people around the world value most highly. The surprising finding is that, higher than wealth, power, pleasure, helpfulness, responsibility, or compassion, what people value most is giving. Most of us reserve giving for our family, and perhaps the religious organization we're involved with, leaving it at the door of the office. Yet if unconditional generosity is what we most want and value in others, it stands to reason that if we offer this in all areas of our lives we will be valued—highly.

Takers see success as a zero-sum equation: they can only win if someone else loses. Givers, on the other hand, do not see success as limited and are always looking for win–win situations. When a giver has a win, it has a multiplier effect: everyone who has benefited from the giver's largesse in the past will also feel good about it, and so more people benefit. Because takers assume that their win involves them defeating someone else, they tend to create ripples of bad feeling. Givers create value, Grant observes, while takers just claim it.

A case study running through *Give and Take* is venture capitalist David Hornik, whose motto is "to demonstrate that success does not have to come at other people's expense." Hornik is considered one of Silicon Valley's most successful investors, with a very high acceptance rate of funding offers to entrepreneurs. Why? Most feel he has their best interests at heart. He is trying to create value, not claim it.

Grant introduces us to the word *pronoia*: "the delusional belief that other people are plotting your well-being, or saying nice things about you behind your back." If you're a giver, he suggests, "this belief may be a reality, not a delusion." Or, as Hornik puts it, "It's easier to win if everybody wants you to win. If you don't make enemies out there, it's easier to succeed."

Failed givers and successful givers: The difference

There is a paradox with the most successful givers: they are obviously very other-directed, yet they are simultaneously *more* self-interested than other other-directed people. How can this be so? Well, successful givers are not doormats; they are as ambitious as anyone else. The only difference is that they want everyone to advance—themselves included. Grant's surprise finding is that people can have other-interest *and* self-interest simultaneously. Indeed, it is only these people who can give consistently over many years, because they know that to do so means looking after themselves.

In contrast, it is the givers with high other-interest and low self-interest who tend to be unsuccessful in their careers. Grant refers to this as "pathological altruism." Barbara Oakley, a researcher in this area, defined it as "an unhealthy focus on others to the detriment of one's own needs." Selfless givers are prone to burnout at work. In contrast, a Dutch study of healthcare professionals found that other-directed people who also look after themselves had lots of stamina to keep contributing.

Grant also points to research by Netta Weinstein and Richard Ryan suggesting that one's motivation for acting does matter. They found that giving has an energizing effect "only if it's an enjoyable, meaningful choice rather than undertaken out of duty and obligation." Clearly, anyone who has a vocation, as opposed to a mere job, finds that a sense of duty and service spurs them on, making them cheerful and effective in their work while others wilt.

Networking styles

Givers and takers have different ways of creating networks and different purposes for them.

One of Grant's examples is the former head of failed energy company Enron, Ken Lay, whom he says was a "taker in the disguise of a giver," a charade that worked for many years. Lay developed a great network of contacts, including the two Bush presidents. He flattered people above him, but cared little for those working under him. Grant is reminded of Samuel Johnson's line: "The true measure of a man is how he treats someone who can do him absolutely no good."

Confirming the gist of James Pennebaker's book *A Secret Life of Pronouns: What Our Words Say about Us*, Grant notes that corporate takers can be spotted by the frequency with which they use "I," "me," or "myself" in their annual report letters, and the size of their portrait photos in those reports. Lay's and that of fellow Enron taker Jeffrey Skilling covered a whole page. In contrast, giver CEOs tend to have very small photos of themselves, if at all, and mention themselves much less in communications.

Grant wonders whether it is harder to get away with being a rapacious taker today, since reputations are easily built or destroyed through social networking and online forums. Networks used to be distinct and separate, perhaps confined to a city or an industry; now, thanks to the internet, they are much larger and more interconnected.

Because a matcher's network is built on the expectation of something in return for whatever they give, their circle tends to be much smaller than that of a giver. And while a taker's network can be large, it is also more likely to be shallow, built on flattery and the pursuit of power. Because there is little goodwill involved, this kind of network is worth much less and can collapse when the person involved loses their position. In contrast, the effect of givers' networks may be longer lasting and more beneficial to all.

Giving, taking, and teams

Both givers and takers rely on the people around them to do well, but givers are much more likely to admit the fact and reward their teams appropriately. Grant gives Frank Lloyd Wright as an example of someone who didn't do this. For many years Wright had a successful architectural practice in Chicago, and then he moved to

Taliesin, the now-famous house he had built in rural Wisconsin. There, his career foundered and commissions dried up. It was only when he brought in a team of architectural apprentices that work began to pick up again. Yet even then he treated his team badly, refusing to give credit where it was due. Wright was a classic taker, Grant argues, seeing himself as a force of creativity against the world. Takers in the creative fields don't value interdependence; the need to collaborate is seen as a weakness.

Grant discusses Jonas Salk, "discoverer" of the polio vaccine, in similar terms. Salk had a team of talented researchers working with him, and when he announced the vaccine at a press conference in 1955, they waited to hear their names mentioned—in vain. They were devastated, but Salk never did credit the team, breaking a fundamental rule of scientific research. This, Grant contends, is why the scientific community never admitted Salk to the National Academy of Sciences and why he never won a Nobel Prize. Why would Salk not have given credit? It's a known psychological phenomenon that people overvalue their own contributions and undervalue those of others. Business relationships and marriages collapse when partners believe the other is not doing their fair share. Yet when marriage partners have been made to list all the things their partner does, they nearly always revise up their estimations of the other's contribution.

In another example, Grant provides a lengthy profile of George Meyer, one of the key comic forces behind *The Simpsons*. Meyer had an executive producer role, so his name rarely appeared on the list of writing credits, yet team members say he provided many of the cartoon series's funniest lines and concepts. Tim Long, who worked with Meyer, says in admiration: "There's something magical about getting the reputation as someone who cares about others more than yourself. It redounds to your benefit in countless ways." In an industry where squabbles over writing credits are common, Meyer's focus on the show's success as a whole helped to give it long-lasting success and *esprit de corps* among its writing team.

Communication styles

Takers are very good at being dominant when it comes to communication. Givers, on the other hand, have a style in which they express doubt, are tentative, and make disclaimers. Yet this kind of communication is more influential on people who are skeptical. Skeptics will resist power talk and dominant communication. Grant mentions a lawyer, Dave Walton, whose stammer seemed to make a jury warm to him and create rapport; he tended to win his cases. In psychology this is known as the "pratfall effect," small blunders or vulnerabilities that make experts seem more approachable and human. Powerful, dominant speech can impress a panel enough to get you a job, but in actual work situations involving teams, it is inclusive, collaborative leaders who get the best results.

Grant did a study on opticians who were also involved in selling pairs of glasses and sunglasses. After surveying them, he found that those opticians with a giving style created 30 percent more revenue than the matchers and 68 percent more than the takers. What was the key to their success? Across many studies, it has been shown that successful salespeople and negotiators spend much more time asking questions and trying to see things from the customer's or other side's perspective. Grant writes:"By asking questions and getting to know their customers, givers build trust and gain knowledge about their customers' needs. Over time, this makes them better and better at selling." In a study of pharmaceutical salespeople, givers came out as the most successful, whether they were extraverted or introverted, conscientious or carefree, open-minded or traditional.

Another subtle form of influence lies in advice-seeking, which is particularly useful when you are in a position lacking authority. Studies across a range of fields and industries have found that simply asking for advice from people is more persuasive than sucking up to superiors or trying to cajole or pressure others (all taker positions), or seeking to pull in or trade favors (a typical matcher position). Benjamin Franklin had a fundamental rule for influencing people and winning friends: appeal to "their pride and vanity by constantly seeking their opinion and advice, and they will admire you for your judgement and wisdom." Grant's caveat: the request for advice must be genuine and spontaneous, not a ploy to gain influence, or people will quickly see through it.

Final comments

Give and Take is a theory of success in the tradition of Malcolm Gladwell's *Outliers*. While both books draw on reams of studies to make their case, Grant gives hints here and there (the words "karma" and "karmic rewards" are mentioned more than once) that he is not just presenting a psychological theory of reciprocity and "prosocial behavior," but is trying to point toward the way the universe actually works. Many parts of the book seem to be simple confirmation of what various faiths have been saying for centuries. Just one example, from the New Testament: "Give, and it will be given to you. A good measure, pressed down, shaken together and running over, will be poured into your lap. For with the measure you use, it will be measured to you." All religions stress the power of generosity, not just in making the world a better place but in greatly improving the life of the giver. Psychology now appears to be confirming this truth.

Adam Grant

*Born in 1981, Grant grew up in Detroit, Michigan, with a lawyer
father and a teacher mother. As an awkward, introverted teenager he
trained compulsively at basketball and spent long hours playing video
games. While an undergraduate psychology major at Harvard, he
worked in advertising sales for its student travel guide company, Let's
Go, bringing in record revenue. As a PhD student at the University of
Michigan, he undertook a study of its alumni fundraising team that
led to significant increases in donations.*

*Grant is Paul Steinberg Professor of Management and Psychology
at the Wharton School, University of Pennsylvania. He has worked
with companies including Google, IBM, and Merck to increase the
productivity of their workers. His other book is* Originals: How
Non-Conformists Move the World *(2016).*

How to Succeed in Business without Being White

"*Money makes people listen. When you have it, then you have something others want and need. When you don't you become invisible. Your needs become irrelevant. Your success, or lack of it, is your problem. How can we build wealth when we have so many obstacles to opportunity? If you pay attention to the challenges we've talked about, it will be difficult to deny you opportunity. If you read and follow the advice in this book, you will make your own opportunities in spite of the nuisances, hatred, and ignorance you encounter.*"

In a nutshell

Recognize and use your background in the service of attaining your goals, and remember to give something back.

In a similar vein

Les Giblin *How to Have Confidence and Power in Dealing with People* (p. 130)
Nelson Mandela *Long Walk to Freedom* (p. 236)

CHAPTER 24

Earl G. Graves

I n 1991, the newly freed Nelson Mandela made a trip to the United States and met a group of the country's top African American businesspeople. Their leader was Earl Graves. As a result of this initial contact, Graves put together a deal to create a $100 million franchise to bottle and sell the soft drink Pepsi in the new South Africa. Though the deal obviously made a great deal of business sense, Graves highlights it as proof of how far black entrepreneurship had come, not merely in the US but internationally.

Graves himself is a symbol of black America's transition from a focus on civil rights to economic empowerment. The era of John F. and Robert Kennedy, then Lyndon Baines Johnson, was a heady time for African Americans, as it seemed that the law would protect their right to live a prosperous life along with everyone else. *How to Succeed in Business without Being White: Straight Talk on Making It in America* conveys the excitement of this period, but also reflects on the difficult realities of trying to do business amid continuing mistrust and prejudice.

Nevertheless, Graves's overall message is reminiscent of Nietzsche's famous line, "That which does not kill us makes us stronger." Being black is an advantage, because African Americans have to be better than the average to stand out, a fact that has been instrumental in the success of many a minority.

Becoming a player

Graves grew up in Brooklyn, New York, his parents the offspring of immigrants from Barbados. At Morgan State University in Baltimore (1953–57) he took business as his major, which some classmates and even professors thought was ridiculous. Though this was only 50 years ago, it was then a given that business was for whites. But Graves had an entrepreneurial bent and his thinking was "basketball was once the white man's game too."

After graduation he became a captain in the Green Berets, then a real estate broker, but politics beckoned. From 1965 to 1968 Graves worked on Robert Kennedy's staff; Kennedy was then a senator of New York and preparing for his bid for the presidency. He had, of course, been a champion of black America in his brother's administration.

The experience of working with Kennedy opened Graves's eyes to the power and wealth of the white American elite, and even though they were in the same camp, Kennedy seemed to him to be from a another world. According to Graves, Kennedy never carried money or a wallet, indeed hardly seemed ever to have to think of money. To someone who had been raised in an environment of lack, this clearly inspired Graves as much as the political agenda, and he began to see how psychologically liberating wealth could be for African Americans.

If Kennedy had not been assassinated and had been elected president, Graves would no doubt have joined his administration in a high-ranking position. As it turned out, the tragedy hastened the development of his idea for a publication focusing on black economic advancement.

After a decade of civil rights reforms under the Democrats, business development was moving on to the agenda, and Graves felt that the time was right to launch a journal celebrating black business achievement. Although originally envisaged as a newsletter, *Black Enterprise* grew into a fully fledged commercial magazine with advertising and was profitable within ten issues.

Waking up to black economic power

Graves describes his efforts in the early days to convince white marketing executives in large companies that they should advertise in the magazine. The familiar refrain was, and in some cases continues to be, "Black people don't buy luxury cars/computers/insurance/financial instruments." Often he was told, "We don't want our product associated with African Americans."

An example he provides is the effort to get Mercedes-Benz America to advertise in *Black Enterprise*, even though he had figures showing that wealthy blacks were five times more likely than wealthy whites to buy a Mercedes. He ended up going to the company's top person in Germany, and only then did ads for the cars start appearing in his magazine. Fittingly, Graves was invited onto the board of the Daimler-Chrysler corporation.

Racism, he found, was more likely in the middle levels of an organization than at the top, but was encountered everywhere in both obvious and subtle forms. Graves relates what tends to happen when a black man sits down in a first-class airline seat: the white person next to him will usually presume he is someone big in sports or entertainment, even if, in Graves's case, he is close to retirement age!

African Americans comprise 12 percent of the American population and earn over $400 billion annually, but as a *Black Enterprise* article (August 26, 2003) noted, black Americans still only make 59 percent of what whites do, which is only 2 percent more than in 1963.

At a time when much affirmative action legislation is being watered down, Graves provides a powerful argument that doing business for nonwhites can still be a struggle. The landmark civil rights march on Washington recently celebrated its fiftieth anniversary, but there was little nostalgia because there is still so much to do.

Graves believes that the answer lies in creating more black-owned businesses and getting those businesses to work with each other where possible. He admires how Irish and Jewish Americans built on their sense of identity to hoist themselves into the upper echelons of American life, and notes that a sense of collective identity is crucial to business success.

Many people are not aware that there is a black business network, but Graves enjoys highlighting some of the success stories. Just a sample includes:

❖ Percy Sutton, theater owner and broadcaster
❖ Clarence Avant, chairman of Motown Records
❖ Howard Naylor Fitzhugh, business professor and first Harvard MBA
❖ The late Arthur Gaston, founder of Booker T. Washington Insurance Company

- John Johnson, publisher of *Ebony* and *Jet* magazines
- Travers Bell and Willie Daniels, co-founders of Daniels & Bell, the first black-owned investment firm listed on the NYSE
- Oprah Winfrey, television host and producer
- Ann Fudge, food and beverage retailer
- The late Ron Brown, President Clinton's Secretary of Commerce

Of course, since Graves wrote his book Colin Powell and Condoleezza Rice have become senior figures in the Bush administration, Barack Obama became president, and business figures such as Franklin Raines (CEO of the huge Fannie Mae mortgage house) are making African Americans seem more commonplace at the top of the corporate world.

The book has a multitude of tips for success, including sections on networking, buying and operating a franchise, creating a business plan, and attracting finance.

This material will be useful for anyone starting out in business or seeking to expand, and indeed, the foreword written by Robert L. Crandall, retired CEO of American Airlines, suggests that the book might well have been called simply *How to Succeed in Business*.

Final comments

Graves's experience, and the lesson for us all, is that while money is the great leveler, color-blind and culturally neutral, it still pays to maintain your links to communities that can provide psychological support as well as business leads.

This book is an eye-opener not merely for African Americans but for anyone who has failed to appreciate the extent of black economic power. Immigration is changing the makeup of traditionally white societies such as the United States, Britain, Canada, and Australia. There is a chance that in the future, white people will not only be outnumbered in many fields but may find themselves outclassed. One of Graves's excellent points is that if you can succeed in business without being white, you will develop a thick skin and a degree of confidence and creativity that your white colleagues may never have needed to develop.

A *New York Times* and *Wall Street Journal* bestseller, Graves's book is not the only work of its type. Consider *Why Should White Guys*

Have All the Fun? by the black Wall Street financier Reginald F. Lewis, and two books by Dennis Kimbro, *Think and Grow Rich: A Black Choice* and *What Makes the Great Great.*

The Compound Effect

"Success strategies are no longer a secret, but most people ignore them."

"You already know what you need to succeed. You don't need to learn anything more. If all we needed was more information, everyone with an Internet connection would live in a mansion, have abs of steel, and be blissfully happy. New or more information is not what you need—a new plan of action is. It's time to create new behaviors and habits that are oriented away from sabotage and towards success. It's that simple."

"As a society, we've been deceived. We've been hypnotized by commercial marketing, which convinces you of problems you don't have and sells you on the idea of insta-fixes to 'cure' them. We've been socialized to believe in fairy-tale endings found in movies and novels. We've lost sight of the good, old-fashioned value of hard and consistent work."

In a nutshell

Success is simple: it involves hard work and habits that compound our value over time.

In a similar vein
Gary Keller *The One Thing* (p. 198)
Orison Swett Marden *Pushing to the Front* (p. 242)
Anthony Robbins *Unlimited Power* (p. 266)
Brian Tracy *Maximum Achievement* (p. 302)

CHAPTER 25

Darren Hardy

*S*uccess magazine was founded by Orison Swett Marden in 1897 and has had a checkered history. In 2008 it was relaunched by Darren Hardy, who had enjoyed a career in personal development media and training, with the motto "What achievers read."

In addition to making a success of the venture, the former real estate agent was keen to turn the journal into a personal laboratory to find out what really worked in personal achievement. As motivational legend Tony Robbins notes in a foreword to *The Compound Effect: Jumpstart Your Income, Your Life, Your Success*, Hardy made himself into a guinea pig to test out the many success strategies, ideas, and tools that were discussed in the magazine's pages. Yet, as Hardy notes in his introduction, though he has been lucky enough to spend time with icons of success including Richard Branson, Steve Jobs, Warren Buffett, Jeff Bezos, and Howard Schultz, it was more important to him that he dedicate the book to his father, a former football coach and "the man who taught me the principles of the Compound Effect." While it is fine to model yourself on successful people, in the end the only models that matter are the people you observe closely not over weeks or months, but over decades, and how they consistently behave. The first truth of success, Hardy learned from his dad—and this contradicts our have-it-now culture—is that success is hard, takes a long time, and is sometimes boring. This is not necessarily the message that readers of *Success* want to hear, but Hardy writes in a way that makes difficulty seem alluring all the same.

One foot in front of another

Hardy's "compound effect" is about the fantastic results that come to pass through "a series of small, smart choices," most of which don't even feel significant at the time. Indeed, because they don't feel significant, we are easily deluded into thinking that they don't matter. A man who gives up running because after a few weeks he hasn't lost weight doesn't realize that only if he keeps it up for half a year will a real transformation of his health begin to take effect. A woman who stops making retirement contributions after a few years because she could use the cash for other things doesn't see that it is only after 15 or 20 years that her ball of contributions starts to gather pace and mass, building on itself. Thanks to the power of compounding, her fund takes on a life of its own, spitting out cash and delighting her in retirement.

Our choices, small and big, create our life, but most of us are barely aware of making them. "Nobody *intends* to become obese, go through bankruptcy, or get a divorce," Hardy observes, "but often (if not always) those consequences are the result of a series of small, poor choices." We should give up our lottery-winner mentality, which says that success just happens to some lucky people. Any "overnight success" is the result of practices and habits put in place years ago, and thinking otherwise is fooling yourself. In an echo of David Brooks's *The Road to Character*, Hardy writes that we need to rediscover the ethic of our grandparents, who knew that only a certain amount of restraint would see them amount to anything. "I want you to know in your bones," he says, "that your only path to success is through a continuum of mundane, unsexy, unexciting, and sometimes difficult daily disciplines compounded over time." In truth, there is no other way.

The task: Take responsibility

If you've ever blamed anyone for anything, Hardy says, it means you are not taking full responsibility for your life. After all, whatever happens with your company, with the economy, whoever is in power, you are still always 100 percent in control of *you*. Realizing this is not a downer, he argues, it is liberating. It makes you very careful only to do things that will bring the results you are after. And remember this: there are so many people in the world who have had fewer opportunities than you, who live in poverty or under autocratic regimes, with poor roads and infrequent electricity or internet. "Luck is all around us," Richard Branson told Hardy. It is just a matter of taking advantage of it. To blame one's circumstances or environment is an affront to your freedom.

When Hardy was involved in a start-up venture that lost him a lot of money, the "cause" was his partner, who squandered and mismanaged most of the cash. Hardy could have taken the partner to court, but the better option (the one he took) was to admit that he had failed to take the time to see what was really happening in the company. It was ultimately no one's fault but his own, so he swallowed the loss and moved on. When you eliminate all excuses from your life, his mentor Jim Rohn taught him, that is the day you finally grow up.

Successful people in every walk of life got that way by becoming extremely accountable for their actions. Sports stars track every calorie they consume, every lap they swim. To be more effective, doctors and lawyers have systems that can tell them exactly how long they spend with each patient/client, at what point in the day. "You cannot manage or improve something until you measure it," Hardy says. The best tool he has found for being accountable is to carry a little book and write down every decision you make. If you have fallen into a financial hole, for instance, every day for a month write down every little or big amount you spend. All your unconscious spending will suddenly become conscious, and you will think twice about buying many things. Do you have a $4 cup of coffee every day? That money, if compounded over a 20-year period, becomes $51,833.79. Wow. The dollar you spend today that wasn't invested is costing you, in 20 years, $5, and in 30 years, $20.

You owe it to yourself and your dreams to get serious about how your time, money, and energy are used. Tracking makes you aware of your habits, and it is habits that make you fail or succeed.

The work: Build great habits

The one thing Hardy noted about really successful people was that they had great *daily routines*. People who are not successful, in contrast, get up at different times, work some days and don't feel like it on others, and lack a core of unbreakable commitments.

Just as pilots know that just a 1 percent change in direction will lead their aircraft to being wildly off course, so a small habit today can end up making the difference between success and failure. Consider two friends. One decides to exercise a little more each week, spend 20 minutes reading a personal development book, and give a little compliment to his wife each day. The other doesn't see the need for any change and just buys a bigger television to watch his favorite programs in comfort. After a year, there won't be much noticeable difference between the two men. But check back on them after five years, and the one who chose a bit more exercise has seen how it benefits him and is doing more of it. He is learning about the power of habits and is getting interested in other stuff to do with the mind and relationships. The second guy is retreating to his man cave, watching an extra show each night, and enjoying an extra beer. Come back in ten years, and the two will have even less in common. The first man has a healthy body, a healthy mind, and a successful marriage. The other is also growing (horizontally). Because he never bothered to learn anything new about relationships, emotions, or basic psychology, or doesn't feel the need for self-examination, he mistakenly thinks that all his problems are due to others, and starts blaming his wife, his boss, and the government for everything. He increasingly looks like a loser.

When Hardy coaches people, he gets them to track every minute and hour they spend over the course of a week. What he has noticed is the incredible amount of time even very senior people spend reviewing the news. One executive would spend 45 minutes each morning reading the newspaper, then another 30 minutes following the news on his commute to work, then another 30 minutes on his way home. He would spend a total of 20 minutes while at work checking news updates, and later at home there'd be the sports news, the local news, and the 10 o'clock news. Three and a half hours in a single day on the news! His job certainly didn't require him to have this kind of deep news awareness. Hardy got him to cancel the newspaper subscription, listen to educational or inspirational material on his commute, and, instead of the diet of evening news, do a little more exercise, spend more time with his family, and do some more reading and planning. The executive's stress levels went way down and he became happier and more focused.

"Habits never lie," Hardy notes. Whatever people say are their priorities, it's their habits and behaviors—what they are doing every minute of every day—that tell the truth. How much time do you spend on the internet or watching television, keeping up with other people's goals and accomplishments? How much money do you spend putting money in other people's pockets, making them rich? Make a decision to spend your time and your resources on your *own* development.

"Success is something you attract by the person you become," Rohn noted. When Hardy started looking for a romantic partner, he wrote in a journal pages and pages of description of his perfect girl, then acknowledged this was the wrong way to go about it. He realized he should be asking what sort of person *he* would have to be to attract a woman like this. His focus went to his habits and behaviors, and he let go of the ones not likely to attract the woman of his dreams. After the hard work on himself was done, his perfect partner walked into his life.

The reward: Momentum

The reward of persevering with good habits is *momentum*. When a rocket is thrust into space, a huge amount of fuel is expended in the first few minutes, but once out of the atmosphere the rocket can glide along at great speed using hardly any fuel. It may be frustrating that it is so hard for you to get your enterprise going, while at the same you can see the rich get richer and big businesses getting bigger, without any apparent effort. Yet the main difference between you and them is that they have already achieved momentum.

You welcome momentum, or "Mo," into your life through repeating small actions, even when you don't feel like it, to create an unbroken chain of effort. One day, things simply take off without there being an apparent cause. Yet the cause is only hard to see because it is spread across thousands of actions over many years. The success that Apple had with the iPod seemed to come from nowhere, Hardy writes, but it was the result of years of innovation and building customer loyalty. The iPod in turn created the momentum for the success of Apple's iPhone and iTunes, and now these provide the platform for future growth.

Speed and intensity of effort are overrated. It is *consistency* of effort that wins the day. Why is consistency so important? It's not the loss of results that comes from failing to perform a single action that matters, it is the loss of momentum that comes from not doing it, the breaking of the *chain* of effort that brings a project to fruition.

Final comments

As many people have noted, in its focus on the power of small things done consistently, *The Compound Effect* is similar to Jeff Olson's *The Slight Edge*. Despite being significantly shorter, Hardy's is the better book, with more references and examples.

Hardy's work is also a very welcome alternative to faddish ideas like "the 4-hour work week" and an antidote to notions that you can "change your life in 30 days." The truth is, no one has ever achieved great success without putting in lots *and lots* of work, Hardy comments. Indeed, though he is a player in the US motivational industry, he is dismissive of motivation itself, which only provides a temporary high. His aim is to get you to create whole new routines and habits that, once established, inevitably and automatically build the life you want.

Success may involve more work than you imagined, but if you grasp the power of compounding, it is also simpler than you think. "When you press on despite difficulty, tedium, and hardship," Hardy writes, "that's when you earn your improvement and gain strides on the competition. If it's hard, awkward, or tedious, so be it. Just do it." Successful people and failures are the same in their dislike of having to do some things. What separates them is that the successful do them anyway.

Darren Hardy

Hardy was born in 1971. His parents divorced when he was a baby, and he and his siblings were brought up by his father, a former university football coach turned salesman who created the expectation that Hardy would excel in school, academically and in sports. He wasn't allowed to take days off school unless he was vomiting, bleeding, or "showing bone." In a wish to please his dad and feel good about having an edge over his classmates, Hardy organized his life for achievement, and by the age of 20 had earned enough to buy his own home. He sold real estate in his twenties in San Francisco before becoming an executive and investor with television networks focused on personal development. He was also involved with The People's Network, a company selling self-development training videos and materials.

Hardy joined Success magazine in 2007 and was its publisher until 2016. He now focuses on public speaking and in 2016 received a Master of Influence award from the US National Speakers Association. He is also the author of The Entrepreneur Rollercoaster (2015).

Think and Grow Rich

"*We live in a world of over-abundance and everything the heart could desire, with nothing standing between us and our desires, excepting lack of a definite purpose.*"

"*I had the happy privilege of analyzing both Mr. Edison and Mr. Ford, year by year, over a long period of years, and therefore, the opportunity to study them at close range, so I speak from actual knowledge when I say that I found no quality save persistence, in either of them, that even remotely suggested the major source of their stupendous achievements.*"

In a nutshell

Wealth comes from increasing your power to think and developing your ability to access the universe's intelligence.

In a similar vein

Robert Kiyosaki *Rich Dad, Poor Dad* (p. 208)
David J. Schwartz *The Magic of Thinking Big* (p. 278)
Wallace D. Wattles *The Science of Getting Rich* (p. 320)

CHAPTER 26

Napoleon Hill

Any book with the word "rich" or "success" in the title has a better than average chance of selling well; money and external achievement are basic to our time, as rank and honor were to the Middle Ages. A compelling title might explain an initial rush to buy a book, but in the last 65 years *Think and Grow Rich* has sold over 15 million copies worldwide. Why?

Hill refused to accept that success was the domain of luck or background or the gods, and wanted to provide a concrete plan for success that depended entirely on oneself. The book also sold because it was not simply Hill's dreamed-up ideas, but a distillation of the success secrets of hundreds of America's most successful men (there weren't many female tycoons in the 1930s), beginning with his patron, steel baron Andrew Carnegie (see p. 56). Carnegie had given Hill letters of introduction to the likes of Henry Ford, Thomas Edison, and F. W. Woolworth, and Hill would spend 20 years synthesizing their experience and insights. Hill's mission was simply to know "how the wealthy become that way," and his systematic approach to success became the eight-volume *Law of Success* (1928).

Think and Grow Rich is a condensed form of this larger work, written while Hill was an adviser to Franklin D. Roosevelt. The prose has a galloping energy to it and the early pages allude to a secret that the book contains but does not spell out. Hill suggests that you "stop for a moment when it presents itself, and turn down a glass, for that occasion will mark the most important turning point in your life." Try to resist that! The book has no shadows or complications, setting out the things that "work," and leaving others, rightfully, to the realm of mystery.

Money and the spirit

Near the end of *Think and Grow Rich*, Hill admits that the main reason he wrote it was "the fact that millions of men and women are paralyzed by the fear of poverty." This was in the America of the 1930s, still scarred by the Depression, when most people were focused on avoiding poverty rather than getting rich. That Hill's book did not stop at poverty avoidance, but dared to be about becoming fabulously rich, may have forever classified it in some minds as a greed manual, but this is precisely what gave it its huge attraction.

The link between spiritual values and making money is something that non-Americans may find difficult to take seriously or even comprehend, yet it is the very expression of American morality. Wealth creation is a product of mind, combining reasoning, imagination, and tenacity. Hill understood that uniqueness, expressed in a refined idea or product, would always eventually meet with monetary reward.

The concept that all earned riches and achievement come from the mind is commonplace now—it is the basis of the knowledge society/information age. Yet in 1937 Hill was already talking about "brain capital" and marketing oneself as a provider of nonphysical services. The sage-like qualities of the book are encapsulated in its title: "Think and grow rich" is effectively the motto not of Hill's era but of our own.

Desire

Hill relates the story of Edwin C. Barnes, who arrived on Thomas Edison's doorstep one day and announced that he was going to be the inventor's business partner. He was given a minor job, but chose not to see himself as merely another cog in the Edison business wheel, imagining himself as the inventor's silent partner. This he eventually did become. Barnes intuitively knew the success secret of willingness to burn all bridges, ensuring that there is no retreat to a former, mediocre life. Having a definite purpose always yields results, and Hill includes a six-step method, developed by Andrew Carnegie, for turning "white-hot desires" into reality.

Hill counsels never to worry if others think your ideas are crazy. Marconi's friends took him to a mental hospital for believing that he could send "messages through the air" (he invented radio). Hill's famous statement is, "What the mind of man can conceive and believe, it can achieve," but his great insight is that no more effort is required to aim high in life than to accept an existence of misery and lack. He quotes the verse:

*"I worked for a menial's hire
Only to learn, dismayed
That any wage I had asked of Life
Life would have willingly paid."*

Infinite Intelligence

A defining feature of this classic is its respect for the ineffable and the suggestion that mental attunement with "Infinite Intelligence" (the universe, or God) is the source of wealth. Hill realized that consciousness was not confined to the brain; rather, the brain was an element of the great unified mind. Therefore, to be open to this larger mind was to have access to all knowledge, power, and creativity.

He mentions Edison's retreats to his basement where, in the absence of sound and light, he would simply "receive" his ideas. A person receptive to this realm is likened to a pilot flying high above where normal people work and play. Such vision allows them to see beyond the strictures of regular space and time.

The subconscious: our connection to Infinite Intelligence

Hill illustrates the concept of Infinite Intelligence through analogy to a radio receiver. Just as you can receive important messages if you are tuned in, thoughts you hold about yourself are effectively beamed out to the world through the subconscious, boomeranging back as your "circumstances." By understanding that your experiences matter only because of how you perceive them and becoming the master of your own thoughts, you can control what filters into your subconscious. It becomes a better reflection of what you actually desire and "broadcasts" to the infinite realm clear messages of those desires.

Since all thought tends to find its physical equivalent, you create the right conditions for manifesting your desires. This is why it is important to write down the exact figure of how much money you want to possess. This amount, once entrenched in your subconscious, is removed from the conscious mind and its doubts and helps to shape your actions and decisions toward its realization.

The concept extends to prayer. Most people give up on prayer because it doesn't work for them, but Hill believed this to be essentially a failure of method. Whatever you seek through prayer has a slim chance of happening if it is merely a heartfelt wish, muttered through the conscious mind. What you desire cannot remain at this level—it must become part of your unconscious being, almost existing outside of you, for it to have real effect.

Final comments

This is a small taste of Hill. Other chapters of *Think and Grow Rich* cover faith, persistence, decision, procrastination, and creating a mastermind of people around you. There is also the classic chapter "The Mystery of Sex Transmutation," which argues that the energy behind all great achievements is sexual.

As readers will attest, the book goes beyond money. Hill makes an effort at the outset to define "rich" in terms of quality friendships, family harmony, good work relationships, and spiritual peace. Further, he warns you not to rely on position or force of authority, remarking that most great leaders began as excellent followers and that you have to learn how to serve before you can achieve.

Yet Hill's central idea, that the source of wealth is nonmaterial, is yet to be fully appreciated. We still tend to worry about our level of education or amount of capital more than about intangible assets such as persistence, vision, and the ability to tap into the infinite and shape the subconscious. Successful people are shy of attributing their wealth or influence to such "spiritual" abilities, but Hill knew their importance. This is why his book continues to be read through decades of economic bust and boom. The source of wealth never ceases to flow and is outside of time.

Napoleon Hill

Hill was born in 1883 in a one-room cabin in Wise County, Virginia, and his mother died when he was only 10. He was apparently one of the roughest boys in the county, but his new stepmother encouraged him to become literate. At 15 he began providing articles for local newspapers.

In 1908, while while working for Orison Swett Marden's Success *magazine, Hill interviewed Andrew Carnegie. The industrialist invited Hill to his estate, where, over the course of three days, Carnegie held forth on his idea that the principles of success should be laid down in writing for anyone to follow. He confronted Hill with the question of whether he would be willing to spend the next 20 years in pursuit of this goal. Hill said yes, although his work, culminating in* Law of Success, *was never funded by his mentor.*

Hill had worked for President Woodrow Wilson as a public relations adviser and returned to the White House under Roosevelt to help write the famous "fireside chats" radio broadcasts to Americans during the Depression. He was also personal adviser to Manuel Quezon before the latter became the first president of the Philippines.

With W. Clement Stone, Hill started the magazine Success Unlimited *and wrote the bestseller* Success through a Positive Mental Attitude *(1960). His last full work was the more philosophical and autobiographical* Grow Rich with Peace of Mind *(1967). After his death in 1970,* Think and Grow Rich: A Black Choice, *for African Americans, was completed by Dennis Kimbro from Hill's notes.*

Michael J. Ritt, president of the Napoleon Hill Foundation in Illinois, chronicled Hill's life in A Lifetime of Riches *(with Kirk Flanders).*

Born to Win

"It takes courage to be a real winner—not a winner in the sense of beating out someone else by always insisting on coming out on top—but a winner at responding to life. It takes courage to experience the freedom that comes with autonomy, courage to accept intimacy and directly encounter other persons, courage to take a stand in an unpopular cause, courage to choose authenticity over approval and to choose it again and again, courage to accept the responsibility for your own choices, and, indeed, courage to be the unique person you really are."

In a nutshell

Enlarge your understanding of success to include self-knowledge and greater connection to others. You have everything in you that you need to succeed.

In a similar vein
Stephen R. Covey *The 7 Habits of Highly Effective People* (p. 84)
Abraham Maslow *Motivation and Personality* (50SHC)
Cheryl Richardson *Take Time for Your Life* (p. 260)
Eleanor Roosevelt (by Robin Gerber) *Leadership the Eleanor Roosevelt Way* (p. 272)

CHAPTER 27

Muriel James & Dorothy Jongeward

James and Jongeward wrote *Born to Win: Transactional Analysis with Gestalt Experiments* for what they believed would be a modest academic psychology audience, but more than 40 years after publication it has sold over four million copies and been translated into 18 languages. In their preface to the 25th anniversary edition, the authors explain its success in terms of readers' desire to understand what makes people tick, whether it is themselves, their family members, or their co-workers. The book not only provides valuable insights into why we do what we do, but adds depth to the success literature in its fine distinctions on what makes a winner.

Becoming an adult

Born to Win is based on two areas of psychology: transactional analysis, developed by Dr. Eric Berne (author of the bestseller *Games People Play*), and Gestalt therapy, developed by Frederick Perls. The authors combine them into a set of ideas that aim to create a responsible, whole person—a "winner."

Transactional analysis is based on the idea that everyone has three "ego states" that produce different types of behavior: the Parent, the Adult, and the Child. In the Parent state you feel a need to be critical or to spout prejudices. In the Child state you are impulsive, excited, or act helpless. In the Adult state you are responsible, fully aware, and rational.

The primary role of the Adult voice is to recognize reality and make decisions. James and Jongeward describe the Adult as the "executive of the personality." Some people may go through most of their adult life avoiding decisions, so when they finally do have to make one it can be terrifying. They may have to defy the internal Parent voice warning them of risks or the Child voice that does not want to leave behind a cocoon of protectiveness. Yet we all come to these points. Winners grasp them and grow, losers shy away from the opportunity and shrink.

Gestalt is a German word roughly meaning "an organized whole." Gestalt therapy is about integrating the personality and developing self-awareness, so that people are able to see their unconscious patterns and behaviors. For instance, a woman whose identity is wrapped up in being a "helpful Hannah" may be closing off another side of herself, the side that sometimes gets angry. You have to be aware of your polarities and be willing to feel things that you may not feel to be "good" or "you." The healthy person, the winner, will be willing to express more aspects of themselves at the appropriate time. They will be more trusting of their own intuition and more willing to renew themselves mentally and physically, in order to give more and be more.

Freedom to write your own script

Together, transactional analysis and Gestalt therapy help a person live fully aware in the present and be responsible for their own life. While this may sound rather like self-help, it is difficult to imagine how you might be considered a success if you have not achieved these two things. While you may think that your games and posturings do little harm, cumulatively they make a big difference to your character, creating a drag on the fulfillment of your potential. By becoming more objective about how you engage with people and how they operate with you, you can be liberated. Where before games and positions may have hamstrung success, now you can see them for what they are and keep your eye on your goals.

The authors discuss "life scripts," the plans you consciously or unconsciously have for how you are going to live your life. Life is often like a play, and humans will adopt roles based on what they have been told about themselves by their family or culture. We begin life, Perls said, as "slaves to our parents," but some people remain so all their lives. Whether we like it or not, we are given a story to act out that may or may not suit us, and the mature human being will feel the need at some point to shake off their script like a skin and write their own story.

Sometimes, the script we have written does not suit the cultural script of the times and we have to take a stand, like Galileo, Martin

Luther, or Rosa Parks, risking punishment or even death. But until we do define our own purpose, separate to upbringing, culture, or genes, we will remain less than what we could be.

Becoming a winner

James and Jongeward describe a winner as being "credible, trustworthy, responsive, and genuine, both as an individual and as a member of society." As winners are not tied up in themselves, their energies can be focused on contributing to a larger cause. When dealing with others, they take pains to preserve their dignity and are not interested in winning at all costs. Yet they are successful in their greater ability to produce "win/win" situations due to a superior understanding of all the parties involved. Winners are not afraid of intimacy, and can be the most spontaneous people in a group because they are not set in their ways. Winners set goals for themselves in order to be able to live in the present.

We are literally "born to win," James and Jongeward say. We have everything within us that we need to succeed. Although we come out of the womb helpless, some of us will proceed to full independence and are not afraid of playing a full part in a community, while others— "losers"—never really take full responsibility for their lives. Such individuals live either in the past or the future, and, because they never bother to crystallize their aims, do not make very good use of their time.

Losers have learned to cope with difficult childhood experiences by manipulating or doing damage to others and denying the truth to themselves. They try to control people, or play the victim or the aloof outsider, in order to preserve a feeling of identity. To others, however, these set mental patterns ("rackets") only make them appear phony.

James and Jongeward sum up the tragedy of the loser thus: "Losers are repeaters, repeating not only their own mistakes, but often those of their families and culture as well." Winning people look, listen, and learn and are able to summon the courage to change when necessary.

Final comments

We have all had the experience of sabotaging our aims by not being in control of what we say and how we react. The successful person has a determination to find out the causes of these automatic reactions and change them, knowing that self-awareness may prevent similar acts in the future.

"Success" may conventionally be thought of as the ability to manipulate other people and events. Napoleon, for instance, was reputed to have said: "Circumstances—what are circumstances? I *make* circumstances." The question is whether you want to have this kind of success, or the sort that Abraham Maslow described as "self-actualized"; that is, the kind experienced by people who achieve things in the world but are also very comfortable with themselves, who have a capacity to give and contribute.

Born to Win could be classed as a self-help book, but the title gives it away as primarily a work of success, different to most in the genre. While the success literature at first glance is about external achievement, in fact its principal concern is fulfillment of potential, seeking to be your best self.

James and Jongeward's ideal of a whole person who has consciously integrated all their "sides" and no longer needs to play games with others is surely the type of person that the world needs now.

Muriel James & Dorothy Jongeward

Muriel James is a psychotherapist, with a doctorate from the University of California, Berkeley, where she taught for many years on the extension faculty staff. She is also a licensed marriage and family counselor, a trainer in transactional analysis, and a past president of the Transactional Analysis Association. Among her 17 books are It's Never Too Late to Be Happy: The Psychology of Self-Parenting, Hearts on Fire: Romance and Achievement in the Lives of Great Women, and The OK Boss.

Dorothy Jongeward is a teacher, counselor, and management counselor specializing in organizational behavior. She also worked at the University of California, Berkeley; is active in transactional analysis circles; and is a licensed marriage and family counselor. Her other books include Everybody Wins: Transactional Analysis Applied to Organizations, and, with Muriel James, Winning Ways in Health Care and Winning with People: Group Exercises in Transactional Analysis.

Becoming Steve Jobs

"The most basic question about Steve's career is this: How could the man who had been such an inconsistent, inconsiderate, rash, and wrongheaded businessman that he was exiled from the company he founded become the venerated CEO who revived Apple and created a whole new set of culture-defining products that transformed the company into the most valuable and admired enterprise on earth and that changed the everyday lives of billions of people from all different socioeconomic strata and cultures? The answer wasn't something Steve had ever been all that interested in discussing. While he was an introspective guy, he was not inclined to retrospection: 'What's the point in looking back,' he told me in one email. 'I'd rather look forward to all the good things to come.'"

In a nutshell

Great business success often follows an arc of personal growth; by facing up to personal and professional failures, we sow the seeds for lasting achievements.

In a similar vein

Henry Ford *My Life and Work* (p. 98)
Bill Gates (by Wallace & Erickson) *Hard Drive* (p. 116)
Sam Walton *Made in America* (p. 314)

CHAPTER 28

Brent Schlender & Rick Tetzeli

Given the fame of its subject, the film *Steve Jobs* (2015) ought to have been a big success. It wasn't, Brent Schlender and Rick Tetzeli argue, because it portrayed Jobs as a sociopath incapable of changing or growing, with a delusional inability to admit the paternity of his daughter Lisa. Yet the remarkable fact about Jobs, they insist, is just how much he *did* change—as a person, a manager of people, and a businessman.

How did "a dying manufacturer of computers," as Apple was in the late 1990s, become the most valuable company in the world? Schlender and Tetzeli argue that it has much to do with the arc of Jobs's personal growth: his realization that he had to make the most of his strengths while limiting his weaknesses. In short, he had to learn how to manage himself. Jobs's marriage to Laurene Powell and his children allowed him to have a rich, meaningful life outside of work. His spiritual life was also important in his unfolding. The Buddhist idea that things are constantly changing, yet we should still pursue enlightenment and perfection, was the unseen driver behind all his work, the authors argue, and the famed beauty of Apple products became an expression of Jobs's metaphysical journey.

Jobs was diagnosed with a pancreatic tumor in 2003, and died in 2011. Most of what was written about him, the authors say, was in the "half-genius, half-asshole" mode. Unlike Walter Isaacson, Jobs's other, more famous biographer, Schlender knew his subject personally for 25 years, writing many stories on him for the *Wall Street Journal* and *Fortune*, so this book has an insider feel that is distinct from Isaacson's biography. The Jobs that Schlender observed was "more complex, more human, more sentimental, and even more intelligent" than he was given credit for. Moreover, Schlender contends that Jobs's "wilderness years"—1985 to 1997, between his first and second periods at Apple, when he started NeXT and Pixar—were in many ways the most interesting:

> *"To overlook those years is to fall into the trap of only celebrating success. We can learn as much, if not more, from failure, from promising paths that turn into dead ends."*

It is on this period that *Becoming Steve Jobs: The Evolution of a Reckless Upstart into a Visionary Leader* focuses.

First steps

Jobs was born in 1955, the child of an American graduate student, Joanna Schieble, and a Syrian PhD candidate, Abdulfattah "John" Jandali, who were together for a time at the University of Wisconsin. Schieble gave the child up for adoption, but insisted that any adoptive parents be university educated. In the event, Steven was adopted by Paul and Clara Jobs, a working-class San Francisco couple who did everything possible to give him a good start, even moving to another area with better schools where his quick mind could fulfil its potential. Mountain View would turn out to be the perfect environment for him: it was the center of an emerging electronics and telecommunications industry, the seedbed of Silicon Valley.

As a teenager, Jobs threw himself into the amateur science and technology scene, where he met Steve Wozniak. "Woz" was far superior to Jobs in technical knowledge and had managed to put together a "personal" computer, one not requiring access to a mainframe and with a keyboard and monitor. Jobs could see the market potential of such a device, and the two formed a company to build and sell the product. The rudimentary Apple I, put together in Jobs's parents' garage with the help of friends and family, sold almost 200 units. Jobs's outlook was more countercultural than businesslike, but he had discovered his mission—bringing the power of computing to the mainstream.

The Apple II, released in 1977 and costing $1,295, or $5,000 in today's money, was the first real personal computer to work right out of the box. Jobs insisted that it not look like an industrial unit, but have a sleek beige exterior. Despite having only one useful program, Visicalc, it was a hit, selling 500 a month. Explosive growth meant sales of $8 million in 1978, $47 million in 1979, and $118 million in 1980. When the company floated on the stock market in 1980, Jobs was suddenly very rich and the first real superstar of computing. The Apple II was in production for 10 years, selling 6 million units.

Unfortunately, the Apple III, which Jobs had wanted to be revolutionary rather than an evolution of the Apple II, was a commercial failure thanks to too many features and poor technical design. This was a shock for Jobs, who had believed he was invincible. Insufferably demanding and petulant as a boss, at the age of 30 he was forced out of the company he had founded. Devastated, he took an unintended holiday wandering around Europe, and sought the advice of old Silicon Valley hands.

NeXT steps

Before long, Jobs was back with a big new idea: powerful computers for engineers, scientists, or academics who needed more power than the home user and who could have their machine networked with other machines. He had this new company, christened NeXT, build an expensive, state-of-the-art factory, when everything could have been outsourced. The projected retail cost of the NeXT computer was to be $3,000, with its actual materials costing no more than $50, but Jobs insisted on magnesium being used instead of plastic, and a paint job that cost $50 alone. These design features made the computer difficult to engineer and much more expensive, but Jobs believed his own press that he was a "genius" and knew better than anyone else how to do things. An "equal-opportunity abuser," as Schlender and Tetzeli describe him at this time, Jobs yelled indiscriminately at top executives, lowly staffers, and external people. Anyone who didn't agree with him was "stupid" or much worse.

With a printer and conventional hard drive (instead of the optical default), the NeXT computer would end up costing over $10,000—over three times more than originally planned. A fantastic launch event didn't hide the fact that it was in a similar price bracket to other, better workstations on the market, such as those made by Sun Microsystems, but without their power, and was too expensive for universities, the intended market. Built to push out 600 computers a day, the NeXT factory never produced more than that in a month.

Microsoft refused to develop software for NeXT machines, which effectively sidelined the four-year-old firm. A deal for IBM to use the NeXTSTEP operating system on its PCs, providing a counterweight to Microsoft's dominance of software, eventually floundered because of Jobs's intransigence over money. It could have been the lifeline that NeXT needed, but Jobs had issues dealing with "Big Blue," for which he had always professed contempt. By 1991, all of the top five people Jobs had taken from Apple to start NeXT had resigned, sick of his overspending, micromanagement, ridiculous demands, arbitrary decisions, and emotional outbursts.

Rescued by *Toy Story*

In 1991, Schlender wrote a piece for *Fortune* on the state of the personal computer industry, interviewing Jobs and Gates together at Jobs's Palo Alto home. Though Jobs was still famous, the two men's fortunes had diverged. While NeXT was going nowhere, Microsoft was dominating the industry with its Windows operating system and Office software suite. Gates, now vastly richer than Jobs, was the world's youngest billionaire. All through the 1990s his star only rose further, with the share price of Microsoft going up 3,000 percent.

A side bet that Jobs made while at NeXT would turn out to be a lifeline. He had bought a small graphics computing company from George Lucas for $5 million, thinking its mastery of 3D graphic manipulation would be useful to NeXT. Jobs kept plowing money and resources into the company, called Pixar, without much return. He watched as Pixar's head, Ed Catmull, brilliantly motivated and managed a group of creative people whose dream was to make a feature-length computer-animated film.

Jobs took on the role of promoting Pixar in the wider world, and reached a deal with Disney to fund a big animation project. The brilliant *Toy Story* would change the film industry. When Pixar went public in 1995, a week after *Toy Story*'s release, Jobs, who owned 80 percent of the stock, became a billionaire. Yet his satisfaction with his role in Pixar's success was much more than financial: he had loved being part of a very creative team, making something he was passionate about, and had learned much from Catmull's management style. Without Pixar, Schlender and Tetzeli say, "there would have been no great second act at Apple."

While Jobs was having success with Pixar, poor leadership had turned the company he had co-founded into a mess. Hemorrhaging money, to stay relevant it needed a new advanced operating system. It became clear that NeXT's was the best fit for its products, and Apple ended up buying NeXT and absorbing its intellectual capital. Jobs now found himself in the strange position of being intimately part of his old company, but not running it. Although disparaging of Apple management, he was reluctant to put his hand up to replace CEO Gil Amelio when the latter was fired. He now had a young family and was too involved in Pixar, and coming back to head Apple would mean unnecessary risk and stress.

However, on further reflection Jobs concluded that he still loved Apple and that it was worth trying to save, even if he failed. When he took on the CEO role, in 1997, he set a dramatic transformation in place. He drastically reduced the product line to two desktops and two laptops and, in place of Apple's many promising technologies in development, the new mission would be a handful of great *products* to serve the high end of the consumer and business markets. Jobs had learned the hard lesson that he shouldn't try to make every product an amazing breakthrough, but simply something that worked brilliantly and that people loved.

Giant steps

The standardization of computing in the PC/Windows era, with one gray-box Compaq, Dell, or IBM looking and performing much like another, left an opening for the possibility of more *personal* computers, ones that would delight people, not just offer them progressively more speed, power, or features.

Jobs's relationship with British designer Jony Ive proved to be crucial in rethinking personal computing. Ive's iconic casing for the iMac, with its bulbous shape and Bondi blue clear plastic to see inside the machine, looked nothing like anything else on the market. It wasn't faster or more powerful, but people *desired* it. Apple reasserted itself as a genuinely personal, creative computer company and sold 2 million iMacs within 12 months. It was back in the business, only a couple of years after facing bankruptcy. "Near death experiences," Jobs put it, "can help one see more clearly sometimes."

Still, the September 2000 earnings report for Apple was poor, and even under Jobs the company's sales across all products were shrinking. *Fortune* called Jobs "the graying prince of a shrinking kingdom." At the time Microsoft was worth over $600 billion, and if anyone had suggested that the next decade of personal computing belonged to Apple, they would have been laughed out of the room. Apple was a financially struggling niche player that made products for creatives.

So the firm's great success from the early 2000s onward surprised everyone in the technology industry, the public, and even Apple staffers themselves. The iMac had reminded people that Apple existed, but it was the subsequent game-changing products, starting with the iPod and iTunes and followed by the iPhone and iPad, that made Apple fantastically cool—and stupendously profitable. With each product, Jobs told Schlender, "We followed where our own desires led us, and we ended up ahead." The iPod and iTunes turned Apple into a leader in the digital music revolution, and the iPhone and iPad pulled together previously disparate technologies of telephony, computing, and touch screens into devices that were hugely powerful and at the same time beautiful and so easy to use. Jobs, says Schlender, had "a belief that the intersection of the arts and technology could lead to amazing things." The technologies all existed, but it was his genius that saw how they could be combined into single, talisman-like objects that could delight people and help make their days much more productive and enjoyable.

Final comments

Business philosopher Jim Collins has said that the mark of a great leader is not just vaulting ambition or raw intelligence, but "deep restlessness," which involves bottomless curiosity and the wish to do something meaningful and powerful with one's life. The things Jobs tried to do, Schlender and Tetzeli note, were all huge and difficult; indeed, what strikes one in reading about his career and life are the many big failures interspersed among the successes.

The caricature of an empathy-free Jobs, whose obsession with his work was such that it made people into replaceable objects that he could use and discard, is at odds with the man he became in his later years—a devoted friend and family man who had created a work culture where many employees often said they had, despite crazy challenges, the time of their lives. In contrast to the publicity-hungry beast of former times, Jobs turned down nearly all media requests, attended only a handful of Mac-related industry events each year, and, despite hundreds of invitations, gave only one college commencement address, his now-famous 2005 Stanford University talk in which he said:

> *"Your time is limited, so don't waste it living someone else's life. Don't be trapped by dogma—which is living with the results of other people's thinking. Don't let the noise of others' opinions drown out your own inner voice. And most important, have the courage to follow your heart and intuition. They somehow already know what you truly want to become. Everything else is secondary."*

In a foreword to *Becoming Steve Jobs*, venture capitalist Marc Andreessen writes that Jobs's real legacy is inspiring people "to be something special and do something special. Good enough was good enough for a long time, but thanks to Steve, it isn't anymore." Jony Ive told the authors how, as Apple became the model company of the 2000s and began raking in mountains of money, Jobs felt vindicated. Not in a told-you-so way, but in this sense:

> *"Given the choice, people do discern and value quality more than we give them credit for. That was a really big deal for all of us because it actually made you feel very connected to the whole world and all of humanity, and not like you're marginalized and just making a niche product."*

Jobs's and Ive's *personal* quests for aesthetic and technological perfection had been writ large on the world.

Brent Schlender & Rick Tetzeli

Brent Schlender was a senior editor at Fortune *from 1989 to 2009, known for his incisive portrayals of people and events in the technology industry. He has degrees in English literature and computer science from the University of Arkansas.*

Rick Tetzeli is executive editor of Fast Company. *He was previously managing editor of* Entertainment Weekly *and covered technology issues for* Fortune.

1998

Who Moved My Cheese?

"He knew he had learned something useful about moving on from his mice friends, Sniff and Scurry. They kept life simple. They didn't overanalyze or overcomplicate things. When the situation changed and the cheese had been moved, they changed and moved with the cheese. He would remember that."

"He realized that the fastest way to change is to laugh at your own folly."

In a nutshell

The ability not only to accept change but to create it is a mark of the dynamic individual.

In a similar vein
Susan Jeffers *Feel the Fear and Do It Anyway* (50SHC)
J. W. Marriott Jr. *The Spirit to Serve* (p. 248)
Ernest Shackleton (by Margot Morrell & Stephanie Capparell)
Shackleton's Way (p. 290)

CHAPTER 29

Spencer Johnson

A group of old school friends is gathered for dinner and the topic of conversation gets on to change: in career, relationships, and family life. One of those present contends that change no longer bothers him after having heard "a funny little story" called "Who moved my cheese?" In this artful way, Spencer Johnson introduces the reader to his fable on how to cope positively with change.

The story involves four characters who live in a maze: the mice Scurry and Sniff and two "littlepeople," Hem and Haw. All is going well because they have found a huge source of their favorite food, cheese. Hem and Haw have even moved their houses to be near it and it has becomes the center of their lives. But they do not notice that it is getting smaller, and are devastated when they arrive at the site one morning and find that the cheese is gone.

This is where the story splits in two. Scurry and Sniff quickly accept the loss of the cheese and go off into the maze in search of other sources. The littlepeople, because they have built their lives around the big cheese, feel that they are the victims of some kind of fraud or theft. Yet this only makes things worse, as their clinging on ensures that they go hungry. Meanwhile, the mice move on and find new cheese.

There will be other cheeses

The fable captures well that moment after you have lost a job or a relationship and you believe it is the end of the world. All the good things were in the previous situation, and all the future holds is fear. Yet Johnson's message is that, instead of seeing change as the end of something, you must learn to see it as a beginning. We have all been told this, but sometimes motivation is lacking. To make himself accept reality, Haw writes this on the wall of the maze: "If you do not change, you can become extinct."

Though Johnson does not mention him, the reader is reminded of people like explorer Sir Ernest Shackleton, whose "cheese" was the expectation that his men would be the first to cross the Antarctic on foot. When his ship, carrying all his men, supplies, and equipment, was slowly crushed by pack ice, instead of panicking Shackleton quickly accepted what had happened; without complaint he focused on what could be done to get his men out alive (see p. 290).

Sudden change can spiral you into self-loathing or depression, because your whole sense of identity has been built around the old circumstances. The surprisingly powerful advice from this story, however, is that you should not take yourself this seriously. Being willing to laugh at your predicament can have a liberating effect, even in the worst situations. You can marvel and even be amused at how weak your attachment had made you.

In a bid to inspire himself, Haw writes another graffiti question on the maze wall: "What would you do if you weren't afraid?" He pushes on and, against all expectations, starts to enjoy the hunt for new cheese. He has no idea where he is going, but feels great just to be moving. Haw also discovers something to help him that the mice do not have: the power to "creatively visualize" the finding of new cheese. This use of the imagination to create a sense of confidence and expectation becomes his savior.

Feeling the fear and doing it anyway

A book about dealing with change is perhaps best categorized as a self-help book, but since change is the basic fact of existence, awareness of it must be crucial to success. The nature of change is that you never think it could happen to you, yet such denial stops you from taking up opportunities for new cheese earlier, or even moving your own cheese before it gets moved by others.

It is not so much that life is short (doctors believe that many people in the twenty-first century will live healthily into their hundreds) but that it goes quickly. For life not to be wasted, it demands a level of risk and adventure. If you are willing to live this way, change loses its horror. In fact, the advancing person purposely creates change because the world is not currently how they would like it. What Hem and Haw discover is that breaking through your fears makes you free. Those who continually seek security, ironically, are racked by the possibility that they may lose it.

Final comments

While *Who Moved My Cheese?* addresses the fact of change in all aspects of our lives, given how many offices the book circulates in, it would be fair to say that its main message relates to work.

Most employees are employees because they prefer the security of a set wage under the apparent protection of a large enterprise. For others, the chief benefit may be that for most of the day they do not have to really think; they "complete tasks." But such dependence restricts personal growth, in the same way that a medieval serf, while given a roof over their head on the estate, often did not stray more than a few miles beyond it and could never expect to be a truly independent person.

The value of *Who Moved My Cheese?* can be appreciated by both the manager and the worker: the boss can get staff to read it to prepare themselves for organizational change or downsizing; and the employee may find the book a spur to understanding our much more fluid working world, in which, even if we choose to remain an employee, mentally we can be in control.

This may be reading too much into Spencer Johnson's book of fewer than 100 pages, which many people will regard as trite. Indeed, there are more inspiring books on how to cope with change, but the lesson from this one is easily remembered: Do you have a "big cheese" in your life that you believe will last forever?

Spencer Johnson

Johnson was born in 1938 and gained a BA in psychology from the University of Southern California and his MD degree from the Royal College of Surgeons in Ireland.

He has been medical director of communications for Medtronic, which invented heart pacemakers; a research physician at the Institute for Interdisciplinary Studies (a think tank); and a consultant to the University of Southern California's School of Medicine.

With Kenneth Blanchard, Johnson co-authored the bestselling The One Minute Manager, *and wrote a number of other* One Minute *books. He was also the creator of the children's series* ValueTales, *based on the life lessons of famous people, and the motivational gift book* The Precious Present. *Publishers claim sales figures of over 18 million copies for* Who Moved My Cheese? *Johnson died in 2017.*

2013

The One Thing

"The ONE thing becomes difficult because we've unfortunately bought into too many others—and more often than not those 'other things' muddle our thinking, misguide our actions, and sidetrack our success."

"It's not that we have too little time to do all the things we need to do, it's that we feel the need to do too many things in the time we have."

"When you see someone who has a lot of knowledge, they learned it over time. When you see someone who has a lot of skills, they developed them over time. When you see someone who has done a lot, they accomplished it over time. When you see someone who has a lot of money, they earned it over time. The key is over time. Success is built sequentially. It's one thing at a time."

In a nutshell

We believe that success requires us to do many things, when all it asks is that we do a single, important thing; the achievement of that unlocks the door to every other good thing.

In a similar vein
Frank Bettger *How I Raised Myself from Failure to Success in Selling* (p. 24)
Andrew Carnegie *The Autobiography of Andrew Carnegie* (p. 56)
Darren Hardy *The Compound Effect* (p. 166)
Napoleon Hill *Think and Grow Rich* (p. 174)

CHAPTER 30

Gary Keller

There was a time in Gary Keller's life when he believed that in order to succeed, he had to do everything the motivational books said: be the first at the office every day, work people hard, "dress for success."

After a time, he realized that this hard-driving approach wasn't really him. He stopped trying to be an overachiever and began looking after his health and having breakfast with his family. By doing less and allowing himself to breathe, the funny thing was that he became more successful than before. "I learned," he says, "that success comes down to this: being appropriate in the moments of your life." Whatever you are doing, you want to be able to say, "This is where I'm meant to be right now, doing exactly what I'm doing." If you can do that, success in all areas of your life will take care of itself.

Written with long-time collaborator Jay Papasan, *The One Thing: The Surprisingly Simple Truth about Extraordinary Results* is one of those deceptively simple books that are easy to dismiss. What does a guy who's done well out of real estate know about the secret of success? In fact, though the concept of the book is simplicity itself— the power of focus— it makes many points that are far from obvious and exposes some myths that may well have held you back from success. Moreover, this is not just another "how I did it" business autobiography, but an attempt at a theory of success supported by academic studies. The book itself is different, with what looks like lead pencil underlining of bits of text throughout. But you have not bought a used book: this is a device to help key ideas sink into the reader's mind, along with the selection of great quotes in the margins.

Go narrow, go small

In the 1990s, everything seemed to be going well for Keller. He built a successful real estate company in less than 10 years, but was hitting roadblocks both commercially and personally. He hired a business coach, who told him he needed to install a new cadre of managers. By putting the right people into 14 key positions, the business would change. Keller doubted this advice, but proceeded to reengineer the company as advised. This focus on key people would turn out to be the seed of his company's success over the following decade.

Yet in the early days of the firm's reengineering, Keller was finding that, although people were clear on the list of things that needed to get done, they were often not doing the most important things. This led him to ask his managers, "out of desperation," he says:

"What's the ONE thing you can do this week such that by doing it everything else would be easier or unnecessary?"

To his surprise, this focus on the one, most important thing began to produce great results for the company. It made Keller reflect on his own life: Every time he had been successful, he said, "I had narrowed my concentration to one thing, and where my success varied, my focus had too."

When you look at people who achieve in a big way, he notes, their success involves a paradox. They are able to get more done with greater effect because they "go small"—that is, they narrow their focus to the single thing that, if all the other things are going to fall into place, they *must* do. People make the mistake of thinking that success is complicated and involves having many irons in the fire at once, but the truth is the opposite. There is a Russian proverb: "If you chase two rabbits, you will not catch either one." Focusing on the one thing that really matters allows your time and energy to be efficiently used, whereas chasing many "rabbits" at once is disheartening when you come back empty-handed. Success is not about being good on many counts, but doing a few things extremely well.

Falling dominoes

You may have seen on television or the internet record-breaking displays of falling dominoes, sometimes involving up to a million pieces. Less well known is the ability of the dominoes to increase in power as the trail moves along. If the dominoes in a line increase in size, each one 50 percent larger than the one before, it turns out that a small domino can, through the movement of energy through the line, end up toppling a domino many, many times its own size. A two-inch domino, seven domino falls later, can topple one that is three feet tall. By the 18th domino, physics tells us that the chain of dominoes could push over something the size of the Leaning Tower of Pisa; by the 23rd, the Eiffel Tower; and by the 31st, an object the height of Mount Everest. And so on, until by the 57th you are talking about a structure that would be the height of the distance between the earth and the moon.

Keller's point is that it is possible to create a similar exponential domino effect in your life. If you keep pushing over the right domino, "success builds on success." Look at every high achiever and you see that at each point in their career, they had a simple focus on getting the *next thing right*. In time, pushing over the small dominoes, one at a time, led to massive successes. It is too easy to look at a successful person and attribute "genius" to them when in reality, Keller says, "Success is built sequentially. It's one thing at a time."

The power of one

Look closely at extremely successful companies, and they all began with a single hit product or service on which everything else was built. Colonel Sanders started Kentucky Fried Chicken with a single, brilliant recipe for fried chicken. The Coors company expanded massively between 1947 and 1967 with a single kind of beer, made in a single brewery. The incredible growth of McDonald's was built on a very small menu of things people loved, not least superior fries. The *Star Wars* franchise, including today's huge merchandise sales, began with the original, lovingly made film. As a company grows, naturally its "one thing" will change in the light of shifts in culture, technology, and competition, but the smart firm is always asking: "What's the ONE thing we should be doing now?" Keller reminds us, for example, of Apple's shifts in focus from Macs to iMacs to iTunes to iPods to iPhones. The company's strategy was not to try out half a dozen products every year and see what worked, but to put all its resources into the next, single thing that it believed could be transformational for users.

Myths of success
Keller goes through what he considers the lies and myths that stop us fulfilling our potential. They include the three outlined below.

Everything matters equally
Keller is a keen observer of the 80/20 principle, first pointed out by Italian economist Vilfredo Pareto, that the relationship between inputs and outcomes is much more uneven than common sense would suggest. A few key efforts produce the lion's share of our results; a handful of people account for most of a firm's profits; a small part of our working day is what generates most of our income.

The problem with to-do lists is that they give all tasks a similar value, when in fact, Keller notes, "some things matter more than others—a lot more." When all your tasks seem equally urgent, when you feel overcommitted and overbooked, you have probably lost your sense of what is really important. "The things which are most important don't always scream the loudest," as Australian prime minister Bob Hawke commented.

Don't have to-do lists, Keller says, have "Success Lists" that state your most important priorities. Time blocking—that is, having a semi-sacred four hours devoted to your One Thing each day—is the greatest tool of productivity there is. If you get into the habit of time blocking four hours a day, working on what really matters, then you will find that everything else is easily taken care of. Get out of the mental habit of believing that "many things have to be done." In truth, there is only *one* important thing you have to do today. A good rule of thumb is to be "a maker in the morning, and a manager in the afternoon."

You need to be highly disciplined to succeed
The fact is, you don't need to have any more discipline than you have now, you just need to direct it better by creating patterns of behavior—habits—that become automatic. Once these habits kick in, results are inevitable.

People who have good habits appear to be "highly disciplined," but they are merely following well-worn behaviors that they began doing long ago; it's not like they have to apply great willpower every day. One of the secrets to swimmer Michael Phelps's extraordinary success was that he was in the pool training 365 days of the year. He didn't even think about whether to train or not, it was automatic. Remember, a habit is only hard when you begin (on average, a habit takes 66 days to become an entrenched part of your life), then it doesn't require much energy to maintain. "People do not decide their futures," said F. M. Alexander (of Alexander technique fame), "they decide their habits and their habits decide their future."

The need for balance

You may assume that you should be seeking "balance," usually between work and life. The problem with balance is that it means you don't really give enough of a time commitment to anything. "In your effort to attend to all things," Keller says, "everything gets shortchanged and nothing gets its due."

It may be reasonable to want a balance between various elements of your life, but it is at the extremes (for instance, lots of time spent with your kids, or on a work project) where great things happen. But how do you achieve success in one thing without allowing the rest of your life to fall apart? Replace the concept of balance with the practice of "counterbalance." If, for instance, you have to spend an intense time on work commitments, make sure that the time you couldn't spend with your spouse or family is not left for too long. Whereas at work you can neglect some aspects or tasks if it means you stick to your long-term goals, with family it's different: the goal is time itself, for which there are no shortcuts. As James Patterson imagined it in his novel *Suzanne's Diary for Nicholas*, work is a rubber ball that will always bounce back, but your family, health, friends, and integrity are like glass balls. If you drop them, they may crack or break for good. "When you're supposed to be working, work, and when you're supposed to be playing, play," Keller advises. An extraordinary life is not a balancing act, and it is certainly not about "multitasking" (which simply means doing a number of things poorly). Success is always a *counter*balancing act, as you swing between things you have identified as very important to you, giving each thing its proper due.

The focusing question

In 1885, steel magnate Andrew Carnegie gave a famous talk to a university on "Success in Business." Carnegie told the audience that the "prime condition of success, the great secret" is *concentration* of energy, thought, and capital. Whatever business you are in, he said, resolve to know the most about it, have the best machinery, and build the best plant possible. The businesses that fail are those in which capital has been scattered, which means *minds* have been scattered, too. "Put all your eggs in one basket," Carnegie advised, "and then watch that basket."

Wise words, but how do you know which basket to focus on? The heart of Keller's book is his "focusing question":

"What's the ONE Thing I can do, such that by doing it everything else will be easier or unnecessary?"

The question forces you to focus on what you *can* do, not what you "could," "should," or "would" do. This is important, because action you can take now is always superior to intentions. Asking what the *single* thing is that, if you achieved it, could unlock the door to everything else you want can lead you to reorganize your priorities and often provides sudden clarity on what really matters. When you have a long-term goal, its achievement may seem so far off that you need to work backwards and work out what you need to do this year, this month, this week, this day, and this hour to get the ball rolling.

Despite his company growing fast, Keller saw that it wasn't getting much industry recognition. His top team sat down for a day to work out what they could do to change this. They came up with 100 good ideas, then the next day narrowed those down to 10. From there, they settled on *one* idea: Keller would write a book on how to succeed in the real estate field. The book was a success, selling a million copies and raising the firm's profile many times over. As another example, Keller was learning to play the guitar, but could devote only 20 minutes a day to practicing. So he asked a master guitarist what would be the one thing he would do, if he only had that time each day to practice. "Scales," he was told; and indeed, working on scales 20 minutes each day proved to be the thing that unlocked guitar mastery for Keller. Before they established their philanthropic foundation, Bill and Melinda Gates had to work out what to do with their fortune. Melinda asked: What's the *one* thing we could do where our money would make the greatest difference? They had many choices, but they settled on the aim of seeing the scourge of infectious diseases end in their lifetimes. What was the *one* thing that would do most to see that goal realized? The evidence said it was the provision of vaccines, so funding vaccination programs became central to their work.

In an age when people judge themselves by how many "friends" they can amass on social media, Keller reminds us that great trajectories of success need only *one* person, a crucial catalyst in the unfolding of our passions and skills. For Walt Disney it was his businessman brother Roy, who got him work at an art studio where he learned animation. For Sam Walton of Walmart, it was his father-in-law, L. S. Robson, who loaned him $20,000 to open his first business, a Ben Franklin store franchise. For Albert Einstein, it was his mentor Max Talmud, who guided the young Einstein's reading of key texts in science, math, and philosophy. The Beatles might never have reached their creative potential or commercial success without George Martin, their record producer. Oprah Winfrey credits her father with saving her, giving her the confidence to pursue her dreams.

None of us is really self-made, Keller says. Ask yourself who is the most important person, or people, in your life and make them even more important, giving them the time, attention, and love they deserve. It is often said that we only change the world one person at a time. By the same token, it may be one person who truly sees our potential and is the seed for our flourishing.

Final comments

"We are kept from our goal, not by obstacles but by a clear path to a lesser goal."

Robert Brault

This quote, inserted unobtrusively in the margin of a page in *The One Thing* to support its arguments, is central to Keller's thinking. The human mind has evolved in such a way that we are continually looking for safety, which in work and life comes to mean hedging our bets. Yet these lesser goals are like the snow that slowly covers up the path that will take us toward a unique and powerful contribution.

We have what Keller calls "megaphobia," an irrational fear of doing big things. We make a mistaken connection between big and bad, meaning that for everything big to succeed it has to come at the cost of much pain and difficulty. According to this view, thinking small seems prudent. However, big things are often easier to achieve than we thought, particularly when our time and energy are liberated by clarity about what is truly important.

When you begin to focus on what really matters, some things will be put on the back burner, Keller warns, and some untidiness and chaos may ensue. Saying no to people may be hard at first, but you must learn to live with not pleasing everyone. However, when you start to achieve success through committing to your One Thing, it will put all smaller worries into perspective.

Gary Keller

Born in Pasadena, Texas, in 1957, Keller grew up in Houston with his schoolteacher parents. He planned to be a rock guitarist, but his parents got him into Baylor University, where he enrolled in a new real estate program. On graduating he sold houses in Austin, Texas. In the 1980s he co-founded the Keller Williams real estate company, which in terms of agents is now the largest in the world. The company promotes itself as an industry leader in the personal development, training, and education of its agents.

Keller's other books, written with Jay Papasan and Dave Jenks, are The Millionaire Real Estate Agent *(2004),* The Millionaire Real Estate Investor *(2005), and* SHIFT: How Top Real Estate Agents Tackle Tough Times *(2008).*

Rich Dad, Poor Dad

"Both men were successful in their careers, working hard all their lives. Both earned substantial incomes. Yet one struggled financially all his life. The other would become one of the richest men in Hawaii. One died leaving tens of millions of dollars to his family, charities and his church. The other left bills to be paid."

"Rule one. You must know the difference between an asset and a liability, and buy assets. If you want to be rich, this is all you need to know."

In a nutshell

Learn how money could work for you; unlearn the expectation that you must work for money.

In a similar vein

Warren Buffett (by Roger Lowenstein) *Buffett* (p. 48)
George S. Clason *The Richest Man in Babylon* (p. 68)
Benjamin Franklin *The Way to Wealth* (p. 104)
Thomas J. Stanley *The Millionaire Mind* (p. 296)

CHAPTER 31

Robert Kiyosaki

*R*ich Dad, Poor Dad: What the Rich Teach Their Kids about Money . . . That the Poor and Middle Class Do Not! became a bestseller during the dot-com boom of the late 1990s. Many ideas and businesses faded away when the bubble burst, but this book has kept going because it has nothing to do with market frenzies and everything to do with our private attitudes about money.

The book's title comes from Kiyosaki's two "dads": his real one, who worked hard all his life as an educator in Hawaii; and a friend's father, who ran businesses and worked for himself. At age 9, the young Kiyosaki decided to follow the advice of the "rich dad," and *Rich Dad, Poor Dad* is the culmination of those teachings.

The rat race

Many people's parents say, or at least strongly imply, that the reason we have to study hard at school is so that we can go on to university and then get a secure job. This is seen as the path to financial success, and anything else is too risky or strange to contemplate.

Accepting this conventional wisdom—a wisdom based on fear— most of us end up "working for the man." The average workplace has a sense of quiet desperation about it. People forever complain about their pay or their boss, but the alternative of quitting seems even worse. If they do go, they have another job lined up so that there is a smooth transition from one pay packet to another.

Thanks to your fear, Kiyosaki says, for the rest of your life you are likely to be dependent on a wage and an employer. As you gain a mortgage, consumer debt, and children, your dependence only increases, and so does your fear of trying something different. Because you can't take any risks with what you do have, your retirement money is placed in mutual funds that emphasize safety and also have low rates of return. And because you are working all the time to get raises to keep up with inflation and debt interest, you have no time to discover alternative investments. To cap it off, Kiyosaki says, you are working from

January to mid-May just to pay your taxes. If you end up with enough to get by in your retirement, you will have done well.

This is the "rat race."

Assets and liabilities

Do you know that there is a difference between money and wealth? Money is a *result* of wealth or real value and sometimes only a symbol of it. What is real is what has generated the money: a business with revenues greater than costs, a property with rent greater than mortgage and upkeep, a creative work that earns royalties.

The poor and the middle class labor under the idea that money (usually a pay packet) is what matters. This equals "security." But the rich don't focus on pay from a job—they are more interested in something that makes money and that will do so even when they are not around. Instead of looking for jobs, they scout for assets that will be a source of income. As rich dad told the young Kiyosaki, "If you look for money and security, that's all you'll get." You might get "money" but not find the *source* of money.

The fundamental difference between the rich and the poor and middle classes is that the rich know the difference between an asset and a liability. Anything that generates money—that actually puts it in your pocket—is an asset. Everything else you own that you think is an asset, be it your home, your car, or your expensive set of golf clubs, is most probably a liability. It takes money out of your pocket.

You can tell someone who doesn't know much about money because they boast about how much they earn in their job. For the savvy, job earnings are almost an irrelevance. What matters is the income coming in from assets that don't even need you to be around to generate cash.

Literate and educated

Would you describe yourself as literate? Your answer may be, "Of course." But do you know how to read a balance sheet? Rich dad told Kiyosaki that accounting was a "story in numbers," and if you could read these stories you had a great advantage. Financial literacy was as important as word literacy. "Illiteracy, both in words and numbers, is the foundation of financial struggle," he said.

People frequently ask Kiyosaki, "How do I start getting rich?" The questioner is then disappointed to hear his response: Before making any investments, educate yourself on all the options and opportunities. The more you know, the better your decisions will be. Lack of financial education teamed with the desire for quick riches leads to disaster. "Most people, in their drive to get rich, are trying to build an Empire State Building on a 6-inch slab," he says. What sort of knowledge foundation do you have?

One of Kiyosaki's fascinating points is the myth that specialization is the path to wealth. The idea goes that if you know more and more about something, you will be paid more for your knowledge. The danger with this is that it may blind you to the business aspects of your profession. Most of us "become what we study." That is, if you study cooking, you become a chef; if you study medicine, you become a doctor or a specialist. As you start to know more about your field, you do become valuable—to whoever employs you. Kiyosaki warns that you can spend so much time educating yourself that you forget to "mind your own business."

Make sure that financial knowledge is not left out of your learning.

Personal development and building wealth

The key to controlling money is controlling your emotions. How many people have won the lottery or gained a big windfall, only to lose it again within a year or two? In these situations, any deficiencies in financial education or self-discipline are magnified.

Becoming rich involves self-discipline and the ability to separate the emotions of fear and greed from a good investment decision. It may seem strange, but self-knowledge is vital to your financial future. That prosperity is intertwined with personal growth is one of the secrets of wealth in the twenty-first century.

Kiyosaki's poor dad was alarmed when he joined Xerox as a salesman. Middle-class, educated people did not go into sales. But Kiyosaki was a shy person and thought that sales training would make him less so. He knew that successful people were not as afraid of rejection, and that to get ahead in life you had to be good at selling, whether it was yourself or a thing. Once he was being interviewed by a journalist, an author herself, who asked him how she could become more successful at it. He told her to quit journalism for a year and take a sales job. He had given her the choice either to be a bestselling author or a best-*writing* author. She didn't like the idea.

Kiyosaki has taken many courses and seminars; one, which cost him $300, made him $1 million when he applied its ideas. If he does not stimulate his mind and learning, he knows he will stand still. Opportunities come from new ideas. Money spent on self-improvement is always a wise investment.

Final comments

This book makes you think. It makes you reflect not merely about investments and assets, but about your whole attitude to work and life. We have all heard it said that the stock market is driven by "fear and greed." Kiyosaki claims that, for most of us, fear is the key influence in our personal economic lives. We are shaped by our attitude toward money, and our attitude toward money is shaped by our fear. If we could change our attitude to risk and wealth, we could begin to think, act, and live like the rich. But first we must become financially intelligent.

Some of the main concepts have been described here, but only some. If you are serious about long-term improvement of your financial situation and are willing to admit that you know little, you should buy Kiyosaki's book.

Robert Kiyosaki

Born in 1947, Kiyosaki grew up in Hawaii, where his father was the chief of education for the state.

After college in New York he worked for Standard Oil in tanker shipping and as a salesman for Xerox, and in his mid-twenties joined the Marines, going to Vietnam as an officer and a helicopter pilot. He also began to buy and sell apartments and invest in stocks, and in 1977 successfully introduced nylon and velcro "surfer wallets" to the United States.

Kiyosaki's real estate portfolio includes thousands of apartments. He is also the owner of several hundred oil wells. Kiyosaki's other books include Retire Young, Retire Rich, Rich Dad, Poor Dad 2: The Cashflow Quadrant *and* The Business of the 21st Century.

Grinding It Out

"In the evenings, I would commute back to Des Plaines and walk over to the store. I was always eager to see it come into view, my McDonald's! But sometimes the sight pleased me a lot less than other times. Sometimes Ed MacLuckie would have forgotten to turn the sign on when dusk began to fall, and that made me furious. Or maybe the lot would have some litter on it that Ed said he hadn't time to pick up. These little things didn't seem to bother some people, but they were gross affronts to me. I'd get screaming mad and really let Ed have it. He took it in good part . . . But perfection is very difficult to achieve, and perfection was what I wanted in McDonald's. Everything else was secondary for me."

"I speak of faith in McDonald's as if it were a religion. And, without meaning any offense to the Holy Trinity, the Koran or the Torah, that's exactly the way I think of it. I've often said that I believe in God, family, and McDonald's—and in the office, that order is reversed."

In a nutshell

Your working life so far may have merely set the scene for your real contribution, but you must be open to the big opportunity that will draw on all your knowledge and skills.

In a similar vein
Henry Ford *My Life and Work* (p. 98)
J. W. Marriott Jr. *The Spirit to Serve* (p. 248)
Sam Walton *Made in America* (p. 314)

CHAPTER 32

Ray Kroc

The movie *The Founder* (2016) brought new attention to the story of how a small fast food stand in California became the dominant restaurant chain of our time, thanks to the vision and wiles of Ray Kroc. Yet the film is a stylized, not always accurate representation of the actual events of Kroc's life. You are best off going back to the source, his autobiography.

You may be a person who doesn't like McDonald's, so why should you bother delving into its history? The tale of its rise is instructive both in personal development and in generic business terms. As a business professor wrote in a preface to the book, the title *Grinding It Out* is not just an amusing take on the creation of hamburger mince, but captures the long slog that was Kroc's working life before he discovered McDonald's and the two decades that the corporation needed to establish itself as a global brand.

Though Kroc was no man of letters (he had journalist Robert Anderson help him do the writing), *Grinding It Out* is an entertaining read. It will make you want to look behind the counter next time you're in a McDonald's restaurant, to see for yourself what a brilliant business system looks like.

Life of a salesman

Born in 1902, Kroc missed the 1890s economic depression, was too young to fight in World War One (he signed up as a Red Cross ambulance driver in World War Two, but the war ended before he was due to ship out), and came of age through the 1910s and 1920s, a period of relative economic stability and even boom times in America.

At school, they thought Kroc was a dreamer because he was always getting excited about some scheme, but in fact he enjoyed working, including helping his parents (Bohemian immigrants who had emigrated to Chicago) around the house; all through school he worked at various jobs.

While still a teenager he opened a music store with a friend, and well into adult life, particularly after he had married and a child was on the way (a daughter, Marilyn), he would play piano in clubs and on radio stations at night to make extra money, while doing sales jobs during the day. Kroc's first really professional job was as a salesperson for the Lily Tulip paper cup company. The idea of selling paper cups would have put many people to sleep. Not Kroc, who notes, "The ten years between 1927 and 1937 were a decade of destiny for the paper cup industry." He did well even in the Depression, and by the time he left the paper cup business he was selling five million cups a year to one account alone, the drug store chain Walgreens.

After 17 years Kroc's imagination had moved on from paper cups; he had discovered the Multimixer, a machine that made it much easier for store owners to produce milkshakes. He saw unlimited potential in this and struck a deal with its creator to sell the machines as the exclusive agent, effectively becoming his own boss. His wife Ethel was not happy, believing he was risking their family's future. In one domestic contretemps, she said: "You are thirty-five years old, and you are going to start all over again as if you were twenty?"

Kroc wished she would get behind him and become involved, perhaps doing the paperwork for the fledgling operation. She refused. Kroc felt this as a betrayal; things were never quite the same between them again. "If you believe in something," he writes, "you've got to be in it to the ends of your toes. Taking reasonable risks is part of the challenge. It's the fun."

Kroc had built up debt to go into the new venture and had to work really hard to pay it off. It was a good product, though, and he gradually moved into the black. Most drugstores or dairy-bar operators needed only one of his milkshake mixers, as their multiple spindles could make five shakes at a time. However, Kroc was intrigued by an operation run by two brothers in San Bernardino, California, that was using no fewer than *eight* Multimixers. Wanting to see for himself what they were doing with them all, he flew out to California to visit.

What he discovered amazed him. In contrast to the usual greasy-spoon cafés that made people wait for a hamburger of varying quality, Mac and Dick McDonald were providing cheap (15 cent) hamburgers of high quality in record time, in a building that was kept scrupulously clean, with an equally well maintained parking lot. The brothers had established a perfect delivery system for the food, combining speed and freshness with a very limited menu. Their french fries were so good that people came back for those alone. The sheer number of customers meant lots of milkshakes too, hence the need for all those Multimixers. Kroc saw the beauty in a brilliant system whose emphasis on speed simultaneously won customers and delivered good profit margins, and in the down-home, almost comforting name of the place—McDonald's.

Epiphany becomes mission

That night in his motel room, Kroc had visions of McDonald's restaurants dotted across America, each of them requiring eight of his machines. As the chief national salesperson for the Multimixer, the financial potential was enormous.

The next day, Kroc went to see the brothers again and put to them the idea that they should open more restaurants around the country. The suggestion was met with stony silence. They were happy with things the way they were, had just built a nice home overlooking the city, and didn't want more worries. Anyway, said Dick, "Who could we get to open them for us?"

A light turned on in Kroc's mind. When he leaned forward, he heard himself saying: "Well, what about me?" He came to an agreement with the brothers that allowed him to copy their concept and system and open stores elsewhere. He opened his first McDonald's in Des Plaines, Illinois, in April 1955. Within three years there were 37 McDonald's restaurants in operation, all of them essentially serving counters in the middle of parking lots. Kroc was 52 when he discovered McDonald's:

> "I was a battle-scarred veteran of the business wars,
> but I was still eager to go into action . . . I had diabetes
> and incipient arthritis. I had lost my gall bladder and
> most of my thyroid gland in earlier campaigns. But
> I was convinced the best was ahead of me."

In fact, Kroc was not the down-and-out salesman that *The Founder* presents, and that motivational writers sometimes like to portray. He had had a successful sales career with a reasonably high salary, enough to buy his own house and support a family.

What did make him different, in contrast to thousands of other men in his position and stage in life, was his belief that "the best was ahead." Throughout his long sales career, he writes, he was always alert to other opportunities and, like Colonel Sanders of Kentucky Fried Chicken fame, always believed that his life to date was simply an apprenticeship to something really great:

> *"People have marveled at the fact that I didn't start McDonald's until I was fifty-two years old, and then I became a success overnight. But I was just like a lot of show business personalities who work away quietly at their craft for years, and then, suddenly, they get the right break and make it big. I was an overnight success all right, but thirty years is a long, long night."*

The years selling paper cups had readied him to start his enterprise as the chief agent for Multimixers, and this in turn had led him to the McDonald brothers. No work had been a waste, and now it all made perfect sense. For example, the detailed knowledge of the geography and demographics of towns and cities across America that Kroc had built up over 30 years of selling paper cups and mixers would ensure that the choice of locations for new McDonald's stores was invariably wise.

From the first day he visited them, Kroc noticed that the McDonald brothers lavished attention on the making of their french fries, including a long curing process when the fries were stored in chicken-wire bins open to the outside air before they were cooked. As these fries were easily the best he had ever tasted, and were to some extent the secret of the restaurant's success, Kroc went to great lengths to replicate the process in the new stores. "The French fry would become almost sacrosanct for me," Kroc writes, "its preparation a ritual to be followed religiously." The words he used were carefully chosen. Having found his mission in life, he would carry it out with the passion of a Jesuit, and thereafter he would often speak of McDonald's—only partly in jest—as if it were his religion.

The pace of growth did not make Kroc an instant millionaire. As with many new businesses, it was a juggling act to keep things afloat, and he did not actually become rich until McDonald's was listed on the stock exchange in 1966. In the last third of his life he was fêted as a hero by the thousands of mom-and-pop franchisees who had become millionaires. He bought a baseball team (the San Diego Padres) and would later move into a mansion in Beverly Hills. Some time after divorcing Ethel, he married the woman he truly loved, Joan B. Smith (who had been the wife of an early franchisee). After his death she became a major philanthropist for disarmament and peace causes, the Salvation Army, disaster relief appeals, and Ronald McDonald houses, and gave over $200 million to the National Public Radio network.

With a little help from my friends

Although Kroc is the name that 99 percent of people associate with McDonald's, he freely admits that it succeeded only through having a team of people who could make it into a professionally managed corporation.

In *McDonald's: Behind the Arches*, John F. Love dissects the Kroc legend. What was his real contribution? He did not invent the McDonald's system, he was terrible at managing finances (he could barely read a balance sheet), and he wasn't great at marketing (nearly all of his many ideas for new food offerings were a failure). His real genius was seeing the potential in people and motivating franchisees, or, as Love puts it, "He succeeded on a grand scale because he had the wisdom and courage to rely on hundreds of other entrepreneurs." As the film *The Founder* so well captures in the scenes where Kroc signs up new franchisees, he understood their dream to escape a humdrum job and create something for themselves. Early franchisees appreciated that Kroc seemed willing to make them rich before he himself became wealthy. His overriding goal was to turn McDonald's into an institution, with the feel of a family, and if that happened the money would surely follow.

Despite its image of obsessive uniformity, Love observes that the management team Kroc put together could not have been more diverse—one could even say odd. He did not hire corporate types but only people who lived and breathed the company, and yet he gave them huge leeway in decision-making.

Key among them was Fred Turner, an affable college dropout put in charge of the grill at Kroc's very first franchise in Des Moines. Three years later, in 1958, Turner became operations manager. Kroc made him CEO in 1973, and by the time Turner retired in 2004, there were over 30,000 restaurants worldwide. It was under Turner that McDonald's added seating, came up with the low-slung classic mansard roof and brick architecture, started the drive-thru service (in 1975), and instituted strict training for new franchisees and employees that became Hamburger University. Turner also oversaw: the introduction of the Filet-O-Fish, to get Catholics into the restaurant on Fridays; the Happy Meal for kids; the Egg McMuffin (Turner's wife came up with the name); Chicken McNuggets (1979), which could be eaten like french fries and became one of the company's great success stories; and the Ronald McDonald charities for children. Finally, it was Turner who moved the famous Golden Arches that symbolize McDonald's from the fascia of the restaurants out to the side of the road, increasing their size so they could be seen from a mile away.

Equally crucial to the rise of the company was Harry Sonneborn, a young finance expert who had experience setting up franchises for the Tastee Freez chain. When Kroc hired him, it seemed touch and go whether McDonald's would even survive. In the early days, profits from taking a portion of franchisees' revenue was wafer-thin. It was only when Sonneborn had the idea of buying and owning real estate and then leasing the sites to franchisees that the money really started rolling in. By 1982, McDonald's was the largest owner of retail real estate in the world. To his credit as a manager, Kroc hired the introverted Sonneborn even though he cared nothing about hamburgers and fries. In Sonneborn's mind, the finest moment for McDonald's was when it listed on the New York Stock Exchange and could begin making money for investors. He could not have been more different to the charismatic Kroc and there was little warmth between them, but, to Kroc's credit as a manager, he put personal differences aside for the sake of his vision.

June Martino had been Kroc's bookkeeper from his Multimixer days and stayed with him as he built McDonald's, taking on senior management roles. She became the glue in a sometimes fractious organization and was known as "Mother Martino" to a generation of new franchisees, not to mention providing a steadying presence for the volatile Kroc. He was no feminist and was famously slow to hire female executives, but Martino seemed to change his mind; he rewarded her loyalty and contribution with an equity stake that made her a rich woman.

Final comments

Today, it is fashionable to paint McDonald's as an enterprise hell-bent on damaging human health and the environment, not to mention the animal welfare aspects of "billions of hamburgers sold."

These accusations may be well justified, yet anyone wishing to start, say, a national vegan food chain would be silly not to study how Kroc's corporation was built. The lessons of McDonald's are not about hamburgers, but about creating a fabulous *system* that gives people what they want. What Kroc saw on that first visit to the McDonald brothers was not just tasty food, served quickly at a low price, but higher standards all-round. His story should make us stop and wonder: What current industry is due for a revolution in standards, and could we be part of it, or even start it? It seemed perfectly obvious to Kroc that the original McDonald's deserved to be writ large across America and the world. In the equation of success, never underestimate the power of doing what seems obvious to you, even if no one else can see it.

The Wealth and Poverty of Nations

"*Round, complete, apparently serene, ineffably harmonious, the Celestial Empire purred along for hundreds of years more, impervious and imperturbable. But the world was passing it by.*"

"*America's society of smallholders and relatively well-paid workers was a seedbed of democracy and enterprise. Equality bred self-esteem, ambition, a readiness to enter and compete in the marketplace, a spirit of individualism and contentiousness.*"

"*If we learn anything from the history of economic development, it is that culture makes all the difference . . . Yet culture, in the sense of inner values and attitudes that guide a population, frightens scholars.*"

In a nutshell

Genuine success is never an accident. The prosperous have a culture of progress that combines curiosity and persistent application.

In a similar vein
Jim Collins *Good to Great* (p. 74)

CHAPTER 33

David S. Landes

S tudents of success, if they are serious about uncovering its secrets
and patterns, must be prepared for fieldwork in unusual places.
Our readings have taken us into the corporate world; now we will
look for the clues that success leaves in the world of nations. This commentary is a little longer than most, but hopefully it will repay the
extra time spent reading.

Medieval Europe

The world has never been a level playing field, David Landes notes.
Climate and geography ("nature's inequalities") have given some countries handicaps, especially in the warmer zones, while temperate lands
have often had the benefit of reliable rainfall, good soil, hardwood
forests, and bearable cold, not to mention the right conditions for rear-
ing livestock. Such elements made for more stable societies and higher
rates of economic development and were major factors in the slow rise
of Europe in the Middle Ages.

A thousand years ago, no one could have predicted continental
Europe's dominance. It was under attack from the Vikings to the north,
the Moors to the south, and the Magyars to the east, and was an intellectual and technical laggard compared to the learning of the Arab
world and Chinese civilization.

Yet Europe had something that would prove to be highly valuable: it
was heir to the classical Roman and Greek tradition, however imper-
fect, of democracy and meritocracy. In contrast, the political culture of
civilizations surrounding it was primarily despotic; Landes describes
them as "squeeze operations" that, when they needed more, did not
hesitate simply to take by force from their own people. Europe had its
fair share of tyrannical rulers, but its concept of private property provided motivation and encouraged enterprise. Medieval Christianity also

223

put limits on the behavior of rulers, since they were subject to God and could not abuse the commoners at will. Good Christian order meant due process, the rule of law, and protection of property rightfully gained.

All of this made Europe different. The water wheel, eyeglasses, reliable clocks and watches, and the printed book were medieval European inventions. Gutenberg had published his Bible in 1452 and by 1501 there were millions of books in Europe. Meanwhile, Imperial China was serene in its isolation and did not bother itself to learn anything new, particularly if it came from "barbarians." Chinese rulers were "control freaks" in today's language, regulating everything and demanding total obedience. Enterprise was seen as a threat.

Thus, Europe overtook China by refining and adapting many of its innovations. Unlike China, Landes says, "Europe was a learner." Despite its feudal structure of kings and queens, nobles and peasants, medieval Europe had vibrant, self-organizing cities and regions. It was essentially a free market, not merely of products but of *ideas*. Literacy was not just a luxury for the rich, Landes says: Europeans read, wrote, and published, private citizens as well as officials. The driving forces were the desire to keep records, but also *curiosity*.

All nations that do well display what Landes calls "buildup"—the accumulation of knowledge and know-how over time; and "breakthrough"—the reaching of thresholds after which things gather their own momentum. He identifies three factors that can account for Europe's success and made it the place of scientific and later industrial revolution:

1. Autonomy of intellectual inquiry from church or state interference
2. Creation of a widely accepted system of proving knowledge
3. Routinization of research as an accepted activity: the "invention of invention"

Nineteenth-century Britain

Why did the Industrial Revolution happen in Britain? First of all, Landes suggests, the country had developed a social, intellectual, and political infrastructure that was conducive to enterprise: a secure system of property rights, basic and higher education, the essential freedom of the people. In these things Britons were better off than every other nation in Europe. Britain had another advantage in that it had relatively few religious constraints, as a result receiving an influx of valuable people from the Continent such as Dutch drainers and farmers, Jewish merchants, and French Huguenot craftsmen. English Catholics could not become Members of Parliament or go to university, but otherwise they were free to prosper.

Despite its famous class system, it was more possible to get ahead in Britain than elsewhere in Europe, and certainly outside it. Napoleon had dismissed England as a nation of shopkeepers, and in a way he was right, because Britain was a country grown rich by consuming. Things were made for average people to buy, not solely for the rich; which is, of course, a hallmark of the modern economy. Even so, you could not have predicted that Britain, as it entered the nineteenth century, would become the industrial powerhouse of the world. As Landes puts it, "Britain had the makings; but then Britain made itself." There is a big gap between having the capacity or the knowledge and acting on it. The country's superiority was "not God-given, not happenstance, but the result of work, ingenuity, imagination, and enterprise."

Imperial Spain and Portugal

To go back in time somewhat, while China was closing in on itself, in the fifteenth century Spain and Portugal were venturing and trading along the coast of Africa and into the Indies. In their lust for gold and silver, the Spanish eventually came upon the Incas. The Inca empire was amazingly efficient, but the rulers were despots and the culture, Landes says, "deprived the ordinary person of initiative, autonomy, and personality." Essentially socialist, the king was the "great divider": all land was his. The empire brought together diverse peoples and established a common language, but because its contact with the outside world was limited (it had no written records either) it misjudged the intent of the Spanish and considered itself too powerful to be overthrown (a familiar conceit of empires).

Landes calls the Spanish "kleptocrats," much more interested in taking rather than making, and often in the name of God. This combination of greed and righteousness unleashed horrible cruelty and exploitation. However, it achieved its purpose: the markets opened up in the New World saw vast wealth return to it, and Madrid became the richest city in Europe.

225

Why, then, did Spain decline? The money was not invested, but instead spent on luxury and war. Because the country had not gained its new wealth through any sort of industry, Landes opines, it was not of the mind to put it to productive use. "Wealth is not so good as work, nor riches so good as earnings," he says. Spain lacked the respect for hard work that the Dutch, English, French, and Genoese had developed, and had a fatal belief in its religious and social superiority. It had to rely on "metics," outsiders, to perform the trades and do the work, and manual labor was scorned.

Landes's view is that Spain became poor because it had too much money, while others had to develop the work habits that begot more enduring wealth. As Spain was deciding how to spend its bullion, elsewhere in Europe people were learning how to weave cloth, forge iron, use timber, process whale oil, and mine coal—less exciting products, but the work needed to produce them ensured that the proceeds were not frittered away.

Portugal's success was a surprise. A nation of only one million people in the fifteenth century, it had colonies from the East Indies to India to Brazil, famously "half the world" carved up with Spain. Yet it shot itself in the foot by adopting the Christian fundamentalism of its larger neighbor. Jews who had fled to Portugal from Spain to avoid persecution found themselves no better off, with pogroms leaving many dead and the rest forced to convert to Christianity. It was a dreadful mistake, as the Jews were the vital traders in the economy and were among the best scientists. They left in droves, and Portugal, Landes says, "descended into an abyss of bigotry, fanaticism and purity of blood." The Portuguese Inquisition followed the Spanish, burning heretics at the stake, and it became worse when the Spanish and Portuguese crowns were united under Philip II.

Portugal lost its scientific leadership and turned inward, with all education and learning strictly controlled by the Church. It held on to its empire, but badly lost ground in the vital sciences of astronomy and navigation and became less productive in agriculture. The new ideas and technology associated with the Protestant Reformation naturally passed it by. By 1700, Landes says, Portugal "had become a backward, weak country."

Thus the simple formula, replayed many times through history and certainly applicable to Spain and Portugal: closed-mindedness = economic failure.

Culture matters

Landes's book was published the same year as Jared Diamond's best-seller *Guns, Germs and Steel*, which argued that Europe's fortunate geography was the main factor in its success. It is for the most part convincing, but Diamond does not really explain why there is such unevenness in prosperity in the *modern* world. Landes argues that although geography has been very important in the development of nations, "it would be a mistake to see geography as destiny." Europe was indeed lucky, but "luck is only a beginning."

Some historians, Landes says, seek "a multicultural, globalist, egalitarian history that tells something (preferably something good) about everybody." In this schema, the European/American success is seen as a lucky accident. But if this is true, how do we account for the industrialization and prosperity of Asian countries like Malaysia, Singapore, and South Korea since the Second World War, when most African and South American countries have stood still or gone backward? Is the progress of these countries merely accidental?

Such an argument surely overlooks the efforts of the *people* who made it happen—and only some of these are leaders and government officials. Another thesis goes: Maybe the other countries didn't *want* to industrialize and adopt western institutions; they are rightly against any form of imperialism. There is something to this, Landes admits, however wealth is wealth and poverty is poverty, whatever country you are standing in, and many of these places have had multiple opportunities to improve. What, then, is the "*x*-factor" that distinguishes dynamic, successful nations from those that languish?

Any scholar of the link between culture and economics cannot ignore Max Weber's famous essay "The Protestant Ethic and the Spirit of Capitalism." Though it has been derided by revisionist historians, Landes says that there is much evidence for its theory that the hard work and honesty ethic of Protestant Europe allowed for the popular accumulation of wealth. The Protestant Reformation also went hand in hand with higher literacy and the questioning of dogma necessary for scientific advance. A culture of popular reading, learning, and questioning—so different, for instance, from imperial China or Spain—was born. A sense of progress replaced somber respect for authority and instead of being criminal offenses, curiosity and innovation were often the way to wealth. Such attitudes, of course, would be instrumental in the success of the United States.

The *x*-factor is therefore a culture of progress that combines curiosity, innovation, and application.

Amazingly, the quest to identify successful economic culture is taboo in some quarters because it appears to be about race and superiority. This attitude is a great pity, because *The Wealth and Poverty of Nations* is essentially a body of knowledge on the basic laws of success, whoever has applied them.

The wealth and poverty of Islamic nations

Islamic civilization had once been Europe's teacher, way ahead of it in learning and culture. But from the triumph of 1187, when the Christian crusaders were driven out of the Middle East, Landes argues, "the course of Islam was mostly downhill." While Europe was separating the religious and the secular, putting a new emphasis on facts, learning, and scientific progress, Islam was insisting on theocracy: a good state was a religious state, and those dedicated to science were not to be trusted.

The legacy? With the exception of oil-rich emirates, the great majority of Islamic countries are economic backwaters, and most are dictatorships of one form or another. Like the Spanish conquistadors, the oil windfalls of many Arabic countries have been a handicap rather than a boon; developing world-competitive industrial enterprises has not been thought necessary.

Today's Islamic countries face another great hurdle to development and prosperity: women continue to be excluded from the work force. Landes argues that "the best clue to a nation's growth and development potential is the status and role of women. This is the greatest handicap of Muslim Middle Eastern societies today, the flaw that most bars them from modernity."

The Arab world likes to blame all its woes on Israel, but Landes suggests that Middle East peace, if it ever comes, will simply further expose the failings of the Islamic economic model.

Final comments

At over 500 pages, *The Wealth and Poverty of Nations* is much more complex and subtle than this commentary can convey, and there is only space here for some examples of Landes's argument. The book really rewards reading twice: once to get the broad sweep, once for the fascinating details.

The title, of course, is inspired by Adam Smith's *The Wealth of Nations* (1776), but Landes decided it was important to look at poverty as well as wealth, because failure can be the best teacher. Did he find any similarities between unsuccessful nations? He admits he is not politically correct in his answer, that it is nearly always a simple failure of application. Of Latin America, for example, he notes that even after 200 years of political independence it is dogged by mismanagement and corruption, kept afloat by borrowing and manipulation of monetary controls. Every ex-colony has had to realize that independence does not guarantee happiness and prosperity; industries must be slowly developed, people properly educated, and institutions built.

Some characteristics of prosperous countries are thus a belief in progress; openness to outside influences; a desire to produce rather than consume; a high value put on learning; emphasis on establishing the facts; and government by the people, for the people. In contrast, fundamentalist quests for purity are diseases that quickly kill off economic health.

The optimistic, hardworking countries will always have the edge, but it is the qualities of individuals that make them this way, and with enough individuals thinking the same way you have a culture. In the wealth or poverty, success or failure of nations, culture matters. In the success or failure of individuals, "culture" is character—honesty, perseverance, diligence, vision, self-education, living by results.

At the end of the book Landes admits that this recipe of self-empowerment sounds like a cliché. Yet at heart, every person, nation, and company knows it is true. Natural aptitudes are always an advantage, but no one is ever born successful, just as nations are not born rich.

David S. Landes

One of the most distinguished postwar American historians, Landes was born in 1924 and educated at City College, New York, and Harvard University. He was professor emeritus of history and economics at Harvard University and has held positions as a professor of history or economics at a number of leading universities in the US and Europe.

His other books include Revolution in Time: Clocks and the Making of the Modern World, The Unbound Prometheus, *and* Dynasties. *Landes died in 2013.*

Lincoln on Leadership

"It was Abraham Lincoln who, during the most difficult period in the nation's history, almost single-handedly preserved the American concept of government. Had he not been the leader that he was, secession in 1860 could have led to further partitioning of the country into an infinite number of smaller, separate pieces, some retaining slavery, some not. He accomplished his task with a naturalness and intuitiveness in leading people that was at least a century ahead of his time."

"[We] here highly resolve that these dead shall not have died in vain—that this nation, under God, shall have a new birth of freedom—and that government of the people, by the people, for the people, shall not perish from the earth."
Lincoln, Gettysburg Address, 1863

In a nutshell

Above all, leaders seek results. Many have wishes, but effective leaders act.

In a similar vein
Nelson Mandela *Long Walk to Freedom* (p. 236)
Eleanor Roosevelt (by Robin Gerber) *Leadership the Eleanor Roosevelt Way* (p. 272)
Ernest Shackleton (by Margot Morrell & Stephanie Capparell) *Shackleton's Way* (p. 290)

CHAPTER 34

Donald T. Phillips

There are now many books that extract leadership lessons from the lives of famous people, but this was one of the first. Phillips had the initial inspiration for it when, in the middle of a week-long management seminar, he realized that the ideas being presented had been enacted in real life by Abraham Lincoln. He was then amazed to discover that amid the thousands of articles and books written on Lincoln, there was very little on his leadership style. It seemed that Lincoln's very genius as a leader and his success as president had made him into a myth, obscuring the fact that his life before becoming president was unspectacular, and that whatever he knew about leading he had, like everyone else, learned.

The unlikeliest hero

Lincoln was born in a log cabin in what was then frontier America. His mother died when he was young and his father remarried. Fortunately, his stepmother encouraged him to read. With a minimal education he went on to try his hand at a number of jobs, including clerk, store owner, surveyor, and postmaster, before becoming a lawyer. Though not particularly successful in his early political career, his views on slavery in the Lincoln–Douglas debates brought him wide attention, and at the 1860 Republican convention he won the party's nomination for the presidency.

Lincoln's election to the White House was not exactly an accident, but he was greatly helped by the fact that the Democrats were split between North and South. Within the Republican party, Lincoln had only been selected over William Seward because he was considered the more middle-of-the-road candidate.

By the time he was sworn in, seven states had broken away from the Union on the slavery issue, yet the outgoing president, Buchanan, had given up trying to control the situation. Congress, though the Union army was in disarray and underfunded, was looking to cut its costs, and only Lincoln seemed to see that action had to be taken if the Union was to survive and be rid of slavery. Decisive and ceaselessly energetic, his determination surprised everyone. He made William Seward, his Republican rival, secretary of state, and Edwin Stanton his secretary of war. While neither man thought much of him, within a relatively short space of time both would change their minds.

Phillips presents us with the amazing fact that Lincoln had never held an executive position before becoming president, yet he proceeded to a total reorganization of the US military, and a constitutionally questionable expansion of the powers of the presidency itself.

Let us look in more detail at some of the points that Phillips makes about Lincoln as president.

The active leader

❖ Lincoln knew that the White House was an ivory tower and spent most of his time out of the office: visiting troops in the field, visiting his staff in their homes, visiting the wounded in hospital, holding cabinet meetings wherever it was convenient. He prized informality and human contact.

❖ Lincoln employed what is now known as MBWA—management by wandering around. He sacked one general for isolating himself from his men, and believed that the best information was found first hand. He took charge of battle situations himself when necessary and remains one of the only US presidents literally to come under fire.

❖ The most accessible US president in history, Lincoln rarely turned anyone away who came to see him, whether top general or lowly farmer. This, and his great ability as a listener, helped build trust in him as a leader.

The scholar of human nature

❖ Lincoln had a "penetrating comprehension of human nature," Phillips writes, which allowed him to take the broad and compassionate view. He was able to forgive mistakes easily and was notorious for his many pardons, particularly of war deserters, who normally would have hanged. Phillips believes that this compassion evoked trust and loyalty, which in a time of war are absolutely crucial to success.

- The president used persuasion, not coercion, to achieve his ends, and was fond of the maxim "A drop of honey catches more flies than a gallon of gall." Only if you could convince someone that you were their friend could you really influence them. Despite periods of depression, Lincoln never underestimated the power of a pleasing personality, and was always ready to compliment or encourage. He rarely lost his temper.
- In terms of managing his own generals, Lincoln was not afraid to let them know what he thought were their bad points, yet he also gave them free rein to perform. Many did not meet his expectations and were given lesser responsibilities, but when the man did come along who could act in the way he wanted—Ulysses S. Grant—he placed the entire US army under his command.

Honest and compassionate Abe

- The nickname "Honest Abe" was accurate. Lincoln's reputation for honesty made people trust him and increased his ability to lead. Top leaders are expected to "do the right thing," and he had this attribute in abundance. "Values motivate," Phillips notes.
- Lincoln sought objectivity: "I shall do nothing in malice. What I deal with is too vast for malicious dealing." He did not have time for retribution, pettiness, or blame. Although he frequently wrote angry letters to his generals who were not doing enough to defeat the Confederate army, he never sent them. To do so would have made enemies, and he was always keen to give people another chance. While some perceived this as weakness, his willingness to overlook mistakes and hold his tongue endeared Lincoln to his staff.
- When the Civil War ended in 1865, Lincoln did not seek revenge on the South, instead offering goodwill. In his second inaugural address, he spoke the famous words:

"With malice towards none; with charity towards all . . . let us strive on to finish the work we are in, to bind up the nation's wounds."

This large view of things helped the South to get on with rebuilding the country without fear, minimizing both guilt and blame.

The great communicator

❖ Lincoln was a brilliant writer but also a remarkable orator. With his high-pitched voice, strange gangly frame, and ill-tailored clothes he did not make good first impressions, but by the end of a talk his audiences were usually rapt. He enjoyed injecting anecdotes, stories, and jokes into his speeches because he preferred them not to be too "high-minded." He wanted them to appeal to the average person.

❖ The same man, with very little schooling, was able to write the almost poetic Gettysburg Address, not to mention thousands of superbly crafted letters. Lincoln's lesson is that every investment we make in increasing our communication skills pays off.

The unmoveable

❖ Lincoln was a master of overcoming setbacks and defeats, because he was supported by the belief that he had right on his side. His assertiveness and refusal to buckle under pressure made him the target of unjust criticism, slander, and abuse, and until he could demonstrate himself in office he was rejected out of hand as a hick country lawyer. Yet he did not often attack his detractors and in fact accepted criticism as part of the job, only worrying when the criticism might affect perception of the Union war effort. He found release in humor and storytelling, both to amuse others and to get him through the dark years of the war.

Final comments

What is remarkable about Lincoln, Phillips notes, is that he actually did what he said he would in terms of preserving the Union and abolishing slavery. This wasn't good luck. He had goals for his time in office and he accomplished them relatively quickly (within four years). Though always ready to admit when he was wrong, he was massively confident about the stance he had taken, and with this certainty of purpose came decisiveness.

Lincoln on Leadership is worth reading to appreciate the nuances of Lincoln's character and for the points that end each chapter, providing an easy reminder of his leadership lessons. It is an inspiring read, because Lincoln himself inspired. He fulfilled the main criterion for a great leader that James McGregor Burns discussed in his seminal work *Leadership*: a person who can "lift others into their better selves."

Next time you find yourself in a quandary about how to deal with someone or how to cope with a crisis, ask yourself, "What would Lincoln have done?"

Donald T. Phillips

Born in 1952, Phillips worked in business before becoming a non-fiction writer.

His other books include The Founding Fathers on Leadership, Martin Luther King Jr. on Leadership, *and* On the Brink: The Life and Leadership of Norman Brinker. *In 2017, Phillips published* Lincoln on Leadership for Today: Abraham Lincoln's Approach to Twenty-First Century Issues.

Long Walk to Freedom

"I never thought that a life sentence truly meant life and that I would die behind bars. Perhaps I was denying this prospect because it was too unpleasant to contemplate. But I always knew that someday I would once again feel the grass under my feet and walk in the sunshine as a free man."

"I am fundamentally an optimist. Whether that comes from nature or nurture, I cannot say. Part of being optimistic is keeping one's head pointed towards the sun, one's feet moving forward. There were many dark moments when my faith in humanity was sorely tested, but I would not and could not give myself up to despair."

In a nutshell

Success is most likely when it becomes a necessity.

In a similar vein

Stephen R. Covey *The 7 Habits of Highly Effective People* (p. 84)
Viktor Frankl *Man's Search For Meaning* (50SHC)
Ernest Shackleton (by Margot Morrell & Stephanie Capparell)
Shackleton's Way (p. 290)

CHAPTER 35

Nelson Mandela

Nelson Mandela grew up in a traditional village in the Transkei region of South Africa, hundreds of miles from either Johannesburg or Cape Town. A member of the Thembu tribe that forms part of the Xhosa nation, his father was both a tribal chieftain and the chief adviser to the Thembu king, and Mandela was groomed to follow in his father's footsteps. The name given to him at birth was, prophetically, Rolihlahla. In his native Xhosa, the colloquial meaning of the name is "troublemaker."

The first member of his family to go to school, Mandela was given the English name Nelson. He recalls an idyllic Transkei childhood of animal herding, stick fighting, and storytelling, but after his father died he was moved to the Thembu capital to live under the wing of the tribal chief.

In his early years, Mandela says, he saw the white man more as a benefactor than an oppressor, and was enamored of British culture and its political system. But he came to realize that the Xhosa was a conquered people, with most of the men having to slave away in the gold mines for minuscule pay or work on white-owned farms. Mandela observed: "No matter how high a black man advanced, he was still considered inferior to the lowest white man."

Early lessons, lifelong contacts

As a student, Mandela was introverted and not brilliant, but worked hard. He was placed in an English-style secondary college for blacks, met young people from other tribal backgrounds, and began to get a sense of being "African" as opposed to simply Thembu or Xhosa.

At Fort Hare University College, run by missionaries and with black professors, he studied English, anthropology, politics, native administration, and Roman Dutch law. At this time his ambition was to be a low-level civil servant, a clerk or interpreter in the Native Affairs Department.

For a black South African, Mandela's education was privileged, and he believed that a BA would be his ticket to prosperity. Only later did he realize that there were many people without degrees who were smarter than him, and that character was the greater ingredient in success. Competing in cross-country running in college taught him that he could make up for a lack in natural ability by hard training. In his studies, he observed: "I saw many young men who had great natural ability, but who did not have the self-discipline and patience to build on their endowment."

Back home from college for a break, Mandela found an arranged marriage waiting for him on which he was not keen, and fled to Johannesburg. After trying to get work in the offices of a gold mine, he eventually found an articled clerkship in a liberal Jewish law firm. He was paid a pittance and often had to walk miles into the center of Johannesburg from his township. Slowly he began to get involved in politics and the African National Congress (ANC), but for a number of years was more observer than activist. It was at this time that he met ANC stalwart Walter Sisulu, a real estate agent when blacks were still allowed to own some property.

A black lawyer was a great novelty, and when Mandela enrolled in the University of Witwatersrand for a bachelor of law degree in 1943 he was the only African student in the faculty. His discomfort was lessened by a circle of supportive whites and Indians, who would later prove to be important in the struggle for black freedom.

Beginning the fight

On a platform of "the nigger in his place," in 1948 the Nationalist Party came to power in South Africa. Though the idea of apartheid ("apartness") had been around for centuries, the Afrikaner Nationalists entrenched it in hundreds of oppressive laws designed to create a brutal hierarchy: whites at the top, blacks at the bottom, and Indians and coloreds in the middle. Afrikaans, the language of the original Dutch farmer-settlers, took over from English as an official language. With race as the basis for South African society, elaborate tests were required that often broke up families. "Where one was allowed to live and work could rest on such absurd distinctions as the curl of one's hair or the size of one's lips," Mandela notes.

The defiance campaigns that the ANC organized, involving stay-at-homes and gatherings to protest against new laws, only made the new government more iron-willed in keeping black people downtrodden. School education was scaled down, whole towns were razed to make way for white housing, and the pass system made it extremely difficult for non-white people to move freely. The 1950 Suppression of Communism Act was only partly related to curbing communism; its real purpose was to allow the government to imprison anyone on a trumped-up charge.

Despite this harsher climate, in 1952 Mandela and Oliver Tambo established the first black law office in South Africa. It was inundated with cases from the first day and was highly successful. In those days, Mandela admits he was a "hotheaded revolutionary" without a great deal of discipline, and that he enjoyed wearing smart suits and driving around Johannesburg in a large American car. He even bought land in the Transkei with a view to moving back home.

Fate had other ideas. At 35 Mandela was banned from any involvement with the ANC, which meant that any work he did for the organization would have to be secret and risk long-term imprisonment. His roles as freedom fighter and family man were never compatible, and from this point on he would live with the constant anguish of having made the people he loved secondary to the larger struggle for freedom.

Criminal and outlaw

In the famous 1958–61 Treason Trial, the Nationalist government charged Mandela and others with trying to overthrow the state. Though the prosecution lacked real evidence, the trial dragged on for years. By this time Mandela's marriage had collapsed, and the time required to be away from the law practice saw that, too, fall apart.

When the members of the group were acquitted, the authorities' embarrassment was so great that it made them even more determined to quell insurrection. In 1960, 70 black demonstrators were killed at Sharpeville, a township south of Johannesburg, when they peacefully surrounded a police station. Many were shot in the back trying to flee the gunfire. South Africa came under a state of emergency in which the rights of blacks were further curtailed.

Mandela knew that he would soon be rearrested for something, so he decided to go underground, moving from place to place with the help of disguises. He grew his hair and wore the blue overalls of the worker and, because he had a car, pretended to be driving it for his *baas* (white master). During this outlaw existence, when there was a warrant for his arrest, the newspapers began calling Mandela "The Black Pimpernel." For several months he actually left South Africa to visit various African states including Sudan, Haile Selassie's Ethiopia, and Egypt to seek support for the ANC's cause, solicit donations, and learn about guerrilla warfare. The trip was the first time Mandela had experienced freedom and had seen blacks either running their own states or being treated as equals, and it only inspired him further. However, back in South Africa he let his guard down, and in 1962 he was captured on a road leading into Cape Town.

Captive revolutionary

At his trial, Mandela tried to put the onus of guilt on the government, and wore traditional clothing to symbolize that he did not recognize the white legal system and the charges it was making against him. He received a five-year sentence without parole. However, much worse was to come. As the ANC's philosophy of nonviolence was clearly not working, Mandela had founded a covert military affiliate that began a sabotage campaign on government property. In 1964 he was charged with sabotage and conspiracy, along with a number of other ANC members.

The death sentence was expected, and in his address to the court Mandela said that he was prepared to die for the cause of justice. Perhaps because of international pressure, however, the men "only" received life sentences. This seemed like a great victory.

Mandela would spend the next 18 years in the notorious Robben Island prison. The first decade involved hard manual labor, terrible food, and a climate of fear and abuse. However, the political prisoners were kept together and so could continue their discussions. Denied virtually all outside contact, the acquisition of a newspaper was prized almost above food. The men's political struggle was reduced to within the prison walls, and they had to fight for any kind of improvement in their daily life. For the slightest infraction they could be thrown into a solitary confinement cell for days on a diet of rice and water. Mandela writes: "It is said that no one truly knows a nation until one has been inside its jails. A nation should not be judged by how it treats its highest citizens, but its lowest ones—and South Africa treated its imprisoned African citizens like animals."

The years on Robben Island made Mandela a virtual stranger to his family, and he often wondered whether the struggle was worth it. His mother died while he was there and he was not allowed to attend the funeral. On the rare occasion that he was allowed family visitors, he was given only half an hour with them. Because of the restrictions on her movements, he did not see his second wife, Winnie Mandela, for two whole years, and his children were not allowed to visit before the age of 15. The nadir of Mandela's time on the island came when he received news that his 25-year-old son had been killed in a car accident.

In the latter years of his imprisonment, as his legend grew, Mandela was moved to mainland prisons and received special treatment, ending up with his own house and cook, and was able to receive visitors.

He had been seeking dialogue with the government for some time, and after 75 years of bitter antipathy white politicians began to listen to his ideas for a fully democratic South Africa. They knew that history was not on their side, and the country was becoming explosive.

Amid great euphoria, Mandela was released in 1990, having spent 27½ years in jail. Four years later, after the country's first nonracial elections, he was elected President of South Africa. In the meantime there had been much bloodshed, but the worst years were behind the country.

Final comments

Long Walk to Freedom is simply but skillfully written, and even at 750 pages you feel that it only skims the surface of one of the twentieth century's great lives. This commentary, in turn, only highlights a few points; reading the book cannot be more highly recommended.

Today we think of Mandela as a gray-haired statesman, a legendary figure, but his memoirs allow us to get behind the image. We see that he was a normal man who was willing to react positively to extraordinarily bad circumstances. He got through his ordeal because he was an optimist and could therefore inspire himself as much as others. The key to his success as a leader was the sense of inevitability he created—the power of his belief. The message he gave out that things would change was so great that even prison warders came around to his way of thinking. The end result was a new nation based on fairness and dignity in the place of a rotten police state.

Though he received a privileged education and was groomed for leadership, neither of these things was a *cause* of his future success as a leader. As the state gave him less and less to work with, he parlayed even these meager opportunities into positive action.

In a tight situation or a long struggle for recognition or success, we would do well to remember Mandela, and to have even an ounce of his mental discipline and bravery.

Pushing to the Front

"*The world does not demand that you be a lawyer, minister, doctor, farmer, scientist, or merchant; it does not dictate what you shall do, but it does require that you be a master in whatever you undertake.*"

"*As the sculptor thinks only of the angel imprisoned in the marble block, so Nature cares only for the man or woman shut up in the human being . . . Nature will chip and pound us remorselessly to bring out our possibilities.*"

"*The slow penny is surer than the quick dollar. The slow trotter will out-travel the fleet racer. Genius darts, flutters and tires; but perseverance wears and wins.*"

"*Don't wait for extraordinary opportunities. Seize common occasions and make them great.*"

In a nutshell

There are few things that cannot be achieved by sheer determination and effort.

In a similar vein
Horatio Alger *Ragged Dick* (p. 12)
Edward Bok *The Americanization of Edward Bok* (p. 36)
Napoleon Hill *Think and Grow Rich* (p. 174)
Samuel Smiles *Self-Help* (50SHC)
Brian Tracy *Maximum Achievement* (p. 302)

CHAPTER 36

Orison Swett Marden

I n their foreword, the publishers of this work boast, "It is doubtful whether any other book, outside of the Bible, has been the turning-point in more lives." The original *Pushing to the Front, or Success under Difficulties* was published in 1894, but was revised and expanded into the two-volume work of 1911. At 70 chapters and close to 900 pages, in its size and scope it could safely claim to be an encyclopedia of success, and has arguably not been overtaken.

Though Horatio Alger inspired many with his poor-boy-makes-good stories, Orison Swett Marden must be considered the real founder of the American success movement. *Pushing to the Front*, which was his first book, was inspired by Samuel Smiles's *Self-Help*, the seminal self-improvement manual, which Marden had discovered in an attic. Though twice the size of Smiles's tome, it is written in a similarly enjoyable style and sticks to the theme of "how men and women have seized common occasions and made them great." Where it differs from Smiles's work is that it has references to successful women of the day such as Jane Addams and Julia Ward Howe, and Marden refers to the dawning twentieth century as "the century of the woman," bringing unparalleled opportunities for young girls. In the second volume, he includes a farsighted chapter on the need for women to express themselves beyond the role of housewife and mother. Marden also shows his understanding of the new world his readers were entering by his praise of black Americans such as Frederick Douglass.

Pushing to the Front distinguished itself from some of the worst attitudes of its times by its strenuous theme of abhorrence of those living only for the dollar. It inspires the reader not to make the most money, but to pursue a career that excites, enriches intellectually, and uses talents to the full.

Overcoming difficulties

Most persistent among the book's themes is that character is built by adversity, or as Winston Churchill put it, "Kites rise highest against the wind—not with it." Marden points out that "poverty and hardship have rocked the cradle of the giants of the race," drawing to our attention such people as:

❖ Horace Greeley (1811–72), who showed up in New York as a penniless printer and became founder of the weekly *New Yorker* and the daily *New York Tribune*, which had a huge impact on American public opinion.
❖ The writer and champion of the poor William Cobbett (1763–1835), a farm boy who taught himself to read and write and became a major English political figure.
❖ Elihu Burritt (1810–79), the Connecticut man known as the "Learned Blacksmith," who during spare moments at the forge began a program of self-study that enabled him to become a linguist, writer, and mathematician. A typical entry in his diary is: "Tuesday, June 19, 60 lines Hebrew, 30 Danish, 10 lines Bohemian, 9 lines Polish, 15 names of stars, 10 hours forging."
❖ Michael Faraday (1791–1867), arguably the greatest experimental physicist, who as a boy in London lived above a stable and made money through lending out newspapers at a penny a piece. Apprenticed to a bookbinder, he read articles on electricity from the *Encyclopaedia Britannica* and began his own experiments. The scientist Sir Humphrey Davy made Faraday his assistant, enabling him to meet some of the great scientific minds of his day.
❖ Frederick Douglass (1817–95), the slave-cum-abolitionist "who started in life with less than nothing for he did not own his own body." Plantation rules forbade slaves to learn reading or writing, but he somehow learned the alphabet from scraps of paper and medicine bottle labels. Later, friends literally bought his freedom (at a cost of $750).

To Marden, necessity is the mother not simply of invention, but of success. "Failure often leans a man to success by arousing his latent energy, by firing a dormant purpose, by awakening powers which were sleeping." Prison, he notes, has often been the rouser of this latent energy. Sir Walter Raleigh wrote *The History of the World* during his 13-year imprisonment; Luther made his translation of the Bible while behind bars; and Dante wrote while exiled. Cervantes took up his pen while in jail in Madrid, producing *Don Quixote*. In more recent times, we think of Nelson Mandela on Robben Island, writing his memorable autobiography and planning a new South Africa (see p. 236).

Jewish people have been oppressed through history, Marden observes, yet they have produced some of the finest music and writing and made cities thrive. It took the plague and the great fire to destroy London before it rose up as a fine city.

Marden recalls Samuel Smiles's simple words on the matter: "If there were no difficulties there would be no success." Burdens make us try harder to lift them and we get stronger as a result, while the person who has none need do little.

Nerve, pluck, persistence, and grit

Marden recalls that Ulysses S. Grant lost an early battle in the Civil War at Shiloh. Every newspaper called for his removal, but Lincoln's final response was, "I can't spare this man, he fights." What Lincoln saw in Grant—a resolve never to let go, "grit"—is what later made him the hero of the war. Lincoln himself was asked what he would do if the rebellion took hold and he could not suppress it, and he replied, "Oh, there is no alternative but to keep pegging away." Both men were not moved by public clamor; they knew what their task was and did it.

Marden notes that Gibbon's *Decline and Fall of the Roman Empire* took 20 years to write, Webster spent 36 years on his dictionary, and Stephenson labored for 15 years to perfect his locomotive. Harvey worked for 8 years before publishing his work on the circulation of the blood, then had to wait 25 before the theory was finally accepted. Cyrus Field spent a decade of heartbreaking setbacks before the transatlantic cable was laid; everyone lost faith in the idea except him, but he believed that instantaneous communication across oceans was a necessity, not an option. The great violinist Gherardini was asked how long it took him to learn to play. His answer: 12 hours a day for 20 years.

Many know the story of Carlyle's *History of the French Revolution*: the manuscript was lent to a friend, who left it lying on his floor. A maid took it as kindling for the fire and it went up in flames in a minute or two. Though this was a great blow, Carlyle went back to his books and spent several more months rewriting the work, better than the original. And the "ease and grace" of Rousseau's style were obtained, Marden says, "only by ceaseless inquietude, by endless blotches and erasures." Thoreau's first book, *A Week on the Concord and Merrimack Rivers,* sold so poorly that the publishers returned most of the copies to him. He wrote in his diary: "I have nine hundred volumes in my library, seven hundred of which I wrote myself." A few years later came the success of *Walden*. One more: Columbus was rejected by scores of kings, queens, and nobles before finding the sponsorship to sail to the New World.

Marden says, "Show me a really great triumph that is not the reward of persistence." Genius, when you look more closely at it, usually turns out to be the result of uncommon dedication to a task.

Vocation and calling

While lauding a university education and the refinements it can produce in a person, Marden criticizes the gap between the high ideals of student years and the cynicism of later adult life. He counsels against graduating students simply taking the highest-paid job. An education should be considered a "sacred trust," not to be looted for your own monetary ends but to be put into the service of humankind. As Marden puts it: "There is something infinitely better than to be a millionaire of money, and that is to be a millionaire of brains, of culture, of helpfulness to one's fellows, a millionaire of character."

Don't enter a profession just because it is respectable, he suggests, or because one of your parents succeeded in it. "The world does not dictate what you shall do," he points out, "but it does require that you be a master in whatever you undertake." With definiteness of aim, or the knowledge that what you are doing is worth your time, you will excel at the task. A job may earn you money, but a vocation earns self-respect.

When Alexander the Great was asked how he had conquered the world, he is said to have replied, "By not wavering." We cleave to the person who has the firmest resolve, who knows who they are and what they stand for.

Final comments

Orison Swett Marden has for a long time been better known as the founder of *Success* magazine, whose revival brought a swing back to recognition of his writing. Copies of his books are not hard to track down on the internet, but they tend to be expensive. If you are serious about building up your success library, however, they are worth the money. These volumes are something to hold on to. It is easy to see how the book electrified audiences of its era, for you cannot come away from its pages without being inspired to greater things, or to stick at what you have embarked on.

The style of *Pushing to the Front*, though tremendously enjoyable, is not as old-fashioned as you might expect—many of Marden's comments could have been made by someone writing today—and in terms of quantity of good content it beats most of today's success and self-help literature. We have only had space here to look at Volume 1, for instance, and even that peremptorily. Marden's references to unfamiliar people will have you reaching for your biographical dictionary, and you will be provided with a history lesson alongside the motivational class.

Orison Swett Marden

Marden was born to New Hampshire farmers in 1850, but both his parents died before he was seven and he lived in a number of foster homes. He managed to go to college, graduating in law from Boston University in 1871, and gained further degrees (LLB and MD) from Harvard University. He also studied at Andover Theological Seminary and at the Boston School of Oratory.

In his college days he worked in catering and hotels, and became an investor in a resort area of Rhode Island. This was followed by the purchase of a chain of hotels in Nebraska, then a stint as a hotel manager in Chicago. In 1890, one of his hotels burned down and a smallpox epidemic ruined the rest of his business. Back in Boston, Marden put together his collection of inspirational stories and notes and, influenced also by Emerson, Longfellow, Oliver Wendell Holmes, Phillips Brooks, and New Thought writers, published the first version of Pushing to the Front in 1894. The retailer J. C. Penney was among the many who ascribed their success to reading the book. In 1897, Marden founded Success magazine, which gained a circulation of half a million copies. Though publication ceased in 1912, six years later he revived the magazine. He died in 1924.

Marden was a prolific writer, averaging two books a year. Titles include Every Man a King; Not the Salary but the Opportunity; Peace, Power and Plenty; Success Fundamentals; and The Victorious Attitude. For an introduction to his thought, see Real Success, by former Success editor Ken Shelton.

1997

The Spirit to Serve

"If you're in the service business and your name is above the door, it's important for people to be able to link a face to the name. I want our associates to know that there really is a guy named Marriott who cares about them, even if he can only drop by every so often to personally tell them so."

"For the key to prospering and adapting in the coming decades amidst an ever-escalating rate of change is to first be clear about and resolutely dedicated to what you stand for and why that should never change. You must then be just as resolutely willing to change absolutely everything else. This rare ability to manage continuity and change is the secret of Marriott's past—and the key to its future." Jim Collins, Foreword

In a nutshell

Hard work, continuous self-improvement, and a sense of building for the future create identity. From identity comes focus; from focus, success.

In a similar vein

Jim Collins *Good to Great* (p. 74)
Spencer Johnson *Who Moved My Cheese?* (p. 194)
Sam Walton *Made in America* (p. 314)

CHAPTER 37

J. W. Marriott Jr.

Often provided as a complimentary copy for guests in Marriott hotels, *The Spirit to Serve: Marriott's Way* may be an unlikely success classic, but in a surprisingly modest way it illustrates some valuable principles that can be applied to personal as well as corporate achievement.

If you travel with any frequency, you have probably lodged in a hotel managed or franchised by the Marriott company. If your stay was enjoyable, it was not by chance. Over several decades, Marriott developed "standard operating procedures" (SOPs)—such as 66-point checklists for room cleaning, recipe cards for the restaurants, and guest satisfaction scorecards—to ensure uniform high standards. J. W. Marriott Jr. makes the startling remark—for an entrepreneur—that building a business can be boring. There is a great deal of grunt work, but you have to put in the hours to create systems that work every time. Without consistency, a service business does not create an enduringly positive reputation. Here we are reminded of Orison Swett Marden's remark, "Success is the child of drudgery and perseverance. It cannot be coaxed or bribed; pay the price and it is yours."

Are attention to detail and hard work the only factors that account for Marriott's rise to industry leader? Let us briefly consider some important points in the company's life.

Laying a foundation

In 1927, J. W. Marriott Sr. moved with his wife from Utah to Washington, DC. Their first step into the hospitality industry was a small franchise selling root beer. Marriott Sr. later established a chain of restaurants called Hot Shoppes, which flourished through the Depression. In 1937, noticing that passengers on the newly emerging airlines wanted to eat, he formed a successful in-flight catering business. This was followed by contracts for cafeterias feeding government workers through the war years, and later for industrial commissaries, including General Motors' and Ford's.

The first Marriott hotel was not opened until 1957, by which time J. W. "Bill" Marriott Jr. had finished college and joined the company. Seeing the potential of the expanding hotel business, he took over the lodging section of the firm and began opening more hotels. By the 1960s, Bill Marriott voiced the hope that one day the company could equal the success of the Howard Johnson chain, which then seemed to line every American highway.

Becoming a player

While Howard Johnson lost its way, Marriott prospered. By the 1980s, it had become one of the biggest real estate developers in the country, in some years opening two new hotels a week. Yet it did not actually *own* the hotels. The family had realized that its greatest profit, and its greatest expertise, was in managing hotels, and as soon as these had been built they were sold to investors. Left with the valuable long-term management contracts, the company enjoyed the flexibility of not having heavy mortgages to service. This system worked because the firm had identified the one thing it could do better than anyone else: design and implement the processes that resulted in a great guest experience.

This narrowing down of purpose paid dividends. Today, Marriott was the world's largest hotelier with over 5,000 establishments in 110 countries. It employs more than 190,000 people.

The people difference

These are impressive figures, but how do we explain the leap from a $50 million enterprise in 1960 to one worth over $12 billion today? In anyone's language, this is a case of "good to great."

The first answer may seem obvious, but Bill Marriott maintains that it is how the company treats staff. He writes that Marriott is in the people business more than it is in the service business, and that "if you treat your people right, they will treat guests right." If they are stressed, dissatisfied, or poorly trained, it is the customers who will feel the effects.

This "employee first" policy is almost a cliché, but the company actually puts its money where its mouth is with a profit-sharing program that has been in place since 1959, better than average training systems, and a free phone line to counselors and experts to solve nonwork problems. This, and a culture of openness ensuring that staff at all levels of the organization are listened to, has led to Marriott's being judged one of *Fortune* magazine's "Top 50 Companies to Work For."

In contrast, hotel chains focused only on making money, which do not try to produce any service "buzz," have had only average growth. Not until someone feels that they are at the front line of a noble idea (in this case, making hotel guests feel welcomed and valued) will they be motivated.

Change amid order, order amid change

Bill Marriott identifies two turning points, what he calls "revolutions," in the company's history. The first was to move from its catering roots into hotels on a large scale. The next came in the 1980s.

The firm realized that its growth would be limited if it only ran "full-service" hotels, and looked into the idea of building other types of lodging, including medium-priced, budget, and long-stay. Since the fear was that these sideways moves would dilute the Marriott brand, there was fierce internal debate about what to do; many Marriott staffers thought that it would be 25 years of work down the drain.

Those in favor won and the company began building the "Courtyard by Marriott" hotels. Suddenly, the huge mid-priced and budget hotel market became its oyster, and it grew exponentially. It was able to do this without harming the full-service Marriott brand, because the cheaper hotels were run on the same strict quality control lines. Unlike other chains, amid the expansion it did not lose its commitment to the customer or its relentless service improvement goals. Marriott quotes Alfred North Whitehead: "The art of progress is to preserve order amid change and to preserve change amid order."

The company certainly found itself in some dead ends: investments in a travel agency, a cruise ship company, theme parks, and home security systems. Yet Marriott says:

"Companies that don't risk anything will inevitably find themselves falling behind those that do. You can lead change or it can lead you."

Risk taking only makes sense when you have a core set of values that do not change.

"Truly great companies maintain a set of core values and a core purpose that remain fixed while their business strategies and practices continually adapt to a changing world." These words from management thinkers Collins and Porras sum up not only the Marriott company, but success generally. If you know who you are, you can be more flexible in what you decide to do, and clearer about what *not* to do.

Final comments

In their groundbreaking *Built to Last: Successful Habits of Visionary Companies* (1994), Collins and Porras overturned conventional thinking by suggesting that great, long-lasting companies are rarely founded on some marvelous new product. Often starting very slowly, these firms put an emphasis on the vitality and philosophy of the firm itself; from this springs great services and products. Hewlett-Packard, for instance, invented excellent things, but it was the fostering of a nonhierarchical culture of innovation and engineering excellence that made it uniquely successful.

In Marriott's case, to answer the initial question of what made it stand out in its industry, we notice its organizational culture of openness; an ethic of continuous self-improvement; an eye on the future; and attention to the little things. In putting good service before money making, it paradoxically guaranteed its own profitability. This bundle of values creates a sense of internal identity even amid massive expansion into new areas. As the French say, "Plus ça change, plus c'est la même chose" (The more things change, the more they stay the same).

The Spirit to Serve is not a trumpet-blowing history of the company. Bill Marriott is candid about the mistakes it has made and the opportunities it perhaps should have taken. But above all, his understated work is about maintaining focus and keeping true to your original purpose.

J. W. Marriott Jr.

Born in 1932 in Washington, DC, Marriott started working for the family firm when he was 14, stapling invoices in the accounting department. He worked for four years in a Hot Shoppe restaurant while obtaining a finance degree at the University of Utah. Graduating in 1954, he spent two years as a supply officer in the US Navy, followed by marriage to Donna Garff.

At 32 he was made president of the Marriott company, and in 1972, when he was 40, his father passed the CEO role on to him. The Marriotts' three sons and a daughter all now work for Marriott International. The Spirit to Serve *was written with Kathi Ann Brown, who provides her own portrait of Marriott in an afterword.*

Marriot has also written Without Reservations: How a Family Root Beer Stand Grew into a Global Hotel Company *(2014).*

1962

The Dynamic Laws of Prosperity

"Let us be done with thinking of poverty as a virtue. It is a common vice."

"There is basically one problem in life: congestion. There is basically one solution: circulation. Systematic giving is, therefore, a powerful practice that blesses every phase of our lives, as it keeps us attuned to the wealth of the universe."

In a nutshell

God does not want you to be poor; appreciate the universe's abundance and your right to prosperity.

In a similar vein
Florence Scovel Shinn *The Secret Door to Success* (p. 284)
Wallace D. Wattles *The Science of Getting Rich* (p. 320)

CHAPTER 38

Catherine Ponder

Catherine Ponder had always been interested in the issue of spirituality and wealth, and when she became a Unity Church minister she decided to study the Bible more closely.

She learned that the identification of piety with poverty had arisen in the Middle Ages, when the feudal system sought to keep people in their place. In childhood she had been given to think that "a poor Christian is a good Christian," but nowhere in the Bible did she find evidence for this. The more she read, the more she realized that it was a textbook for prosperity.

Teaching prosperity

In 1958, when America was in a recession, members of Ponder's congregation were asking her for guidance on how to get through it. She started giving prosperity classes, teaching that prosperity was first and foremost a *state of mind*; a mindset of lack could only manifest negative results.

Many of her members experienced dramatic turnarounds—unexpected raises, promotions, debts paid—yet what struck Ponder was how many people wondered whether it was "right" to seek prosperity; that is, whether it was consistent with spiritual values. Didn't the Bible say, "You cannot serve God and Mammon" (Matthew 6:24)? Didn't Jesus say, "How hard it is for them that trust in riches to enter the kingdom" (Mark 10:24)?

Ponder responded to the first question by making a distinction: Mammon is wealth that is worshiped for its own sake; it is wealth without God. Prosperity thinking, on the other hand, puts God first as the source of your supply. She agreed that Jesus had told a wealthy man to go and sell everything he had, but it was because he was still attached to his riches; he did not yet recognize God as the source of his supply.

The Dynamic Laws of Prosperity is generally considered to be Ponder's classic work, a carefully and compassionately written compendium of the secrets and techniques of prosperity. The following is a sample of her ideas.

Desire + visualization and affirmation = success

The brain works in terms of mental images, Ponder writes, and whatever images it has are likely to become reality. You can, therefore, literally see your way to success. When you create prosperous images from scratch, don't be "reasonable," think big. Project thoughts of increase onto others, and you will find that they do prosper in health and monetary terms. Send positive thoughts to those with whom you are in conflict, and watch them soften their stance. That this could work may at first seem incredible, but is simply an extension of the "speaking well of others" that you were taught to do as a child. Denouncement has a way of bouncing back on you, but pointing out someone's good points while keeping quiet about their bad is both truthful and prospering.

Ponder tells of a man who "dared to write out hundreds of times how he wished things to be, rather than fretting about how they appeared at the moment." The man was not deluded, but was simply "affirming his good"; that is, making firm a desire through the power of speech or writing. Desires are healthy, Ponder says: they are like God knocking on the door of our mind, the means by which we can develop our full potential. You cannot expect to be successful, she adds, when you "idly drift in a stream of small events and small expectations."

The secret of turning desires into reality is to *write them down*. You must be specific about what you want and when exactly you would like to achieve it, because the fuel of the imagination is detail. Remember the phrase "Fortune favors the bold." Life does seem to clear a path for those who know what they want. Nature respects purpose. Writing things down clarifies your purpose in a way that idle thought cannot.

Prosperity is circulation

To attract prosperity, don't ever think about yourself as poor or say that you can't afford something. Count your blessings, focus on abundance, look only for opportunities. If you don't have something that you desire, use the "vacuum law" of prosperity and create room for it by throwing out old goods. Make way for growth.

Ponder talks in terms of radiation and attraction; that is, the thoughts that you give out coming back to you in some form. You engage in radiation and attraction all the time, but because you are not properly aware of it you don't see the error in radiating thoughts of negativity and lack. A person trained in prosperity thinking will be very careful only to think thoughts of prosperity, knowing that nothing but these can attract success back to them. Appreciate the prosperity principle that you've got to give to get. You should expect the very best in life, but you must "give full measure for the good you wish to receive" in advance. Emerson's famous essay "Compensation" highlighted this basic law of prosperity.

Ponder describes a law as "a principle that works." The practice of tithing, she argues, puts you in tune with the universal law of circulation. Many people think it old-fashioned, but giving away the first tenth of your income demonstrates to yourself that the universe is an abundant place and that in acknowledgment you are returning some of it to its source—"just as the farmer returns one-tenth of his seed for soil enrichment."

She notes that some of the magnates of the twentieth century—John D. Rockefeller and the Heinz, Colgate, and Kraft families—attributed their amazing success to tithing. Between 1855 and 1934, Rockefeller gave away over $500 million, and when asked why, his standard line was, "God gave me my money." Ponder also recalls the words of Moses: "Thou shalt remember Jehovah thy God, for it is He that giveth thee power to get wealth" (Deuteronomy 8:18).

The key point about tithing is that it is *systematic* giving, not the ad hoc giving that we normally associate with charity. In systematically giving the first 10 percent of whatever you earn, you will discover that the remaining money goes further, and that the universe will want to give back to you systematically. Tithing is much more than dutiful giving to charity, it is also, Ponder points out, an act of personal growth (it does, after all, require courage!) "by which one evolves into larger giving (and larger receiving)."

How to see money

People often have a funny attitude about money, Ponder says. They are quick to say that money doesn't mean a lot to them, but spend their lives working to get it. Why not admit that money is important and that it is basic to living a good life, wonderful if rightly used?

Money reacts to your attitudes about it, Ponder comments, therefore if you think well of it and admire what it can do, you are much more likely to enjoy more of it. See it as a tyrant and it will be so. Continually remind yourself of the relationship between money and thought. Think of and expect lavish abundance for the day ahead when you wake up in the morning. You may be surprised at what happens.

Ponder includes a fascinating reference to Einstein, saying that he shook up the scientific world by proving that substance (or energy, the unformed) is convertible to matter (the formed, which includes money). Einstein showed that the physical and nonphysical worlds are convertible and interchangeable. Prosperity thinking acknowledges the connection between the invisible substance or energy that makes up the universe and your thoughts. By connecting the two, you have greater control over the creation of matter.

Final comments

This discussion is merely an appetizer. Most of the 20 chapters of *The Dynamic Laws of Prosperity* deal with a different prosperity law, covering health, debt, work, persistence, intuition, and a truly unusual chapter on the prospering power of charm. Though the book was mostly written in the late 1950s, many of its ideas were ahead of their time. In the face of the conformity of her era, Ponder dares the reader to be different, noting that uniqueness always pays and it is your duty to be like no other.

If you are an academic Bible scholar you may not agree with Ponder's interpretation of biblical stories, but the book is best read for inspiration and for its quiet good sense about thinking prosperously. *The Dynamic Laws of Prosperity* may be one of the more unusual success classics, but could be the most valuable to you if you are willing to have an open mind. (The chapter on overcoming debt may on its own justify the price of the book.) Consider it a spiritual complement to the more "nuts and bolts" books on financial success.

Catherine Ponder

*Born in 1927, Catherine Ponder studied education and business in
North Carolina before being ordained as a nondenominational Unity
Church minister in 1958. Her first ministry was in Birmingham,
Alabama, followed by Austin, Texas, then San Antonio. In 1973 she
moved to Palm Desert, California, where her ministry continues to this
day.*

Ponder has written 16 books, including The Prosperity Secrets of the
Ages, The Dynamic Laws of Healing, The Millionaires of Genesis, The
Millionaire Joshua, The Prospering Power of Prayer, *and her memoir,* A
Prosperity Love Story. *She has lectured across the United States.*

Take Time for Your Life

> "I've grappled with the same issues my clients are dealing with. I've worked ridiculous hours, built a successful business, made plenty of mistakes in relationships, and paid little attention to my health. Over the last several years, I've used the process in this book to improve my own life. I know it works."

In a nutshell

Achievement is more meaningful when it springs from a base of physical, emotional, and spiritual well-being.

In a similar vein
Stephen R. Covey *The 7 Habits of Highly Effective People* (p. 84)
Muriel James & Dorothy Jongeward *Born to Win* (p. 180)
Thomas Moore *Care of the Soul* (50SHC)

CHAPTER 39

Cheryl Richardson

Originally a tax consultant, Cheryl Richardson found that her clients needed advice and support on making decisions on the nonfinancial aspects of their lives. Eventually she stopped doing people's tax returns and gave workshops on the "secrets of success."

Life planning or personal coaching is now a well-established field, but Richardson, one of American's top life coaches, was an early practitioner. *Take Time for Your Life: A Seven-Step Program for Creating the Life You Want* is her bestselling introduction to what she does. It is different to most success titles in that she focuses on *life* instead of simply career or personal goals. Outward achievement is all well and good, but if it is not balanced by what she calls "extreme self-care" you will burn out and be no use to anyone.

Slowing down to succeed

The best part of *Take Time for Your Life* is its vignettes of people with whom Richardson has worked. Most of her clients seem to live fast-paced lives and dream of more time for themselves, more fun, and more authenticity in their existence. They feel that it is time to step off the merry-go-round and take stock.

Richardson identifies the seven common obstacles these people seem to face in living their best lives:

1. They generally have difficulty putting themselves first.
2. Their schedule does not reflect their priorities.
3. They feel drained by certain people or things.
4. They feel trapped for monetary reasons.
5. They are living on adrenalin.
6. They don't have a supportive community in their life.
7. Their spiritual well-being comes last.

You may feel that to get ahead or simply maintain your current success you have to work very long hours, sacrificing everything. This is a myth, and Richardson shows how altering even small things about your daily existence can make a big difference. She mentions one woman, for instance, who tried leaving work by 5.30 P.M. each day and found, to her surprise, that her business did not fall apart; she achieved the same amount through greater focus and delegating.

Yet Richardson's book is less concerned with time management than it is with *self*-management. She does not suggest abandoning your responsibilities, merely that you need to devote much more consideration to the renewal of your energies. In his book *The 7 Habits of Highly Effective People* (see p. 84), Stephen Covey calls this "sharpening the saw." Without frequent sharpening you become blunt in a productivity sense and lose the ability to connect with the people you love and influence those you work with.

Tipping the scales in your favor

One of the many ways to regain balance is to create what Richardson calls an "Absolute Yes" list, a ranking of what you feel are the most important aspects of your life. One client of Richardson's, Joan, put at the top of her list daily time to herself to read, meditate, or exercise. Second was time spent with her husband each evening. Next came quality time with her children, then study to complete her degree, time with friends, and finally household chores. She had to reorganize her life to fit these priorities, but the result included much better moods and greater harmony. Note that the elements in her life did not change, just the order of priorities.

The gift of *Take Time for Your Life*, through its hundreds of ideas for self-care, is the feeling that you do not have to be hurried along by circumstances. You can regain control of your life simply by making more conscious decisions. The seven obstacles to a balanced life mentioned above are the springboard for Richardson's strategies to "win back" your life. The following gives a taste:

❖ Regular "downtime" is important for your sanity. At first you may feel very edgy in doing "nothing" but, as Richardson puts it, "We all need a holiday from thinking too much."
❖ Pay people to do services you normally do. Though it costs money, "sharing the wealth" allows you to care for yourself and think at a higher level, both of which can bring you greater success.

- ❖ Go through old stuff and papers and throw much of it out. This makes way for what you really want to come into your life.
- ❖ Don't fret over spending a little less time working. The world has a way of rewarding those who are focused and make better use of their time.
- ❖ Identify the drains on your life; that is, the people, places, and situations that tax your mental and physical energy. Eliminating or lessening their impact is the beginning of successful living and abundance.
- ❖ Stop running on caffeine and adrenalin. "Fuel your body with premium fuel and it will provide you with the strength and stamina to live well." Caring for your body is essential to living a high-quality life.
- ❖ Consciously engineer more "amazing moments" into your life: bring back the soul.
- ❖ Tell people when you are grateful for what they have done.
- ❖ Write a journal.
- ❖ Notice your dreams.
- ❖ Follow your intuition.
- ❖ Have the courage to seek your highest purpose instead of simply looking for another job.

Taking time for financial health

As you would expect from a former financial consultant, Richardson includes a useful chapter on "Financial health." She manages to bridge practical financial skills with a more spiritual attitude toward money. Her thesis is that once you decide to take more responsibility for your finances (paying bills on time, paying off your debts, keeping an account of spending), money stops being a source of frustration and begins to flow more freely into your life. You have to get more serious about money before it gets serious about you.

She identifies all the attitudes you may have toward money that prevent you from attracting more of it, and disabuses the reader of such ideas as "I am a creative person, I shouldn't have to worry about financial stuff." A person can be both spiritually and financially rich, Richardson says. She includes a list of books at the end of the chapter that can help you appreciate this, covering the practical and spiritual aspects of wealth, including authors such as Catherine Ponder (see p. 254), Thomas Stanley (see p. 296), and Robert Kiyosaki (see p. 208).

Final comments

With her emphasis on spiritual well-being Richardson may not seem too practical for some readers, but her definition of "spiritual" is fairly loose. It simply means the sense of calm that comes to you when you are willing to stop and contemplate. Though uncomfortable at first, the practice reconnects you to what is important and therefore puts your life on more solid ground.

You need to appreciate the truth that success should not be "at all costs," that you don't want to achieve something if it leaves behind a trail of poor health, ignored spouses and children, and the hollowness of never having any time for yourself. In *The Richest Man in Babylon* (see p. 68), George Clason's message for a lifetime of financial security is that when you receive money you must "pay yourself first." Richardson's principle of "extreme self-care" is similar. It allows you to go into the world refreshed and with priorities sorted. If you don't do this, you become an empty reflection of other people's wishes. Despite the pressures, don't forget who you are and what you love doing in life.

With its checklists, wealth of ideas, and warm, friendly style, *Take Time for Your Life* is as close as you will get to a personal coaching relationship in a book. Sometimes you need a person outside your regular circle of friends, family, and co-workers if you are to see your true worth. While therapy will focus on your problems, a good life coach will work with you on your possibilities. The elements of success are already there—you simply need to identify them and bring them to the fore.

Cheryl Richardson

Richardson has been a frequent guest on US television shows such as Oprah *and* The Today Show *and is a professional speaker and seminar leader.*

Take Time for Your Life *was a No. 1 New York Times bestseller. Her other best-known books are* The Art of Extreme Self-Care *and* You Can Create an Exceptional Life.

1986

Unlimited Power

"*The movers and shakers of the world are often professional modelers—people who have mastered the art of learning everything they can by following other people's experience rather than their own.*"

"*Often we are caught in a mental trap of seeing enormously successful people and thinking they are where they are because they have some special gift. Yet a closer look shows that the greatest gift that extraordinarily successful people have over the average person is their ability to get themselves to take action.*"

In a nutshell

Success leaves clues, but they must be acted on.

In a similar vein
Darren Hardy *The Compound Effect* (p. 166)
Anthony Robbins *Awaken the Giant Within* (50SHC)
Brian Tracy *Maximum Achievement* (p. 302)

CHAPTER 40

Anthony Robbins

I n the early pages of *Unlimited Power: The New Science of Personal Achievement*, Robbins tries to define power. He quotes John Kenneth Galbraith, who said, "Money is what fueled the industrial society. But in the informational society, the fuel, the power, is knowledge."

How many of us really appreciate this? We are still so used to thinking that power is in money or position that it is easy to overlook that power is in the *person*. Our ability to influence and persuade others, our capacity to build something out of nothing, our strength to reason for ourselves, all make up the capital of our personal power.

The chief skills we must learn for success, Robbins says, are communicative. Successful people are master communicators, but they also communicate masterfully with themselves. They decide what meaning an event will have for them and as a consequence tend not to divide their life's experiences into "successes" and "failures" but look more to *results*.

Refinement based on feedback about results is the basis of all progress, but it requires a certain open-mindedness. Robbins discusses the seven traits of successful people: passion, belief, strategy, clarity of values, energy, bonding power, and mastery of communication. All link in to each other, but by applying each to yourself you can begin to realize that there is an "anatomy of success" that can be studied.

Modeling the best

The easiest way of becoming successful is to model the behavior of an already successful person. This is an NLP (Neuro-Linguistic Programming) concept based on the premise that every human being has the same neurology, therefore "anything you can do I can do"—by copying it. Robbins mentions Blanchard and Johnson's bestseller *The One Minute Manager* (see p. 30), which was based on modeling some of America's top managers, to make his point that "success leaves clues." Robbins himself modeled the best shooters in the US army so that he could give courses in shooting accuracy—even though he had never held a gun before in his life. Even if you have no expertise or knowledge of something, with the right models you can learn—and quickly.

Everyone models, but most do it unconsciously. If you are able to choose the inspirational people and skills that can assist you, your destiny comes under control. Robbins suggests that the real horror of ghettos and poverty-stricken places is not the daily struggle to survive, but the effect of these environments on personal ambition and belief. "If all you see is failure, if all you see is despair, it's very hard for you to form the internal representations that will foster success," he writes.

It is great to have personal mentors, but they are not absolutely necessary. If you can read, you have a whole universe of accomplishment arrayed before you, and it is difficult for it not to rub off. Never listen to bar-room wisdom or sit around at "coffeepot seminars," Robbins warns. If you want a better life, don't seek gossip, seek great models and mentors, in real life and in books, whose behavior you can follow. Let these people, not simply your friends or family, be the standard by which you gauge yourself.

Running your brain

Robbins devotes a chapter to "submodalities," the types of visual, auditory, and other forms of sensory experience that you can manipulate in your mind in order to change the way you see something. One method, the "swish" pattern, involves replacing existing negative images in your mind with positive ones. When you run through the "film" in your head of this happening a few times, it is difficult to have the same view of what you thought was an addictive or destructive behavior. This may sound dubious, but try it. You need to learn how to "run your brain."

Robbins puts the idea before us that "Misfortune is a point of view." There are always different ways to perceive something, and by "reframing" an experience you have much more choice in how to respond to things in life. Remember, successful people see things less in terms of good or bad, but as results. The result is the fact, not your emotional response to it. Your response is your *choice*.

At the practical work level this sort of thinking is valuable, for what is an entrepreneur, Robbins asks, if not someone who sees existing resources through a different lens, reframing them so that they become something new and valuable. An entrepreneur is an expert reframer.

To appreciate NLP, you have to appreciate that, even though you think of yourself as a person or perhaps a soul, your brain still operates as a machine. In contrast to "deep" therapy such as psychoanalysis, NLP holds that change can happen in an instant. In quantum physics, Robbins notes, particles do not slowly change and develop over time—they make quantum leaps. Start to think of your brain in an impersonal way; it is your servant to program in order to achieve your highest goals and live by your highest values.

Great goals produce action

Robbins uses a biblical quotation to explain the life and death power of quality goals: "Where there is no vision, people perish" (Proverbs 29:18).

The brain and nervous system work in a way that means you tend to live up to the private images of your life that you carry around with you. Whatever you ask for in life is most likely what you will get. Robbins suggests, "People are not lazy. They simply have impotent goals."

Late one night after a seminar, he encountered a homeless person who asked him for a quarter. Although he had more money, that is exactly what he gave him, saying to the man, "Life will pay whatever price you ask of it."

Perhaps this was somewhat mean, but the anecdote illustrates a powerful principle. Ask for great success and joy, and you'll probably get it. Don't ask for anything in particular, and you will get whatever life throws at you. Be precise in your everyday language, but particularly when it comes to goals. Use what Robbins calls the "power of precision," because language shapes thought and thought shapes action.

The magic of rapport

All successful people know how to create rapport. They have inbuilt ways to get themselves into the mindset of whomever they encounter so that the encounter will have real value. Some people spend a lifetime developing their interpersonal skills, but there are skills of rapport that have the same effect and that you can learn in a few minutes, if you can be bothered.

Robbins's point is that you can become a persuasive person more easily through establishing agreement than through competition. Competition is one of many patterns you have in your brain that you let run without really thinking whether you could replace it with something more effective. The route to unlimited power is continually to look for a different, better way to do something. If you always stick to the same techniques, you will always get the same results. This is a foundational idea of NLP, but Robbins explains it well.

Final comments

Written when Ronald Reagan was president, some of *Unlimited Power*'s references are a little dated, but even the seasoned success scholar will be reminded why Robbins is the world's No. 1 motivational guru. The book is less refined than the later *Awaken the Giant Within*, but remarkable for the fact that Robbins wrote it when he was only 25.

If you have had little experience with NLP it is a great introduction to some of the concepts and techniques, including modeling. One of Robbins's great points is: "No matter how grim your world is, if you can read about the accomplishments of others, you can create the beliefs that will allow you to succeed." The apparently innocuous activity of reading the success stories of people you admire, availing yourself of centuries of life experience, has been the springboard of many illustrious people.

Fortune doesn't shout or beckon, but it does leave clues for those who are interested. Yet as Robbins points out, unlimited power is not yours until you develop the skill of *action*. His book is as good a starting point as any to help you become a person of distinction; that is, someone who acts.

Anthony Robbins

Now in his early fifties, Robbins grew up in Los Angeles in modest circumstances. He earned a reputation as a master salesman selling tickets to motivational events, and his first mentor was guru Jim Rohn. Discovering NLP in 1983, Robbins toured America with the boast that he could cure people of phobias in 15 minutes. For a time he was a partner of John Grinder, one of the founders of NLP.

Robbins is best-known for his weekend seminars that involve participants walking over beds of hot coals. He has worked with IBM, AT&T, American Express, and the US Army as well as sports teams and Olympic athletes, and been a personal coach to Bill Clinton, Mikhail Gorbachev, and Andre Agassi.

His foundation runs programs to help the elderly, young people, the homeless, and people in prison. Robbins lives in Palm Beach, Florida with his wife, Sage. A 2016 documentary film, Tony Robbins: I am Not Your Guru, *directed by Joe Berlinger, depicts Robbins at one of his "Date with Destiny" seminars.*

Leadership the Eleanor Roosevelt Way

"It is true that I am fundamentally an optimist, that I am congenitally hopeful. I do not believe that good always conquers evil, because I have lived a long time in the world and seen that it is not true . . . It is not wishful thinking that makes me a hopeful woman. Over and over, I have seen, under the most improbable circumstances, that man can remake himself, that he can even remake his world if he cares enough to try."
Eleanor Roosevelt, You Learn by Living

In a nutshell

One of the duties of the leader is to lift up those who are not able to advance themselves.

In a similar vein
Warren Bennis *On Becoming a Leader* (p. 18)
Abraham Lincoln (by Donald T. Phillips) *Lincoln on Leadership* (p. 230)
Nelson Mandela *Long Walk to Freedom* (p. 236)

CHAPTER 41

Robin Gerber

Eleanor Roosevelt was one of the most admired people of the twentieth century, put on the cover of *Time* magazine three times. We think of her now as a vital force in her husband's administration, protector of the dispossessed, and UN stateswoman, but for the first four decades of her life she was comparatively anonymous, living up to the expectations of those around her and acting fully in accordance with her class and upbringing. Her story is interesting precisely because she was not overly ambitious or achievement oriented, but with time and circumstances became so.

Robin Gerber's book, *Leadership the Eleanor Roosevelt Way: Timeless Strategies from the First Lady of Courage*, is not a full biography of "ER," but traces some of the key points in her life to illustrate how she came to lead and why she inspires a new generation.

From orphan to young mother

Anna Eleanor Roosevelt was born into upper-class New York society in 1884, with future president Theodore Roosevelt as an uncle. Her mother, Anna, was a society beauty who was cold toward her plain daughter. Her father, Elliott, adored Eleanor and she him. He was a popular man but had a drinking problem.

While Elliott was exiled to a clinic for recovering alcoholics, Anna grew ill and died of diphtheria. Six months later, Eleanor's four-year-old brother died. Having succumbed to depression, drugs, and alcohol, Elliott then passed away a few months before Eleanor's tenth birthday. He was the center of her world and she was shattered. As Gerber suggests, this painful childhood would leave Eleanor with an empathy for those who were suffering that was basic to her personality and achievements.

After boarding school in England, Eleanor returned to the United States and before her twenty-first birthday married the dashing young

Franklin Delano Roosevelt ("FDR"), a distant cousin. For the next 12 years Eleanor was a dutiful wife and devoted mother, having six children, one of whom died in infancy. The family lived at Hyde Park, Franklin's family home in New York, and the young Eleanor had to live uncomplainingly under the command of her mother-in-law, Sara Delano.

While Franklin became a senator, the outbreak of the First World War gave Eleanor a chance to step outside the gilded cage and do some volunteer work for the US military. As a newly appointed assistant secretary of the US Navy under Woodrow Wilson, her husband was spending a great deal of time away.

Out of the chrysalis

Thirteen years into the marriage, the bottom fell out of Eleanor's world when she discovered that FDR was having an affair with her social secretary. Devastated once again, she emerged from a time of mourning and reflection with a decision to continue with the marriage. She "chose life," as Gerber puts it, and moved on. In her book *You Learn by Living*, Eleanor wrote:

"Courage is more exhilarating than fear, and in the long run it is easier. We do not have to become heroes overnight. Just a step at a time, meeting each thing that comes up, seeing it is not as dreadful as it appeared, discovering we have the strength to stare it down."

This courage was tested again in the summer of 1921 when the family were staying at their holiday home in Maine. Franklin had been swimming and that night felt tired. The next day he could not move his legs. He had been stricken by polio and would not walk properly again.

Eleanor developed a new, separate sense of identity, creating her own circle of friends and shedding the influence of her mother-in-law. Already in her forties, she discovered her "leadership passion": social reform issues. Women had only recently been given the vote, and Eleanor became involved in organizations to make the most of the women's voice. She had a retreat built, Val-Kill, where she could entertain friends and hold meetings, and in 1926 began to teach history and government classes at the Todhunter School for Girls in New York City, which she had purchased with friends. Leadership involves openness to the new, Gerber notes, and in these years ER hungrily sought out experiences and people outside her established circle.

In 1928 FDR was elected governor of New York, and Eleanor's campaigning for the women's vote was an important factor in the victory. In the presidential race four years later, Eleanor and her team, who coordinated an army of women "grass trampers," were instrumental in increasing female support for the Democrats. FDR would be in office for an incredible 12 years, taking the couple through the Great Depression, the Second World War, and three more elections.

First lady of America

ER held the first ever press conference for the wife of a president and admitted only women to it. She published a feminist-leaning book, *It's Up to the Women*, which sold well and was instrumental in the appointment of the first woman cabinet member, Frances Perkins, as secretary of labor. A forceful, active First Lady was something new, and ER came in for a lot of criticism, attracting tags like "Eleanor Everywhere." But she developed a tough skin; one of her sayings was, "A woman is like a teabag. You never know how strong she is until she gets in hot water."

Eleanor became FDR's "eyes and ears," going out into the country to see the grinding poverty and joblessness that had overwhelmed the nation. Her desire to bond with housewives, mine workers, soldiers, and struggling farmers, to make friends with black and Jewish Americans, would make her seem like a bleeding heart to opponents and a traitor to her class, but her nose for suffering and oppression made her a much-loved figure for many ordinary people. She was able to empathize instead of merely offering patrician sympathy.

ER gave strong support to improvements in labor laws and contributed to the foundation of the civil rights movement by highlighting the lynchings still taking place in the South. She enjoyed entertaining prominent black Americans in the White House. When her friend Marian Anderson, the great American contralto, tried to book a concert in Washington, DC at a hall owned by the Daughters of the American Revolution, this WASPish organization refused to let a Negro perform. In protest, Eleanor—a longtime member—resigned and helped organize a huge concert for Anderson at the Lincoln Memorial. The black voters that Eleanor attracted away from the Republicans, Gerber notes, would stay with the Democrats for the rest of the century.

First lady of the world

After FDR's death while in office in 1945, Eleanor was on her own. President Truman offered her the opportunity to join the American delegation at the first meetings of the United Nations. With great trepidation she went, and was given responsibility for helping to develop the Universal Declaration on Human Rights. Her work to get the declaration passed, which UN Secretary-General U Thant described as "the Magna Carta of mankind," is perhaps her greatest achievement.

In the 1950s she became a roving ambassador for the US government, visiting many nations in the Middle East and Asia and creating enormous goodwill. ER overcame suspicions of American motives because she made clear that her trips were for listening, not preaching. These travels, and the impression she gave of being a "friend to humanity" instead of simply a voice of America, gave her the nickname "first lady of the world." In another testament to her liberal values, she fought against the witch-hunt conducted by Senator Joseph McCarthy's House Un-American Activities Committee to identify supposed communists.

In her last years she continued to campaign for the Democratic party, supporting Adlai Stevenson and then John F. Kennedy, and also hosted a television show, *Prospects for Mankind*. When Martin Luther King was jailed in 1962 for opposing segregationist policies, ER persuaded Robert Kennedy, the attorney general, to get the charges dropped. She died the same year.

Final comments

If a mark of a great leader is the ability to create others, Eleanor Roosevelt certainly did this, fostering women's leadership within and outside America and providing an inspiration to African American leaders.

While her husband was commander in chief with the ability to change millions of lives at will, she had a daily syndicated column, "My Day," to work with. Yet this piece of writing, summing up each of her very full days, was influential and became a platform for her political views. Without formal powers, her leadership on issues came from the power to persuade, and her journey from shy mother to master of UN debate is remarkable.

Robin Gerber's book is different to other works on Eleanor Roosevelt because it attempts to apply the lessons of her life to women today. The book interweaves the ER story with the actual experiences of contemporary women, and provides many tips on mentoring, networking, and public speaking drawn from ER's life. While you may find a full biography or some of ER's own writings more satisfying, the worth of Gerber's work is that it is an easy-to-read introduction to the subject, attracting a new generation of admirers who wish to know why she inspired so many. Breaking the mold in many ways, today's leaders such as Hillary Clinton are much in her debt.

Robin Gerber

Gerber has a background as a Washington lobbyist and a women's leadership trainer and has worked with the Democratic National Committee, the UN, and the State of New York. She is a noted professional speaker.

Leadership the Eleanor Roosevelt Way *includes a foreword by James McGregor Burns, author of the seminal study* Leadership.

Gerber is also the author of a biography of Ruth Handler, creator of the Barbie doll: Barbie and Ruth *(2009).*

The Magic of Thinking Big

"Believe Big. The size of your success is determined by the size of your belief. Think little goals and expect little achievements. Think big goals and win big success. Remember this, too! Big ideas and big plans are often easier—certainly no more difficult—than small ideas and small plans."

In a nutshell

Much of the difference between failure and success lies in what you believe you are entitled to, so you may as well think big.

In a similar vein

Frank Bettger *How I Raised Myself from Failure to Success in Selling* (p. 24)
Claude M. Bristol *The Magic of Believing* (p. 42)
Napoleon Hill *Think and Grow Rich* (p. 174)
Brian Tracy *Maximum Achievement* (p. 302)

CHAPTER 42

David J. Schwartz

Think of people who earn five times as much as you. Are they five times smarter? Do they work five times harder? If the answer is no, then the question "What do they have that I haven't?" may occur to you. In a book that has sold several million copies, David Schwartz suggests that the main factor separating them from you is that they think five times bigger. We are all, more than we realize, the product of the thinking surrounding us, and most of this thinking is little, not big.

Plenty of room at the top

In the course of researching *The Magic of Thinking Big*, Schwartz spoke to many people who had reached the top in their field. Instead of getting detailed responses, he was told that the key factor in personal success was simply the desire for it. Rather than there being "too many chiefs and not enough Indians," the opposite is true. Some people choose to lead, others to follow. Success is not primarily a matter of circumstances or native talent or even intelligence—it is a choice.

From the many little comments and asides that have been made to you throughout your life, you may have unconsciously written a log of the things you can or can't have, the person you can or cannot be. These daubs of paint may even have been applied by people who loved you very much, but the result is that it is not your picture. *The Magic of Thinking Big* tries to show that in fact the canvas you work on is vast. Schwartz delivers the right quote by Benjamin Disraeli: "Life is too short to be little." You must enlarge your imagination of yourself and act on it.

"Thinking big" does work in relation to career goals, financial security, and great relationships—but it is more significant than that. You are challenged to see yourself in a brighter light, to have a larger conception of life. This is a choice that is no more difficult than the choice to keep doing what you're doing, laboring in darkness.

You may feel that some of the ideas and suggestions are somewhat obvious or basic compared to more recent success writing, but, like the other older success classics, *The Magic of Thinking Big* contains simple and powerful messages that do not date.

The quiet route to success

Schwartz's book is basically about "getting ahead," with a fair amount of attention given to increasing your income exponentially, making that dream home a reality, and getting your children a first-rate education. It tells us how to think, look, and feel "important."

Is it simply a bland 1950s product of an achievement-oriented consumer society? Well, it does have some amusing passages about moving out of one's "crummy apartment" to a "fine new suburban home." Readers presumably continue to be attracted because of its materialist promise, but the paradox of Schwartz's message is that to get the material results, you must know the immaterial; that is, you must spend time alone with your thoughts. Decisions arrived at in managed solitude, he says, have a habit of being 100 percent right. Action drives out thought, whereas leaders set aside time for solitude to tap their supreme thinking power.

Belief is everything

There is nothing mystical about the power of belief, but you must draw a distinction between merely wishing and actually believing. Doubt attracts "reasons" for not succeeding, whereas belief finds the means to do the job. Schwartz was in conversation with an aspiring fiction writer. When the name of a successful author came up, the aspiring writer quickly said, "But I could never equal him; I'm not in his league." Knowing the writer in question, Schwartz pointed out that he was neither super-intelligent nor super-perceptive, merely super-confident. The writer had at some point decided to believe that he was among the best, and so he acted and performed accordingly.

Most of us believe that the result of an event is the best indicator of how successful we are, yet events are much more likely to reflect our level of confidence. In Schwartz's words: "Belief is the thermostat that regulates what we accomplish in life." Turn the thermostat up and witness the results.

Excusitis, the failure disease

Never depend on luck to get what you want. The only vaccination against "excusitis," as Schwartz calls it—"commonly known as failure's disease"—is conscious self-belief. Schwartz knew that as soon as you hit a rough spot your thinking is likely to shrink back to its normal size, yet this is exactly when it is crucial for it not to do so. Sporting champions do not collapse when, in the course of a game, they are being beaten. Instead of building a case against themselves, they remember that they are champions. Tennis great Boris Becker tells up-and-coming tennis players that talent is not enough: you must walk, talk, and think like a champion.

Staying big

While it is said that a large vocabulary is a big determinant of success, what really counts is the effect that your words have on how you think about yourself. Instead of trying to use long words, Schwartz says, use positive language, and see how it transforms your mood and the perceptions of others. Don't see yourself merely in terms of how you appear now. You may have an old car, dingy apartment, debts, job stress, and a crying baby, but they are not truly a reflection of you as long as you are working on the vision of what you will be two years from now. Concentrate on your assets and how you are deploying them to change the situation, and avoid getting mired in petty recriminations. Absorbing the blows is a quality of greatness.

Schwartz also reminds you that every big success is created one step at a time, therefore it is best to measure yourself against the goals you have set, rather than comparing yourself to others.

Improving the quality of your environment

Or as Schwartz phrases it, "Go first class." This does not mean always getting the most expensive ticket. It does mean getting your advice from successful people and not giving the jealous the satisfaction of seeing you stumble. Spend time with those who think on a large scale and are generous in their friendship. After a while, the base level of what you think possible will rise. People make assessments of you whether you like it or not, and the value the world gives you matches the one you give yourself.

Schwartz has many more useful tips on how to think and act success, backed up by case histories. They include:

- ❖ Don't wait until conditions are perfect before starting something. They never will be. Act now.
- ❖ Persistence is not a guarantee of success. Combine persistence with experimentation.
- ❖ Goals, once in the subconscious, provide energy and an invisible guide to correct action.
- ❖ Walk 25 percent faster! Average people have an average walk.

Final comments

This stalwart of the success literature was written in the golden age of postwar American industrial society. The focus is on sales, production, executives, getting a great job in a good company. It may be a product of its age, but it transcends it too. *The Magic of Thinking Big* has literally been worth its (hardback) weight in gold for many people. It is one of the great examples of the success literature's call to break free of self-imposed limitations, to recast your idea of what is possible.

The desire for success, Schwartz argues, begins with a willingness to find the tools that can deliver it. Amazingly, although no one likes crawling in mediocrity, not everyone is seriously interested in finding and using these tools. Thinking larger thoughts is a kind of magic, since the effort put in is small compared with the long-term results.

In the 1890s, a person named Gottlieb Daimler drew a three-pointed star on a postcard to his family and wrote next to it, "One day this star will shine down on my work." He co-founded Daimler Motoren Gesellschaft, now DaimlerChrysler. Great accomplishments such as these demonstrate Schwartz's claim that a person is best measured by the size of their dreams.

David J. Schwartz

Born in 1927, Schwartz was a professor at Georgia State University, Atlanta, and was considered a leading American authority on motivation. He was also president of Creative Educational Services, a consulting firm specializing in leadership development.

His other books include The Magic of Getting What You Want, The Magic of Thinking Success, *and* The Magic of Selling.

Schwartz died in 1987.

The Secret Door to Success

"Your big opportunity and big success usually slide in, when you least expect it. You have to let go long enough for the great law of attraction to operate. You never saw a worried and anxious magnet. It stands up straight and hasn't a care in the world, because it knows needles can't help jumping to it. The things we rightly desire come to pass when we have taken the clutch off."

In a nutshell

Dissolve the walls around your success through positive expectations. Trust ultimately in God for your prosperity.

In a similar vein

Catherine Ponder *The Dynamic Laws of Prosperity* (p. 254)
Florence Scovel Shinn *The Game of Life and How to Play It* (50SHC)
Wallace D. Wattles *The Science of Getting Rich* (p. 320)

CHAPTER 43

Florence Scovel Shinn

Jericho seemed like an impenetrable fortress to the Israelites, a walled city containing a great deal of treasure that separated them from the Promised Land. They had been decades in the wilderness and were discontented. Yet Joshua is told by God that, if they blow their trumpets in a certain way and give a great shout in unison, the city will be theirs. Amazingly, it works; they walk in and Jericho is taken with ease.

All Bible stories have metaphysical or second meanings, Florence Scovel Shinn says. "Jericho" is simply the success that you may feel has been denied you, but is closer to being yours than you think. It is possible that you have unknowingly built a wall around your success, which may fall once you come to certain realizations.

Expecting the best

If you have been hammering away at a goal for years without much apparent gain, unless you are unusually strong of mind, resentment and envy will have started to eat away at you. This outlook can sabotage your success just as it is getting close to being realized.

Scovel Shinn devoted her life to helping people recognize the link between their attitudes and their level of happiness. A relaxed state of expectancy, she taught, is the best mindset for bringing success into your life. Sometimes, intensity of desire can actually turn away things that are good for you because it suggests faith only in yourself and not in the higher power that has created you. Few understand the success law that deeply felt, even burning ambitions and desires are most easily realised by *allowing* them to be realized—a case of "set and forget."

It is hard for the driven person to accept the biblical suggestion to "Have no thought for the morrow." Yet instead of madly pursuing something night and day, it is much more efficient to have a relaxed knowledge that the achievement you desire is pulling you toward it. Be clear about what you want and then have the faith that it will come. Employ what she calls the occult law of indifference: "Your ships come in over a don't care sea." We have all observed that success has its own time frame and often comes quietly when we least expect it.

Preparing for good things

While it is good to change your outlook so that you expect good things, you must also *prepare* for them.

You can read as much as you like about prosperity thinking and make affirmations, but this is only "armchair faith," Scovel Shinn says, unless you act prosperously in real life. She recounts the story of a woman who wanted to send her two daughters to college, but clearly did not have the money. However, against her husband's objections that the idea was unreasonable, she went ahead with plans for their enrollment, stating that "some unforeseen good" would occur. As it happened, a rich relative sent her a sum of money that covered all the girls' tuition costs.

Doubt, worries, and living in the past only buttress the walls around your Jericho. Life has a way of shaping itself to our expectations, good or bad, Scovel Shinn says, therefore let your thoughts and actions express relaxed, unwavering faith.

Intuition

While Scovel Shinn describes prayer as "telephoning to God," she says that intuition is "God telephoning you."

Some people are careful reasoners, relying only on their intellect to solve problems. They "weigh and measure the situation like dealing in groceries," but the solutions they come up with are far from perfect. How often do you wish that you had gone with your hunch on an issue? At Christmas time a house can be filled with presents, but none is felt to be quite right for the recipient. Consumption without intuition is inevitably wasteful. Asking for guidance, Scovel Shinn says, "always saves time and energy and often a lifetime of misery." Intuition seems magic, because it has the power of Infinite Intelligence behind it. "Unless intuition builds the house, they labor in vain who build it."

Many of the great achievements have been guided by intuition. Scovel Shinn mentions Henry Ford, who never gave up on his feeling that the motor car could be for everyone. Despite his boss and his father thinking it a crazy idea, he persevered, hearing only the voice inside him that said "Do it." When you come to a fork in the road, follow the voice of intuition. If it is God's role to give you hunches, it is yours to be awake to them and not waste them.

Relieved of the burden

Many times in your life you will feel overwhelmed. This is the perfect time to practice faith over fear.

A woman came to Scovel Shinn with a mess of complications in her life and was simply told, "Let God juggle the situation." The woman took a leap of faith, imagining the matters out of her hands, and things quickly cleared up. Try to juggle everything yourself and inevitably you drop the balls; what you find so difficult is of course nothing to God. Perfect faith leads to perfect outcomes.

It is easier to have faith with things that matter less to you, but the real successes come when you entrust the big things. How can you remember to buttress this confidence when you need it? If you are beginning to doubt, Scovel Shinn says, say this to yourself: "His ways are ingenious, His methods are sure." Let God take up the burden.

Abundance

The Secret Door to Success tells the story of a priest on a visit to a French convent, which every day fed many children. However, it had run out of money and the nuns were despairing. Holding up a single piece of silver, one of them told the visitor that this was all they had left to buy food and clothes for the children.

The priest asked for the coin and the nun handed it to him.

He promptly threw it out the window, saying, "Now rely entirely on God." Soon after, people arrived bearing gifts of food and money.

The moral? You don't have to throw away your money or close your bank account, but do not *depend* on the money you have. Whenever you feel "short," remind yourself: "God is the source of my supply." You don't need to know exactly how you will be provided for;

don't limit the channels by which you might receive. The one caveat is that you should ask for what is yours by "divine right."

Many people achieve wealth but then quickly lose it, because it was grasped, not given. To maintain ownership of your investments, remember that they are a manifestation of God for which you must be grateful. Scovel Shinn recalls an old Arabic saying: "What Allah has given cannot be diminished." If you happen to lose money you will not be shattered, knowing that God will soon provide other opportunities.

Don't underestimate the power of words to make or break you financially, Scovel Shinn says, for "Your world is a world of crystallized ideas, crystallized words." Those who speak only of what they lack will therefore end up with little. "You cannot enter the Kingdom of Abundance bemoaning your lot." Instead, you will enter it by being more and more aware of the world's abundance; you can never really feel a state of lack, knowing the truth of the statement that "The Lord is my Shepherd; I shall not want" (Psalms 23:1).

Final comments

Most people give up just before something great is about to happen to them. Success is a system, Scovel Shinn claims, in which courage and perseverance are important elements. A friend once took her to a New York City park to see the sun rise, and she found this simple thing to be a wondrous experience. You may be so used to your daily habits and patterns that you wear yourself into a rut. You cease to be aware of the opportunities that arise through being fully present in the moment, and you stop expecting great things.

If there is one overall message to *The Secret Door to Success*, it is that you must avoid being overwhelmed by life and realize that there is something larger than you that is willing to shoulder the burdens. It is a simple fact that you are constantly "fooled by the darkness before the dawn." If you can live by faith instead of fear, you have found Scovel Shinn's secret door.

Florence Scovel Shinn

Born in 1871 in Camden, New Jersey, Florence Scovel was the daughter of a lawyer. She was educated in Philadelphia and attended the Pennsylvania Academy of Fine Arts from 1889 to 1897, where she met Everett Shinn (1876–1953), a well-known painter. They married after her graduation and moved to New York City to pursue their artistic careers, living near Washington Square.

Florence became an illustrator of popular children's literature in magazines and books and also a teacher of metaphysics. Her classic, The Game of Life and How to Play It, *was self-published in 1925, followed in 1928 by* Your Word Is Your Wand. The Secret Door to Success *was published shortly before her death in 1940.*

Shackleton's Way

"It was suddenly clear they were going to face an extraordinary challenge just to stay alive. The men had expected to be working in relative comfort in a base camp, or to be doing ship's work. Instead, they were stranded on a vast, unstable layer of ice that was their only refuge from the depths of the Weddell Sea or, even worse, the jaws of a killer whale or a sea-leopard. And it was −16° Fahrenheit."

In a nutshell

The true leader brings out the best in people in even the toughest situations.

In a similar vein

Warren Bennis *On Becoming a Leader* (p. 18)
Spencer Johnson *Who Moved My Cheese?* (p. 194)
Martin Seligman *Learned Optimism* (50SHC)

CHAPTER 44

Margot Morrell & Stephanie Capparell

S ir Ernest Shackleton never led a group larger than 27 men and
failed to achieve most of his own exploration goals, yet, as
Morrell and Capparell point out in *Shackleton's Way: Leadership
Lessons from the Great Antarctic Explorer*, he has been hailed as one
of the great leaders of all time.

Shackleton was selected to go on the 1902 *Discovery* expedition
with the explorer Robert Scott, but it fell short of the South Pole by
460 miles because the men were racked by scurvy. Six years later, on
his own expedition, he made it to within 97 miles of the Pole before
having to turn back. Polar explorers were the heroes of the time, so
even this failure was rewarded with a knighthood from Edward VII.

Scott and Shackleton were both beaten to the South Pole by
Norwegian Roald Amundsen in 1911. Shackleton, though, came up
with the idea to be the first to traverse the still largely unexplored
Antarctica on foot, an 1,800-mile journey. With the outbreak of war,
1914 was not the best time to go, but the British government allowed
the expedition to proceed. Shackleton had a talent for raising money for
his adventures and acquired a ship that he renamed *Endurance*, after his
family motto "Fortitudine Vincimus" (By endurance we conquer).

The story in brief

The *Endurance* sailed for Buenos Aires, then South Georgia and into
the Antarctic Circle, plowing through 1,000 miles of ice-strewn waters
toward its goal of a base camp on the Antarctic continent from which
the men would begin the trek. Everything was going well until within a
day's sail of land the *Endurance* got caught in ice—"like an almond in
a chocolate bar"—and refused to budge.

The fierce winds and strong currents gradually dragged the ship
north for ten months, but just as it seemed the ice was loosening up the

floes caught the ship in a vise-like squeeze. The *Endurance* was irreparably damaged and the men were forced to camp on the ice. One day, the ice crushed the ship and it sank in front of their eyes. They would now have to spend months on the frozen sheets, which threatened to crack open at a moment's notice. All of this happened 1,000 miles from any civilization, and they were without any form of contact. Not least of Shackleton's many challenges were boredom and isolation. If they did happen to survive, surely they would go mad.

After months on the shifting packs of the Weddell Sea, using up their rations, the men realized that they would have to move closer to land and the attention of other ships if they were going to live. Throwing gold coins, expensive instruments, and books onto the ice, they set off dragging three small lifeboats across the icefields, making a series of camps.

The time came when they knew they had to make a break for uninhabited, storm-swept Elephant Island, which they managed to do. It was a miserable place and they knew that their supplies of food would quickly run out. So Shackleton and a small party, in their leaky wooden lifeboat, made an 800-mile, 17-day dash over bitterly cold, tempestuous seas to reach South Georgia, where they knew there was a whaling station. This trip, including giant waves and a hurricane, is now considered one of the epic boat journeys. But even then the ordeal was not over: the men had landed on the wrong side of the island and faced a freezing trek across mountains and glaciers to find the station.

People manager par excellence

The expedition is most famous for the fact that Shackleton did not lose a single man, and in fact all of them returned in good physical and mental health. How was this possible, at a time when horrible deaths from starvation, disease, and exposure were a normal part of polar exploration? How did the crew maintain a degree of optimism and cheerfulness despite a number of weak links and sour characters? When Lionel Greenstreet, the first officer, was asked some years later why they had survived when so many polar expeditions had ended in disaster, he replied with a single word: "Shackleton."

He had bravado and vision, yet he was not careless. The safety of crew members came above everything. Whereas Scott was a British Navy man used to hierarchy and command-and-control leadership, and treated his men accordingly, Shackleton believed that the crew *was* the expedition. Though a long apprenticeship in the merchant navy had toughened him and finely developed his leadership skills, he was genuinely interested in people and was ahead of his time in his close personal attention to each member of the expedition.

"Flexibility" and "teamwork" have become jaded management terms, but in 1914 this approach to management was daringly new, and though Shackleton respected the differences between the seamen, the scientists, and the officers under his command, he tried to make the atmosphere as egalitarian as possible. If there was a job to be done, no one could be "above" it. He was forward thinking also in realizing the importance of exercise and relaxation: games and various entertainments, plus a careful schedule of mealtimes, gave order to the day and staved off boredom in the months they were stuck on the ice or huddled together under upturned lifeboats.

Shackleton could be a soft touch if it contributed to crew harmony, nursing men who fell sick in his own cabin and "flattering the egomaniacs." A friend described him as "a Viking with a mother's heart," and Shackleton acknowledged that his way could be very feminine (he had grown up in a female environment, the protective older brother of no fewer than eight sisters). As a captain he could be tough, but because each man felt valued order never broke down. Polar environments are a strange combination of pressure cooker and isolation, and it is common for warring cliques to sabotage expeditions, yet for two long years Shackleton's leadership was never questioned. Though it may seem minor, part of the explanation was that he gave men tasks they were interested in, and encouraged them to express themselves through their work. In the long Antarctic nights he had them write and perform verse, held parties, and encouraged reading from a well-stocked library.

Shackleton inspired such loyalty, the authors suggest, because he wasn't willing to win at all costs. He saw life as a serious game, but you were successful only if you could win "honorably and splendidly." If he had succeeded in the planned traverse across Antarctica and even one man had died, it would not have been worth it to him.

Optimism is courage

Top leaders are set apart by a calm wisdom. It is gained through experience, obviously, but also through active knowledge gathering. Shackleton loved nature and adventure, but he also loved books. He had traveled the world in the merchant marine, "but nothing opened his mind to the vastness, richness and complexity of the world the way his books did," Morell and Capparell note. His voracious reading had given him a sense of perspective that would prove crucial on the *Endurance* expedition.

Shackleton's personal motto was "Optimism is true moral courage." While the expedition's predicament looked dire on paper, the men seemed to exist under a happy illusion—conjured up by their leader— that everything would be all right and they would get out alive. While other leaders might have been challenged by mutinous resentments, Shackleton engineered the vital camaraderie that kept spirits up. He knew that optimistic people tend to bring unity to crews and was later not surprised when the more pessimistic members of the expedition performed the worst (despite seeming more hardy at the beginning), while apparently weaker but more upbeat men flourished.

When a school headmaster subsequently asked the explorer to give a message for his boys, Shackleton replied: "In trouble, danger and disappointment never give up hope. The worst can always be got over." This example of what Claude Bristol called "the magic of believing" (see p. 42) should be remembered every time we face an obstacle; it, above all else, seemed to save the expedition from perishing. Shackleton was a natural psychologist and had intended to write a book on the mental side of the *Endurance* ordeal, as this was what had fascinated him most about it.

Final comments

Shackleton's Way is not meant to be a definitive account of the *Endurance* expedition. Alfred Lansing's gripping *Endurance* provides this, and there are good accounts written by members of the crew. What Morell and Capparell give the reader are the lessons of a great leader in easily digestible form, lessons that they emphasize can be *learned*. Each chapter has a list of pointers: Shackleton's way of "Hiring an outstanding crew" or "Creating a spirit of camaraderie," for example. The chapters are also interspersed with snapshots of contemporary leaders whose lives and careers have been inspired by Shackleton.

The book is clearly a product of its times, with references to how the internet is throwing out old ways of business and what this means for today's leader, but the timeless part of it is Morrell and Capparell's identification (after many years of study) of leadership secrets forged under the most difficult conditions. These are useful to anyone required to manage people.

The rescue of the *Endurance* crew made news, but because a war was on and people were dying the crew were not greeted as heroes, and after Shackleton's death in 1922 (age 47, on his fourth Antarctic expedition) his name slipped into obscurity.

Why the upsurge in interest in this man? Morrell and Capparell describe the expedition as a "successful failure"—while failing utterly to achieve its goals, it managed something much more glorious, the survival of its 27 crew against all odds. The Shackleton story only confirms the cliché that the journey is often greater than the destination, and that the camaraderie of fellow travelers is always more satisfying than prizes.

Margot Morrell & Stephanie Capparell

Margot Morrell became a Shackleton scholar after first coming across the Endurance *story in 1984. Her work includes transcribing two of the diaries of the ship's crew members.*

In 1998, business journalist Stephanie Capparell wrote a Wall Street Journal *article on the* Endurance *expedition, with reference to Morrell's research into Shackleton's leadership skills. The article sparked renewed interest in the story, and a year later the two began work on* Shackleton's Way, *which has been a bestseller. Both authors live in New York City.*

2000

The Millionaire Mind

"They live in lovely homes located in fine neighborhoods. Balance is their approach to life. They are financially independent, yet they enjoy life—they are not 'all work, no play' type of people. Most became millionaires in one generation."

"Some millionaires do feel that their IQ was a factor in their successful achievements, although most others feel just the opposite."

In a nutshell

People are not born with a millionaire mind. It is a set of attitudes and knowledge that anyone can adopt and acquire.

In a similar vein

CHAPTER 45

Thomas J. Stanley

*T*he *Millionaire Next Door* was Thomas Stanley's runaway bestseller, revealing to the world a most unexpected picture of
America's millionaires. *The Millionaire Mind* is a more thoughtful
and insightful look into the psychology of millionaires, the "soft" factors in terms of attitudes and beliefs that have made these people financially successful.

The research base was broadened to encompass an even wealthier
set of millionaires (including many "decamillionaires," with a balance
sheet value of $10 million or more). In all, the author received 733
responses to his carefully targeted questionnaires, and the sum effect of
this book is a little like being invited into the living rooms of 733
wealthy people for a fireside chat.

The key question asked is: Is it possible to have a very enjoyable,
balanced life but still achieve millionaire status? Stanley's surprising
answer is that while money can't buy happiness, millionaires are perhaps more aware than most that the best things in life are free. Rather
than, as you might expect, spending their nonworking time visiting
glamor spots or engaging in expensive hobbies, the great majority of
millionaires prefer to spend time with family and friends. If they are
not doing this they are involved in community activities or playing a
round of golf. As the author suggests, most millionaires are a "cheap
date"—but they are not miserly personalities.

Vocation, vocation, vocation

The way to sustainable wealth and an enjoyable life is simple: Do work
that you love to do. The more you love your work, the more likely you
are to excel at it, and the more rewards will accrue to you. You are
also much more likely to create a profitable niche through the process
of deepening your skills, knowledge, and contacts in your chosen area.

Millionaires are happy to make a life out of truck spare parts or car
washes if they see opportunities, no matter what others think. Compare
this to people who don't particularly like what they do but were led to

the belief that it would give them financial and career security. Ironically, this perception leads many to choose similar business opportunities, with the result that they find stiff competition. Above all, millionaires "think differently from the crowd": they spend much of their time looking for things that others have overlooked, overturning assumptions and creating profitable niches within generic industries.

Still haven't found your vocation? Against the conventional view that you go directly into a field after school or college, stick at it, and eventually do well, most millionaires did a variety of jobs and had a good spread of life experiences before they found their vocation. Looking at the data, Stanley concludes, "It's hard for a person to recognize opportunities if he stays in one place and remains in one job."

Risk, reward, and self-belief

Stanley notes the strong correlation between willingness to take financial risk and financial success. While most of us would see starting a business as a great risk, the financially successful see working 9 to 5 for someone else as risky. You are dependent on your employer for your livelihood, and your income is related to how much time you spend working. Millionaires tend to choose a career in which there is no ceiling on how much money they can make if they are successful at it.

You may ask, what about all those among Stanley's respondents who don't own businesses? Surely the list includes doctors, lawyers, accountants, and people who have done well as employees in large firms? There are indeed many, but they tend not to be among the decamillionaires surveyed. Even if a person is at the top of the profession in one of these areas, they are required to give the service personally in return for a fee, one client at a time. As an employer, you can always get other people to put in the time, but you reap more and more of the fruits.

One of the book's most fascinating chapters concerns the link between courage and wealth. The millionaires in Stanley's surveys all seemed to have one thing in common: a belief in their ability to generate wealth. People talk ad nauseam about the importance of investing in the stock market, but, as Stanley rightly points out, few really think about the *source* of wealth: generally an idea turned into a business, initially owned by a small group of people. Real wealth creators focus on creating a prosperous business instead of gambling on public companies about which they can never have all the information. This may seem like putting all your eggs in one basket, but those eggs can be watched like a hawk.

School

A good proportion of self-made millionaires worked hard in school but were not the top students. What they learned most in school was how to judge people well and get along with them, and that hard work could bring a surprising level of success. Many were judged not intelligent enough to succeed because they lacked the high levels of analytical intelligence or IQ to get them into medical school or law school. Yet later in life, most of the millionaires admit that these judgments only made them more determined to achieve. Knowing that they would never run with the "beautiful people," they sought to prove their worth in other ways. They became very good at dealing with people and scoping out opportunities.

People often put success down to good luck, but Stanley's millionaires rate luck quite low on the scale of success factors. "The harder you work, the luckier you get" seems to be a consensus view.

Spouse

Nine out of ten married millionaires say that their marriage has been a significant factor in their success. A spouse provides on-tap psychological support and advice that is likely to be honest.

After love, attractiveness, and sharing common interests, most millionaires chose their spouses for a certain "x-factor": small things they noticed that indicated self-worth, integrity, even compassion. It turns out that millionaire spouses have the sort of qualities that would be helpful in running a business: intelligent, honest, reliable, cheerful. Millionaires choose their lifelong partners astutely, knowing that it will greatly affect their own success.

Every little helps

Becoming wealthy involves a set of habits and ways of doing things, some of which seem of minor importance or common sense, although many of us don't do them:

❖ Acquiring antique furniture or quality reproductions, which can be reupholstered instead of buying cheaper pieces every few years.

❖ Investing in better-quality shoes and getting them repaired or resoled when necessary, instead of buying a new pair.

❖ Buying household items at bulk discount stores. Half of the millionaires surveyed always make a list before going supermarket shopping.

❖ The typical millionaire from the survey has never spent more than $41,000 on buying an automobile (a good proportion buy quality used cars at much less than this figure), nor spent more than $38 on a haircut.

❖ Millionaires are frugal, but are not into DIY. They get other people to paint their house because they know their time is better spent focusing on their investments. They employ top experts to sort out their tax and legal matters. Big accountancy and legal firms cost more, but their better advice and contacts make their cost low over the long term.

Final comments

The Millionaire Mind could have been better edited (many statements are repeated), but it is not for lovely, elegant prose that you will buy this book. At less than the price of a main course at a good restaurant, its insights may prove an insanely good investment.

There are a multitude of revealing facts and ideas, including the five "foundation stones" of financial success most often mentioned by millionaires, and enjoyable case histories and anecdotes of specific millionaires. Forty-six tables display the research data in a manner that even the numerically challenged can understand.

What is the millionaire mind? Not living a spartan lifestyle and making money your god, but staying free from reliance on credit and being in control of your finances. The great self-discipline of the average millionaire means that they can't help piling up wealth long after their modest needs have been satisfied. The millionaire mind evokes the famous biblical saying, "To them that hath, more will be given." Not only do these people have money, they love their work. Most people will think, "Of course they love their work, they can do what they want," but few appreciate that it was their love of their vocation that helped to make them wealthy in the first place.

Thomas J. Stanley

Born in 1943, Stanley had a doctorate in business administration from the University of Georgia and was formerly a marketing professor at the same institution. One of his colleagues there was David J. Schwartz, author of The Magic of Think278Big (see p. 246).

Stanley's research into wealthy people began in the early 1970s. His books include Marketing to the Affluent and The Millionaire Next Door.

He lived in Atlanta, Georgia, and died in a car crash in 2015.

Maximum Achievement

"*The way for you to be happy and successful, to get more of the things you really want in life, is to get the combinations to the locks. Instead of spinning the dials of life hoping for a lucky break, as if you were playing a slot machine, you must instead study and emulate those who have already done what you want to do and achieved the results you want to achieve.*"

"*The primary cause of success in life is the ability to set and achieve goals. That's why the people who do not have goals are doomed forever to work for those who do. You either work to achieve your own goals or you work to achieve someone else's goals.*"

In a nutshell

Measuring your life daily against written goals is a fundamental of success.

In a similar vein
Maxwell Maltz *Psycho-Cybernetics* (50SHC)
Anthony Robbins *Unlimited Power* (p. 266)

CHAPTER 46

Brian Tracy

Brian Tracy grew up in a poor family and had to wear charity store clothes. After dropping out of school he worked in a succession of laboring jobs, living in boarding houses. At 21 he found work on a Norwegian freighter ship and traveled around the world, living and working in 80 countries over the next eight years.

He finally found himself in straight commission sales, and though not an outward success himself, Tracy had always been interested in the question "What makes some people successful and others not?" As a freshly minted salesman, he started to read voraciously on selling techniques and what makes the best salespeople the best. He copied what they did and, slowly, his results improved. Six months later he was the top salesperson in his company.

When he moved into management, he read everything he could on managing people and built a large sales organization across several countries. Entering the real estate industry, he "hit the books again" and talked to successful developers. His first project was financing, building, and leasing out a $3 million shopping center. At night Tracy completed a high school diploma and eventually gained entry to an MBA program to study business theory and marketing, which enabled him to become a management consultant.

To learn about happiness, he read what he could find on metaphysics, psychology, and motivation, and when he married learned all he could about parenting. To get a sense of perspective and find out why some countries were rich and others poor, he read widely on history, economics, and politics.

After two decades of thinking about the question of what makes some people more successful, Tracy decided to put everything he knew into a "success system" that could help others. He designed a seminar, but it took about three years to really catch on. Then he released an audiotape program, *The Psychology of Achievement*, which went on to sell half a million copies. *Maximum Achievement: Strategies and Skills that Will Unlock Your Hidden Powers to Succeed* is the written version of this program.

The master skill

Tracy provides us with this potted biography to show how he moved from being a wanderer to a focused person. His varied work roles became his means to continue his real love: studying success itself.

As he came to synthesize everything he knew, he realized that there was a "master skill" that could produce brilliant results across a person's life: the ability to set goals and achieve them. When he discovered goal setting at 23, for the first time Tracy felt that he could have control over his future. Human beings, he learned, are teleological: we are shaped by our ambitions, adapting ourselves to meet the image of an imagined end state. Maxwell Maltz's famous *Psycho-Cybernetics* told Tracy that humans are really goal-setting machines, requiring goals in order to live to the full. Maltz compared people to self-guided missiles, which constantly adjust their path to hit a target; in the same way, we can program ourselves to achieve our desires through constant self-feedback.

What is interesting about goals, Tracy found, is that they are value neutral: whatever desires you set for yourself, you are likely to achieve them whether they are good or bad. Therefore, why not take the time to create wonderful, life-enriching goals?

The skill's value

Fewer than 3 percent of people have written goals, and fewer than 1 percent regularly review them, Tracy notes. Yet most of us know that it is good to have goals, and we may even have been to seminars or read books on the matter. We spend a dozen years being schooled, but the most important contributor to success in life—how to make our wishes and ambitions concrete—is rarely learned.

So why don't we take the step of setting goals for ourselves? Tracy lists reasons, but one that stands out is that we aren't willing to accept full responsibility for our lives. If we don't set goals, then we don't have to reach them. The more mundane reason is that goal setting has never been part of our family or social background. As a result, we may end up mixing with people who have no clear idea where they are headed, becoming a person who "follows the followers."

The payoff of goal setting is that as you achieve each goal you feel in charge of your own destiny, with every moment taken up productively. Self-esteem increases and it is easy to remain motivated. You suddenly see the meaning of the saying, "Nothing succeeds like success."

Becoming an expert goal setter

For goals to work, they must stretch you but not be unrealistic. When he was earning $40,000 a year, Tracy set a goal to earn $400,000 within 12 months. The problem was, the goal was so huge that deep down he did not really believe he would meet it. Revising the goal down to $60,000 within 12 months—still a 50 percent increase—he achieved it within six.

Goals must be written down. Although this requires some discipline, there is something magic about putting things on paper that increases the probability of a goal becoming fact. The more detail about the goal the better, because the subconscious needs details to shape action. "You can't hit a target you can't see," Tracy says. You don't need to worry about the details of how the goal will be achieved, however; what is important is to be certain and exact about what you want. Without this you are leaving your life up to chance.

Goals can be divided into the tangible and intangible. Intangible ones, for instance relating to an increased ability to be patient, do not need deadlines. Tangible ones, such as meeting a sales quota, do, because they make you work backward to ensure that the goal is achieved. A sales trainer friend of Tracy's commented, "There are no unrealistic goals, only unrealistic deadlines." If you fail to make the one you've set, don't conclude that goal setting doesn't work. Instead, seek to increase your knowledge of it. Remember that clear goals provide the strength to keep going; without them it is easy to collapse at the first obstacle.

The goal of meaning

Any achievement, Tracy says, is worthless if it is not congruent with a sense of inner peace, so whatever your goals are they must revolve around a single meaningful purpose for your life. You are only successful to the extent that you can achieve your own happiness, so you must pursue goals that you are vitally interested in—only then can you really be of use to others.

Loving relationships should feature highly in your goal setting. Only when these are going well, Tracy reminds us, "can you turn your thoughts toward the self-expression and self-actualization that enable you to fulfill your potential." Very few people have definite goals to improve the quality of their love life.

One of Tracy's other key ingredients for success is financial freedom. Money worries are the cause of around 80 percent of relationship breakdowns, therefore you owe it to yourself and your partner to develop the skills and get the education to make yourself more valuable.

Final comments

Maximum Achievement is a straightforward success manual and many of the book's ideas may seem like nothing new, but go beyond the cover and you may find yourself deeply inspired. The dozen chapters cover almost every aspect of personal development. We have focused here on only the central element of Tracy's philosophy, goal setting, but there is a wealth of material answering his original question: "What makes some people successful and others not?"

One of the answers is that they are great readers. The motivational gurus like Tom Hopkins, Anthony Robbins, and Tracy never seem to miss an opportunity to relate how books opened their eyes to what was possible. This is because the more you read about the lives and actions of successful people, the more likely it is that you will set the bar higher for yourself.

Brian Tracy

Born in Canada in 1944, Tracy is a leading motivational figure and holds frequent seminars for sales forces, executives, and individuals. His company, Brian Tracy International, is based in San Diego, California.

Audiotape programs include The Psychology of Achievement, The Psychology of Selling, Peak Performance Woman, Million Dollar Habits, *and* How to Master Your Time. *Books include* The 100 Absolutely Unbreakable Laws of Business Success, Create Your Own Future, *and* Focal Point.

The Art of War

"Sun Tzu said:
In general, the best method for using the military force is to conquer an
entire country; to destroy the country is inferior. Ancient warriors who
knew how to use the military well defeated the enemy's army, but not
by battle. They overpowered the enemy's country, but not by force. The
goal was to take things whole. In this way, soldiers were not killed and
our lord gained the largest booty. Therefore, a general who wins all his
battles by destroying other armies is not the ultimate warrior. The
ultimate warrior is one who wins the war by forcing the enemy to
surrender without fighting any battles."

In a nutshell

The successful person has unusual skill at dealing with conflict and
ensuring the best outcome for all.

In a similar vein
The Bhagavad-Gita (50SHC)
Chin-Ning Chu *Thick Face, Black Heart* (p. 62)
Lao Tzu *Tao Te Ching* (50SHC)

CHAPTER 47

Sun Tzu

Sun Tzu lived in the same era as Confucius, in northern China. He was a brilliant military strategist in the warring states period. Known in China simply as the Sun Tzu, *The Art of War* is a record of his ideas for survival and success in a difficult time. For a long period only communicated orally, it was later written on bamboo sticks and eventually became a book.

The Art of War was not the only military leadership text of the time, but came to be considered the greatest. As the authors of an excellent recent translation (Denma Translation Group, Shambhala, 2002) argue, other military books of the time were simply technical manuals. *The Art of War* "emphasizes knowledge as a means of attaining victory, and its principal weapon is the power already existent in the natural and human worlds." This attention to the personal—knowledge, character, attunement to the Tao (the guiding spirit of the universe)—is why it is still relevant and valuable.

Winning through nonaggression

"One hundred victories in one hundred battles is not the most skillful. Subduing the other's military without battle is the most skillful."

The Art of War is a different way of seeing conflict, transcending the instinctual "fight for your life" approach. With enough intelligence, it says, a conflict can be prevented from developing into something nasty—or developing at all. The wise general knows that actual battle is only one way to achieve a victory. This is the concept of "taking whole": conquering with a minimum of force and with little destruction. The resources of both parties are left intact.

Such an outcome we would describe today as "win/win," not merely defeating someone in an argument but bringing them over to our way of thinking. Because we have taken the larger view, pride and dignity are undamaged. In contrast, if we believe in the need for "win/lose" outcomes then we are dependent on aggression and force. The Sun Tzu way is to think less in terms of "the enemy," but rather the Tao of the whole situation—that is, the way it seems to be moving—so that you and the other actor almost become one. You control the situation even amid apparent chaos. As the Denma translators put it: "This is not a matter of belief in strange forces. Rather, it is about how things work."

A modern example

Most people will never have to engage in a war, but we do have to deal with conflict. The best way to approach conflict—as difficult as it sounds—is in a detached manner. *The Art of War* teaches that "The angry general loses." Anger creates chaos and even greater suffering than is necessary, while self-control makes for detached but powerful action.

In his biography of Warren Buffett (see p. 48), Richard Lowenstein recounts a crisis in the legendary investor's career in which he fought to save the Wall Street firm Salomon Brothers. The firm, in which he was a major investor, was in danger of being closed down by the US government because one of its traders had lied to the Treasury. Buffett cooperated to a fault with the investigators and ended up getting them to drop charges. His lawyer argued that going ahead with charges would make it seem like cooperation had been penalized. Instead, it should be rewarded. Lowenstein writes of Buffett:

"Instinctively, he shrank from confronting his adversaries, but he was superb at winning them over without a fight. He did not so much convince; he disarmed, he co-opted."

Buffett's way is the perfect example of Sun Tzu's message that the best warrior gets what he wants without even having to fight. By giving respectful acknowledgment to your adversaries, they become less antagonistic and a better outcome is achieved for all.

Leadership through character

To be a Sun Tzu leader requires not only thorough information about the other, but knowledge about yourself.

To be invincible, you must make yourself so. You cannot rely on the other's weakness. Victory comes to those who have developed an ethic of constant refinement and improvement, not those who worry about the competition. You cannot control the other, but by developing your own strength of character, knowledge, and insight you can build invincibility. Donald Krause—whose *The Art of War for Executives* (1995) applies Sun Tzu to success in managing people, growing your business, and thriving in changing circumstances—notes that in Chinese philosophy leadership is character. People with great character, developed over time, naturally become leaders.

> *"Knowing the other and knowing oneself,*
> *In one hundred battles no danger."*

Through such self-knowledge, plus the development of strategic insight through close observation of others, you can become a "wise general," or what the Denma translators describe as a "sage commander."

Taking the larger view and seeing clearly

The smaller view is always the false one, the vulnerable one. To take the larger view is to open yourself to all pieces of information, which gives you a more accurate picture of what is going on (the Tao of a situation). The smaller view tends to be driven by fear, the larger view is driven by an objective that you pursue in a detached way.

The Art of War puts the highest value on current information. It says: Do not act according to beliefs or dogma but within the information arc of the situation or moment. Always challenge conventional wisdom.

A master of timing

With the ability to see what is happening also comes skill in picking the direction and speed of movement. Because you see the whole and have patience, you have the genius of timing. You can read the flow of a situation and react accordingly. The opposite of this is action based on unconscious habit and rigidity of mind. Even good habits can stand in the way of reading a situation correctly.

Sun Tzu's strategies are about building up momentum and then striking hard and getting away quickly. "And so the military values victory/It does not value prolonging." The actions of the sage commander are quick and decisive. Some further attributes of such a leader:

❖ Controls the form of engagement instead of reacting to it.
❖ Moves quietly and without arrogance in order to achieve the objective.
❖ Lets the enemy wear itself out trying to get advantage, then lets its own force throw it off balance.
❖ Seems formless, everywhere and nowhere.
❖ Decides on victory, rather than wishing for it.
❖ Is a master of uncertainty and chaos.
❖ Is orthodox in some things, so as to be able to surprise in others.
❖ Is practiced in the art of deception; that is, lets others see what he or she wants them to see.
❖ Insistently seeks knowledge about the other side.
❖ Develops a closeness to the organization so that it can move as one piece and with one spirit.

Final comments

It has taken a long time for the West to fully appreciate *The Art of War*. This is partly because the text itself is so enigmatic. There is no building up of an argument and, like the *Tao Te Ching*, the order in which ideas are presented often seems to make no sense or be contradictory. Most translations are more like interpretations.

Nevertheless, many leaders in history have attributed their success to Sun Tzu's strategies. Among the first was the Chinese warlord Cao Cao, who managed to unite all of China, and the influence continued right up to Mao Tse-Tung. And as the Denma translation notes, the US Marines manual *Warfighting* bears a striking resemblance to many passages in *The Art of War*.

Yet today it is in the more prosaic situations of everyday work and life that the book is most used. *The Art of War* will be found in the hands of the businessperson as much as the military leader or politician.

Sun Tzu's manual was forged at a time of great instability when the old beliefs and morality were under threat. It is therefore not about "morality"—that is humanity's invention—but about being aware of what works, going with the grain of the universe.

The Art of War offers strategies for success that have been proven over thousands of years. As is the nature of true wisdom, it is not bound by time or place.

Made in America

"It is a story about entrepreneurship, and risk, and hard work, and knowing where you want to go and being willing to do what it takes to get there. It's a story about believing in your idea even when maybe some other folks don't, and about sticking to your guns. But I think more than anything it proves there's absolutely no limit to what plain, ordinary people can accomplish if they're given the opportunity and the encouragement and the incentive to do their best."

"I always wanted to be the best retailer in the world, not necessarily the biggest."

In a nutshell

Be the best at what you do and the world will beat a path to your door.

In a similar vein

Andrew Carnegie *The Autobiography of Andrew Carnegie* (p. 56)
Ray Kroc *Grinding It Out* (p. 214)
J. W. Marriott Jr. *The Spirit to Serve* (p. 248)
Thomas J. Stanley *The Millionaire Mind* (p. 296)

CHAPTER 48

Sam Walton

I n 1985, *Forbes* magazine named Sam Walton the "richest man in America." 30 years later, the same magazine ranks four members of his family among the richest people in the world, and their company, Wal-Mart, turns over more than any other on the planet.

The media were always going to be interested in a family of such vast wealth. As Walton puts it:

"The media usually portrayed me as a really cheap, eccentric recluse, sort of a hillbilly who more or less slept with his dogs in spite of having billions of dollars stashed away in a cave."

Made in America, written in the couple of years before Walton died, is his attempt to explain the philosophies and strategies behind Wal-Mart's rise from nothing to be the largest retailer in the world in one generation.

Beginnings

Sam Walton had grown up in the Depression, going with his father, a loan appraiser, to witness the repossession of family farms. His boyhood ambition was always to be a salesman, but after college and military service he began his retail career with the retailer J. C. Penney. After marrying Helen Robson, whose father put up some money, the young couple opened a Ben Franklin variety store franchise in Newport, Arkansas.

The store turned out to have very high rent and strong competition, but Walton still managed to multiply sales and profits. When the day came for the renewal of the lease, the owner refused to do so; he wanted his son to take over the store. Walton was devastated.

The couple started over again in Bentonville, an even smaller town in northwest Arkansas. Walton's Five and Dime adopted the brand new idea of self-service with checkouts at the front and fluorescent lighting, and the store did well. Walton had discovered that there was huge untapped demand in small towns and their hinterlands if the prices were right. People were willing to travel tens of miles for a bargain.

Expansion

Postwar America was changing rapidly. People were moving to suburbs and commuting into cities and the car was king. Fast food joints and motels sprouted to service the freeway traffic, which usually bypassed the towns. In these towns retailing stayed much the same: small specialty stores (butchers, drapers, etc.) and variety stores. The Waltons began to challenge this cozy arrangement by offering much lower prices, greater variety, satisfaction guaranteed, and long opening hours—all now taken for granted.

Walton tried always to buy direct from manufacturers, cutting out the middleman. If you buy goods at a high price, he believed, "you've just bought someone else's inefficiency." The Wal-Mart strategy—not obvious at the time—is that you have higher profits from selling more things at a lower price, compared to selling fewer at a higher price.

By 1960, Sam and his brother Bud Walton had built an "empire" of nine variety stores. When asked how much further they would expand, Sam Walton's answer was "probably very little"—any more and they would not be able to supervise them all personally. The purchase of a small light plane, however, enabling the brothers to visit stores quickly and scout new locations, left this prediction in the dust.

Outsider becomes giant

The first store called Wal-Mart was not opened until 1962, by which time Walton was 44. S. S. Krege Co.'s Kmart opened for business the same year.

Walton emphasizes his company's outsider status. For much of its history, it was viewed as a hick upstart from Arkansas and not taken very seriously. By the early 1970s, Kmart had 500 stores and the Waltons fewer than 70. By 1976, Kmart had doubled to 1,000, while Wal-Mart still had only 150.

The first Wal-Marts were quite ugly and chaotic, but prices were generally 20 percent lower than other stores and this alone caused the customers to flock in. With improved distribution, the company had found a way to grow at 30 to 70 percent a year, and competition with

Kmart began to heat up. The figures say it all. By 1980 there were 276 Wal-Marts, and by 1990 the company hit $1 billion in profits with 1,528 stores.

In the year that Sam Walton wrote *Made in America*, Wal-Mart sold 27 million pairs of jeans and 280 million pairs of socks, enough for every man, woman, and child in the USA.

Wal-Mart today

Wal-Mart is now often criticized for being closed to unions and for having a third of workers who are only part-time. Another accusation concerns the company's comparatively small charitable giving.

Walton's defense was that his overriding aim is to save customers money, and through these savings to raise the standard of living wherever his stores are located. Neither higher wages nor an expansive charity program would serve this purpose. Wal-Mart's policy of using American suppliers where possible, Walton believed, created hundreds of thousands of jobs and made US manufacturing more competitive. He had also made sure that the Wal-Mart organizational structure allowed ideas to filter up from the grass roots; the company had only got so big by "thinking small." On these points it is clear that Wal-Mart could not be more different from the Enrons of this world, whose operating style Walton referred to (years before the problems in some of America's largest corporations was revealed) as "looting from the top."

The Sam Walton way in business and life

❖ Copy other businesses' ideas and successfully adapt them ("most everything I've done I've copied from somebody else," Walton wrote).
❖ Competition forces refinement. Welcome it.
❖ Embrace technology, but only to reduce costs and serve the customer.
❖ Never stop looking for ways to save. Wal-Mart's executive offices are cramped, and Wal-Mart executives famously sleep two to a hotel room when traveling.
❖ Never pass up a market because it looks too small.
❖ Treat your employees (Wal-Mart calls them associates) well. Happy

associates will treat customers well and customers will come back.
(Wal-Mart's profit-sharing program has made a lot of associates well
off, while "shrinkage"—stealing by employees or their friends—is
half the industry average.)

❖ Never be satisfied with how things are. "To succeed in this world,
you have to change all the time." This, not money, drove Walton.

❖ Your job in life is to create value where there was none before. To
gain money, enrich the world in some way.

❖ Don't be afraid of being wrong, and never worry about changing
your mind. Walton enraged other managers by going back and forth
on big decisions.

❖ Speak to people before they speak to you. Acknowledge them.

❖ Have goals and set them high.

❖ Retain an underdog attitude.

Final comments

Walton's dedication and determination were notorious. For his
Saturday morning meetings with managers, he would get up at 3.00 or
4.00 A.M. to go over the week's figures, giving him the best overview of
anyone in the company. Wal-Mart would never have expanded at the
pace it did without the founder's emphasis on action: "getting it all
done in record time."

Yet at the end of *Made in America*, written when he did not have
long to live, the driven Walton asks: Was it all worth it? Was building
Wal-Mart worth the time he couldn't spend with his family? His
answer is yes, for the simple fact that everyone has a role to play in life,
and his was as a merchant. His family was extremely important to him,
but this was his calling.

The book is a classic because it is not an ego trip. Walton takes
pains to point out that Wal-Mart is a collective success story, and even
if you have zero interest in retailing you may be fascinated by the tale
of what a single family can achieve. Helen Walton, who had a degree in
finance, was clearly a major factor in her husband's success beyond the
stable home life she provided. He had originally wanted to go into
partnership with a friend and open a store in St. Louis, but she over-
ruled him: no partnerships, no living in a town with more than 10,000
people. The seed of Wal-Mart's success—a family-based company with
a small-town focus—was thus sown by Helen Walton.

Get the book to read Sam's "10 rules for building a business," equally appreciated as 10 personal success rules, and for the many anecdotes from Wal-Mart family members, managers, and associates. If you are considering starting a company, you should read *Made in America* to rethink what might be possible.

Sam Walton

Walton was born in Kingfisher, Oklahoma, in 1918, and when he was five his parents moved to Missouri, finally settling in Columbia. He sold magazine subscriptions and ran paper routes through school and into college, where he was making $4,000 a year while doing a business degree. He made efforts to be well liked and became president of the student body.

When America went to war in 1942, a minor heart irregularity meant that Walton was put on limited duty. While living in Oklahoma, where he was working at a gunpowder plant, he met his future wife, Helen Robson, daughter of a prominent banker and lawyer. They would have four children, Rob, Jim, Alice, and John. Walton Enterprises, the Walton family partnership, owns over a third of the company's publicly listed stock. Walton decided to go public in order to free the family from debt.

In 1992, aged 74, Walton died of a form of bone cancer. He had recently received the Presidential Medal of Freedom. Walton had wanted to spend his last weeks visiting stores, but immobility and the encouragement of associates and family provided the opportunity to finish Made in America, *which was co-written by John Huey.*

The Science of Getting Rich

"Life has advanced so far, and become so complex, that even the most ordinary man or woman requires a great amount of wealth in order to live in a manner that even approaches completeness . . . To understand the science of getting rich is therefore the most essential of all knowledge."

"Riches secured on the competitive plane are never satisfactory and permanent; they are yours today, and another's tomorrow. Remember, if you are to become rich in a scientific and certain way, you must rise entirely out of the competitive thought. You must never think for a moment that the supply is limited."

In a nutshell

It is natural and logical that you should become rich through the use of your creative powers.

In a similar vein
Claude M. Bristol *The Magic of Believing* (p. 42)
Shakti Gawain *Creative Visualization* (50SHC)
Catherine Ponder *The Dynamic Laws of Prosperity* (p. 254)
Florence Scovel Shinn *The Secret Door to Success* (p. 284)

Wallace D. Wattles

When you come across a book with a title like *The Science of Getting Rich*, you may be forgiven for suspecting that it is a greed manual by an author of questionable motives. It is worth keeping an open mind, however, as Wattles's classic is essentially a metaphysical work that deals with a very earthly issue.

The monistic view of the universe, on which the book is based, says that everything in the universe is linked up and part of the whole. It is the basis of East Asian philosophy and religion, and in addition, Wattles argues, the foundation for Descartes, Spinoza, Leibnitz, Schopenhauer, Hegel, and Emerson—philosophers whom he spent years studying. It is also the faith of the New Thought churches, which are remarkably light on dogma and strong on the betterment of humanity.

Whereas the traditional Christian church linked spirituality with poverty, the religion of Wattles emphasizes the naturalness of abundance. He took this to its logical end by saying that a person could not really fulfill their potential if they had to struggle financially—in fact, the evolution of the world depended on each of us seeking riches in an honest way.

Let us go further into this short but intriguing work, one of the twentieth century's early prosperity classics.

Tapping in to the flow

What is the source of wealth? All the great prosperity writers say that the origin of wealth is thought, rather than things. Napoleon Hill called this source Infinite Intelligence, Deepak Chopra (see 50SHC) named it the "field of pure potentiality," and both Wattles and Catherine Ponder describe the formless stuff from which all matter springs as "substance."

Can abundance really emerge from apparent nothingness? Consider what the great inventor Thomas Edison said:

"Ideas come from space. This may seem astonishing and impossible to believe, but it is true. Ideas come from out of space."

This comment is found in *The Magic of Believing* (see p. 42), whose author, Claude Bristol, remarked, "Surely Edison should have known, for few men every received or gave forth more ideas."

The premise of Wattles's science is that if you purposely place a clear thought in the formless substance, it cannot help but find material expression. Through visualization of what you desire on a repetitive basis, the thing will come into being through the organization of existing modes of production. This is the secret shortcut to gaining what you need.

Yet humanity, through most of history, has approached this from the other way around, by trying to create only from existing materials, applying thought to things through manual labor. Wattles notes that we have only just begun to operate as God does, who is after all continually creating something from nothing. Through the science of mind, we are now starting to see that we can manifest things more easily and more perfectly by first impressing the idea of them on formless substance.

If you accept that everything comes from something immaterial, how you live and act will be different from someone who believes that the foundation of everything is matter. Appearances alone will cease to form the basis of your decisions, because your underlying knowing will be that the universe is abundant and ever-renewing. In Wattles's words:

"To think health when surrounded by the appearances of disease, or to think riches when in the midst of appearances of poverty, requires power; but he who acquires this power becomes a master mind. He can conquer fate; he can have what he wants."

The fact of increase

Nature always seeks expression and increase—this is the one reliable fact of the universe. It seeks greater sophistication and refinement; in short, progress. Therefore, Wattles argues, "there can be no lack unless God is to contradict himself and nullify his own works." It is natural for you to want more, and the desire to be rich must be understood in terms of organic growth and progress.

The caveat: What you seek must be in harmony with the universe. It should be to further your fullest expression, not merely for excitement and entertainment. "You do not want to get rich in order to live swinishly, for the gratification of animal desires; that is not life." You want wealth so that you can pursue your interests and develop your mind, travel, surround yourself with beauty, and be in a position to give generously.

Creation, not competition

Wattles reminds you that the substance that creates the evolving universe does not pick and choose who it will favor: its power is open to all and its flow of riches is endless. There is no need to be fearful of what you will "get" — "You do not have to drive sharp bargains," he says — and no sense in trying to take things away from others.

These ideas of competition do not reflect the reality of an abundant universe. The concept of competition rests on the belief that there is one pie to be carved up, whereas creation rests on an acknowledgment of infinite riches. You need to become a creator rather than a competitor.

However, what about all the people who have become rich on the plane of competition? They are like the dinosaurs of prehistoric eras, Wattles says, in that they have been a vital part in an evolutionary process of organizing production, but are invariably brought down by the same logic of competition that thrust them to the fore. Their riches were neither satisfying to themselves nor enduring in a wider societal sense.

Consider that other people can't "beat you to it" if you are creating something unique out of the imagination, skills, and experience that make up your unique personality. Big organizations cannot shut you out of prosperity if you follow your own path to it. Wattles's further tip for real-world prosperity is that you must endeavor to provide something that buyers feel is greater in value than the price they have paid for it. To use a contemporary term, you must "overdeliver."

Harmonious gratitude

Many will attest that the best way to draw something to you is to give thanks that you already have it. Because the nature of the universe is abundance, it rewards those who are actively aware of the fact and are continually grateful for it.

When you are attuned to the source that creates all things, it is natural that it will provide you with the things you need. Gratitude will prevent you from falling on to the plane of competitive thought and lack, and make you realize the blessings that are already yours. Wattles refers to the Bible's words, "Draw nigh unto God, and He will draw nigh unto you," as a statement of fact, because thanks cannot fail to move the giver and indeed will inspire them to give more.

Wattles further advises you not to spend your time complaining about the world, railing against magnates and politicians. These people are part of Earth's evolution, and their actions allow you physically to pursue your opportunities efficiently and in peace. Instead, cultivate gratefulness.

Never talk about your past financial troubles, Wattles says: "If you want to become rich, you must not make a study of poverty." Do not care how poverty is created or sustained, even if you have an interest in the history of tenement dwellers or hunger in developing countries—look only for what makes for riches. The poor need inspiration more than charity, and so you should endeavor to show them the path to wealth rather than trying to alleviate poverty.

Final comments

The question must be asked: Why seek to be rich? Some will say that we should want less, settling for a standard of living that is less taxing on the earth. This is no doubt true, but it fails to take account of human nature. What is a person if not a bundle of aspirations?

Desire is the engine that drives the world, and without ever-increasing wealth there would be a miserable gap between what is wanted and what can be afforded. The nature of life is growth and increase, so it would be contradicting nature to restrict the urge to plenty.

It is also a fact that you cannot seek the higher things in life if you have to fight for the basics. "Moral and spiritual greatness," Wattles says, "is possible only to those who are above the competitive battle for existence." You will not be able to pursue what fascinates you or fulfill your intellectual potential if you have no money to buy books or free time to read. It is also much easier to have a positive view of life when you are able to surround yourself with items of beauty. And not least, Wattles points out, to live soulfully a human being must have love, and it is difficult to love when you are poverty stricken.

In the twenty-first century we seem much more open to the idea that spirituality and wealth go together. For this we partly have to thank the pioneers of prosperity consciousness, who have removed the possibility of personal riches from the realm of guilt to rightful expectancy. *The Science of Getting Rich* will be dismissed as quaint by some, but it was actually ahead of its time. Despite its mystical language, it is profoundly practical.

Wallace D. Wattles

Biographical information on Wattles is scant, but we know that he was born in 1860, died not long after the publication of The Science of Getting Rich, *and was an active socialist and Christian. For more information, see my introduction to* The Science of Getting Rich *(Capstone, 2010).*

His other books include Health through New Thought and Fasting, The Science of Being Great, The Science of Being Well, *and a novel,* Hellfire Harrison.

1992

Coaching for Performance

"Coaching is not merely a technique to be wheeled out and rigidly applied in certain prescribed circumstances. It is a way of managing, a way of treating people, a way of thinking, a way of being. Roll on the day when the word coaching disappears from our lexicon altogether, and it just becomes the way we relate to one another at work, and elsewhere too."

"All instruction, all criticism, every reduction in choice, every manifestation of hierarchy, every act of secrecy subtly lowers people's self-belief. Coaching, trust, openness, respect, authentic praise, freedom of choice and, of course, success raise it."

"To use coaching successfully we have to adopt a far more optimistic view than usual of the dormant capability of people, all people."

In a nutshell

Consider changing your way of learning and relating to others, and reap the performance benefits.

In a similar vein
Stephen Covey *The 7 Habits of Highly Effective People* (p. 84)
W. Timothy Gallwey *The Inner Game of Tennis* (p. 110)
Abraham Maslow *Motivation and Personality* (50SHC)
Cheryl Richardson *Take Time for Your Life* (p. 260)

CHAPTER 50

John Whitmore

This modest-looking work on the elements of coaching in the business setting has sold a million copies and been translated into 20 languages. Revised and updated editions help to keep it selling, but it is a classic because it calls for a transformation in how we relate to others and run organizations, and was the first work to apply coaching principles to the business world.

Though it includes an array of useful techniques for increasing your own performance and bringing out the best in others, *Coaching for Performance*'s deeper message of awareness and responsibility makes you realize that coaching is *a way of seeing things*: it contains within it the seeds of great cultural change, from a world driven by instruction and institutions to one shaped more by self-learning and equality between people.

What *is* coaching?

Coaching is based on the ancient Socratic principle that you can never really teach a person something, they must learn it for themselves. It is about helping them to become aware of how they do things, to increase both their awareness and their responsibility.

Coaching is easily learned, and you may feel that you do it already and that it is common sense. Yet it goes against much of what our culture has instilled in us: judgment, criticism, punishment, and reward. Its premise is that each of us is a success-in-waiting, and the coach's role is simply to draw out a person's own solutions through questioning. The questions seek to reveal the details of a situation (the what, when, who, and how much) but not the why. "Why" questions can involve judgment and provoke defensiveness, and make the whole process too analytical. The demand for more detail increases the focus and awareness of the person being coached. They are compelled to go deeper into a situation to discover their own answers. In place of the traditional imparting of knowledge from one person to another, coaching is about optimizing individuality and uniqueness. It is therefore a more positive way of seeing people.

The coaching organization

Whitmore gives us the alarming statistic that most people only fulfill their potential at work about 40 percent of the time, either due to lack of opportunity within the organization, or lack of self-confidence or self-belief. This produces an organization working at much less than full capacity, and to counter it management nearly always imposes a technical or structural fix. The real answer, however, lies in improving human psychological performance.

Traditional managers exploit their position of being in charge of pay, promotion, and firing (the carrot and the stick) to get things done. In this context, they do not see any problem in telling people to do things. But Whitmore suggests that telling or dictating demotivates people and creates an "us and them" environment. Staff members are afraid to reveal their true feelings and ideas, and the absence of non-judgmental feedback stifles innovation and improvement.

Coaching lies "on a different plane altogether," Whitmore says. While a traditional boss, if someone comes to them with a problem, will either take charge of the situation themselves or scold the person for getting into the situation, a coach-boss will ask brief questions about what is happening that get the employee to think about it for themselves. This gives the employee ownership of the problem and prompts them to find a solution. Occasionally, in an emergency, it will be quicker for the boss to tell rather than coach, but in a supportive environment this won't be a problem.

You foster self-belief in people by changing your *expectations* of them. Whitmore mentions tests showing that a pupil's performance generally measures up to the beliefs about their ability that a teacher has conveyed to them. In the same way, employees generally perform up to expectations. Whitmore suggests:

"Only when coaching principles govern or underlie all management behavior and interactions, as they certainly will do in time, will the full force of people's performance potential be released."

This is the difference between an organization with *esprit de corps*, with a unity of purpose in which everyone's contribution is maximized and validated, and the more common kind in which there is a gap between stated purpose and performance and disaffection in the ranks.

Jim Collins (*Good to Great*, see p. 74) has noticed a remarkable similarity among the best companies: they are not simply focused on creating great products, but *first* on creating a great organization in which everyone can flourish. If people feel that they have room to reach their potential, great products or great service emerge almost automatically. This blend of business achievement and personal development is what coaching aims for.

GROWing your people and your business

Some bosses will say that coaching is all very well, but it takes time that they don't have. However, once you have a coaching *environment* in place you can grow the business and devote time to your people simultaneously. Whitmore provides a well-tested sequence of questions to be used in coaching sessions that can achieve personal and business growth simultaneously. The GROW sequence involves Goals, Reality checking, Options, and Will.

You might expect that coming to grips with harsh realities faced by an individual or an organization should be first on the agenda, but Whitmore points out that setting goals based only on current reality will result in solutions framed by past performance. In coaching, goals need to be formed around what might be possible, not what is likely. To be inspired by a goal, it must express an image of ourselves or our company that takes us to a whole new level. Once you are aware of what is possible (Goals) and where you are currently (Reality), you are ready to explore the alternative routes and strategies (Options) that can get you to your goal. The final set of questions to be answered involve action: once a path has been chosen, who is going to be involved and when will it be done (Will)?

Though simple, this sequence has a transforming effect because the task of achievement loses its mystery. The clarity of expectation produces Whitmore's twin performance pillars of greater responsibility and awareness.

Beyond performance: coaching for meaning

Timothy Gallwey's seminal coaching book *The Inner Game of Tennis* (see p. 110) came out at a time when the very model of how human beings work was being challenged, Whitmore notes. The business world had been in thrall to behaviorist psychology, which saw us as blank slates in which everything we knew must be taught or instructed, and assumed that money was the prime motivation for working. But Abraham Maslow's humanistic psychology offered an alternative: a more optimistic view of human beings in which the satisfaction of basic needs (food, shelter) led us on to want to satisfy higher needs such as belonging, prestige, self-esteem, and finally, a sense of meaning or purpose.

The company of the future, Whitmore says, will go out of its way to provide people with money, security, and a sense of community, but will also have values that a person feels are worthy of the time they spend working for it. Could a more spiritual—higher-purpose—business be the ultimate competitive advantage? Whitmore believes so. People want to love the organization for which they work. Those that are socially responsible, rated on everything from whether they recycle to whether suppliers are treated well, will naturally be more desirable to work for than those that are not. Staff motivation will not be a problem.

What is the role of coaching in this transformation in our attitudes to work? Whitmore believes that stress is a symptom of lack of meaning and purpose, therefore coaching must not simply seek efficiency or attainment of goals, but draw out people's highest values so that the work they do can be a way to express themselves fully.

Final comments

This commentary has touched only on some themes. You should get *Coaching for Performance* for:

❖ A valuable chapter on goal setting.
❖ Actual questions that you can use in coaching situations and examples of coaching conversations.
❖ A section on providing valuable follow-up and feedback.
❖ A chapter on improving team performance.
❖ A chapter (in the 2017 edition) on measuring the results of coaching in a business context.

Why has coaching become popular? Whitmore suggested in an interview that it is "a manifestation of the decline in external authority." We don't trust governments, organized religion no longer gives us the answers we need, and we cannot rely on the companies we work for to provide security or values. In this secular vacuum it is clear that we must develop our own codes of ethics, and coaching is a way of aligning our goals and values with daily life.

Moreover, in this age of personal development and individualism, coaching is a means of changing the world through *people*, not institutions, Whitmore believes. Though many have paid lip service to coaching ideas, they are still to be truly understood, and *Coaching for Performance* goes a long way toward reminding us what it is really about. If the discipline succeeds in becoming a part of our culture, the number of individuals who are truly empowered and responsible will explode, and the results of that we can only imagine.

John Whitmore

Born in 1937 in the UK, Whitmore was educated at Eton College, Sandhurst Royal Military Academy, and Cirencester Agricultural College.

As a professional racing driver in the 1960s, he won the British and European Saloon Car Championships and drove in the winning Ford team at Le Mans. He retired in 1966 to run an agribusiness and became a director of a Ford dealership, then moved to Switzerland and later the US to study physics, psychotherapy, and sports psychology.

In 1978, Whitmore returned to the UK and set up a tennis, golf, and ski school based on Inner Game principles that he had adopted from Timothy Gallwey. He discovered that this new type of sports coaching could be applied to the business context, and his firm Performance Consultants became a leader in corporate coaching in Europe.

He died in 2017.

Chronological List of Titles

Sun Tzu *The Art of War* (4th century BCE)
Baltasar Gracian *The Art of Worldly Wisdom* (1647)
Benjamin Franklin *The Way to Wealth* (1758)
Horatio Alger *Ragged Dick* (1867)
Orison Swett Marden *Pushing to the Front* (1894)
Wallace D. Wattles *The Science of Getting Rich* (1910)
Andrew Carnegie *The Autobiography of Andrew Carnegie* (1920)
Edward Bok *The Americanization of Edward Bok* (1921)
Russell H. Conwell *Acres of Diamonds* (1921)
Henry Ford *My Life and Work* (1922)
George S. Clason *The Richest Man in Babylon* (1926)
Napoleon Hill *Think and Grow Rich* (1937)
Florence Scovel Shinn *The Secret Door to Success* (1940)
Frank Bettger *How I Raised Myself from Failure to Success in Selling*
    (1947)
Claude M. Bristol *The Magic of Believing* (1948)
Les Giblin *How to Have Confidence and Power in Dealing with People*
    (1956)
David J. Schwartz *The Magic of Thinking Big* (1959)
John Paul Getty *How to Be Rich* (1961)
Catherine Ponder *The Dynamic Laws of Prosperity* (1962)
Muriel James & Dorothy Jongeward *Born to Win* (1971)
W. Timothy Gallwey *The Inner Game of Tennis* (1974)
Ray Kroc *Grinding It Out* (1977)
Kenneth Blanchard & Spencer Johnson *The One Minute Manager*
    (1981)
Anthony Robbins *Unlimited Power* (1986)
Warren Bennis *On Becoming a Leader* (1989)
Stephen R. Covey *The 7 Habits of Highly Effective People* (1989)
Chin-Ning Chu *Thick Face, Black Heart* (1992)
Donald T. Phillips *Lincoln on Leadership* (1992)

James Wallace & Jim Erickson *Hard Drive: Bill Gates and the Making of the Microsoft Empire* (1992)
Sam Walton *Made in America* (1992)
John Whitmore *Coaching for Performance* (1992)
Brian Tracy *Maximum Achievement* (1993)
Nelson Mandela *Long Walk to Freedom* (1994)
Roger Lowenstein *Buffett* (1995)
Earl G. Graves *How to Succeed in Business without Being White* (1997)
Robert Kiyosaki *Rich Dad, Poor Dad* (1997)
J. W. Marriott Jr. *The Spirit to Serve* (1997)
Spencer Johnson *Who Moved My Cheese?* (1998)
Cheryl Richardson *Take Time for Your Life* (1998)
Jim Collins *Good to Great* (2001)
David S. Landes *The Wealth and Poverty of Nations* (1998)
Thomas J. Stanley *The Millionaire Mind* (2000)
Margot Morrell & Stephanie Capparell *Shackleton's Way* (2001)
Robin Gerber *Leadership the Eleanor Roosevelt Way* (2002)
Malcolm Gladwell *Outliers* (2008)
Darren Hardy *The Compound Effect* (2010)
Adam Grant *Give and Take* (2013)
Gary Keller *The One Thing* (2013)
Brent Schlender & Rick Tetzeli *Becoming Steve Jobs* (2015)
Angela Duckworth *Grit* (2016)

Credits

Please note that the dates in brackets are the date of publication of these editions. Original publication dates are stated in each of the 50 commentaries.

Alger, H. (1962) *Ragged Dick and Mark, the Match Boy*, New York: Macmillan.

Bennis, W. (1989) *On Becoming a Leader*, London: Arrow.

Bettger, F. (1992) *How I Raised Myself from Failure to Success in Selling*, New York: Fireside.

Blanchard, K. & Johnson, S. (1981) *The One Minute Manager*, London: HarperCollins.

Bok, E. W. (1921) *The Americanization of Edward Bok: The Autobiography of a Dutch Boy Fifty Years After*, New York: Charles Scribner's Sons.

Bristol, C. M. (1948) *The Magic of Believing*, New York: Simon & Schuster.

Carnegie, A. (1986) *The Autobiography of Andrew Carnegie*, Boston: Northeastern University Press.

Chu, C.-N. (1992) *Thick Face, Black Heart: The Asian Path to Thriving, Winning and Succeeding*, London: Nicholas Brealey Publishing.

Clason, G. (1955) *The Richest Man in Babylon*, London: Plume.

Collins, J. (2001) *Good to Great: Why Some Companies Make the Leap . . . and Others Don't*, London: Random House.

Conwell, R. H. (1921) *Acres of Diamonds*, Marina del Rey, CA: DeVorss & Co.

Covey, S. R. (1989) *The 7 Habits of Highly Effective People*, London: Simon & Schuster.

Duckworth, A. (2016) *Grit: The Power of Passion and Perseverance*, London: Ebury.

Ford, H. (1996) *My Life and Work*, Manchester, NH: Ayer Co. Publishing.

Franklin, B. (1993) "The Way to Wealth" in *Benjamin Franklin: Autobiography and Other Writings*, O. Seavey (ed.), Oxford: Oxford University Press.

Gallwey, W. T. (1975) *The Inner Game of Tennis*, London: Pan.

Gerber, R. (2002) *Leadership the Eleanor Roosevelt Way: Timeless Strategies from the First Lady of Courage*, New York: Prentice-Hall.

Getty, J. P. (1966) *How to Be Rich*, London: W. H. Allen.

Giblin, L. (1956) *How to Have Confidence and Power in Dealing with People*, New Jersey: Prentice-Hall.

Gladwell, M. (2008) Outliners: *The Story of Success*, London: Allen Lane.

Gracian, B. (1992) *The Art of Worldly Wisdom: A Pocket Oracle*, New York: Currency.

Grant, A. (2014) *Give and Take: Why Helping Others Drives Our Success*, New York: Penguin.

Graves, E. G. (1977) *How to Succeed in Business without Being White: Straight Talk on Making It in America*, New York: HarperCollins.

Hardy, D. (2010) *The Compound Effect*, Boston: Da Capo Press.

Hill, N. (1960) *Think and Grow Rich*, New York: Fawcett Crest.

James, M. & Jongeward, D. (1996) *Born to Win: Transactional Analysis with Gestalt Experiments*, New York: Perseus Books.

Johnson, S. (1998) *Who Moved My Cheese? An Amazing Way to Deal with Change in Your Work and in Your Life*, London: Random House.

Keller, G. (2013) *The One Thing: The Surprisingly Simple Truth Behind Extraordinary Results*, London: John Murray Press.

Kiyosaki, R. with Lechter, S. (1997) *Rich Dad, Poor Dad: What the Rich Teach Their Kids about Money . . . That the Poor and Middle Class Do Not!* London: Time Warner.

Kroc, R. (2012) *Grinding It Out: The Making of McDonald's*, New York: St Martin's Press.

Landes, D. S. (1998) *The Wealth and Poverty of Nations: Why Some Are So Rich and Some So Poor*, London: Abacus.

Lowenstein, R. (1995) *Buffett: The Making of an American Capitalist*, London: Orion.

Mandela, N. R. (1994) *Long Walk to Freedom: The Autobiography of Nelson Mandela*, London: Abacus.

Marden, O. S. (1997) *Pushing to the Front, or Success under Difficulties, Vols. 1 & 2*, Santa Fe, CA: Sun Books.

Marriott, J. W. Jr. with Brown, K. A. (1997) *The Spirit to Serve: Marriott's Way*, New York: HarperCollins.

Morrell, M. & Capparell, S. (2001) *Shackleton's Way: Leadership*

Lessons from the Great Antarctic Explorer, London: Nicholas Brealey Publishing.

Phillips, D. T. (1992) *Lincoln on Leadership: Executive Strategies for Tough Times*, New York: Warner Books.

Ponder, C. (1962) *The Dynamic Laws of Prosperity*, Camarillo, CA: DeVorss & Co.

Richardson, C. (1998) *Take Time for Your Life: A Seven-Step Program for Creating the Life You Want*, Bantam: London.

Robbins, A. (1986) *Unlimited Power: The New Science of Personal Achievement*, London: Simon & Schuster.

Schlender, R. & Tetzeli R. (2015) *Becoming Steve Jobs: How a Reckless Upstart Became a Visionary Leader*, London: Sceptre.

Schwartz, D. J. (1959) *The Magic of Thinking Big*, New York: Simon & Schuster.

Scovel Shinn, F. (1978) *The Secret Door to Success*, Camarillo, CA: DeVorss & Co.

Stanley, T. J. (2000) *The Millionaire Mind*, Sydney: HarperCollins.

Tracy, B. (1993) *Maximum Achievement: Strategies and Skills that Will Unlock Your Hidden Powers to Succeed*, New York: Fireside.

Sun Tzu (2002) *The Art of War*, Denma Translation Group, Boston: Shambhala.

Wallace, J. & Erickson, J. (1992) *Hard Drive: Bill Gates and the Making of the Microsoft Empire*, New York: John Wiley & Sons.

Walton, S. with Huey, J. (1992) *Made in America: My Story*, New York: Bantam.

Wattles, W. D. (1976) *Financial Success through the Power of Thought* [*The Science of Getting Rich*], Rochester, VT: Destiny Books.

Whitmore, J. (1992) *Coaching for Performance: GROWing People, Performance and Purpose*, London: Nicholas Brealey Publishing.

About the Author

A graduate of the London School of Economics and the University of Sydney, Tom Butler-Bowdon was 25 years old and working as a political advisor in Australia when he read his first personal development book: Stephen R. Covey's *The 7 Habits of Highly Effective People*. Captivated, he came to the view that this was an underrated field of writing. At 30, he left his career to write the bestselling *50 Self-Help Classics*, the first guide to personal development literature and winner of the Benjamin Franklin Award.

The follow-up, *50 Success Classics*, celebrated the great writings in motivation and success, from Horatio Alger to Napoleon Hill to Anthony Robbins. Tom completed the personal development trilogy with *50 Spiritual Classics*, which provides insights into the thinking of Gandhi, Mother Teresa, Carl Jung, and Eckhart Tolle, and 46 other great minds.

USAToday described Tom as "a true scholar of this type of literature." His award-winning *50 Classics* series has sold over 300,000 copies and has been translated into 23 languages.

Visit his website www.Butler-Bowdon.com

THE GREATEST BOOKS DISTILLED

by Tom Butler-Bowdon

The *50 Classics* series has sold over 300,000 copies

50 Economics Classics 978-1-85788-673-3

50 Philosophy Classics 978-1-47365-542-3

50 Politics Classics 978-1-47365-543-0

50 Psychology Classics, **2nd ed** 978-1-85788-674-0

50 Self-Help Classics, **2nd ed** 978-1-47365-828-8

50 Success Classics, **2nd ed** 978-1-47365-835-6

50 Spiritual Classics 978-1-47365-838-7

50 Business Classics 978-1-85788-675-7 (coming 2018)